Advances in Educational Psychology 2

edited by Mia Kellmer Pringle and Ved P. Varma

Advances in Educational Psychology 2

University of London Press Ltd

ISBN 0 340 11580 7

Printed and bound in Great Britain by
T. & A. Constable Ltd, Edinburgh EH7 4NF

Foreword

It is both an honour and a pleasure to have the opportunity to write the foreword to a book dedicated to Professor W. D. Wall and thereby to express my admiration for a very good friend. I knew him personally and saw him at work at UNESCO and I believe I was partly responsible for his appointment to that great international organisation. The high quality of the work he did there will always be remembered. However, I must confess complete failure in my attempts to persuade him to come and work with me in Geneva. He felt that he could make a greater contribution to education in the United Kingdom. He has possibly forgotten my vain efforts on that occasion, but I am pleased to recall them now as evidence of my high regard for him.

What is really remarkable about Professor Wall is the combination within him of two qualities rarely found in one person and which are often mutually exclusive even in otherwise distinguished teachers: on the one hand, a passionate personal involvement in education so that every problem is approached as though he were dealing with his own children; on the other hand, a scientific mind (as befits one who has studied under that excellent psychologist, Professor Valentine) which allows nothing to be asserted unless it can be proved and no scheme to be proposed unless the necessary psychological research has been carried out in advance.

It is the combination of these two basic qualities which has made the National Foundation for Educational Research in England and Wales, of which he was the director for about twelve years, so successful and world famous. It is amazing that he managed to secure continuous and effective support and financial aid from the Ministry of Education, when it is well known how often authorities are reluctant to spend money on research. They are usually more interested in actual teaching than in research, which is too often regarded as a luxury with only dubious practical implications. The story is told (and has been told so often that Professor Wall's name is frequently left out) that his usual tactic for persuading the Minister to agree to important and costly decisions was to have the following question put to him beforehand by the press: 'On what proven scientific data have you drawn before making a decision which will affect the future of our children and the whole nation?' In this way he always managed to get adequate financial backing for his work at the NFER. In fact he was so successful that the Foundation is now one of the most important educational research centres in the world.

Professor Wall's activities have not however been confined to the NFER and UNESCO. His publications are many and varied, covering all branches of education. He has frequent lecture invitations (in particular to the International Children's Centre in Paris, but to many other European countries as well) and he is often to be heard stirring the consciences of teachers, headmasters, parents and even pupils. He presents an argument clearly and forcefully. He can be so direct, open-minded and forthright that the whole audience is stirred. (I once saw this happen in Switzerland!) He speaks on radio and television in England and even gives lectures on psychology to London policemen—and they are world famous for their qualities of understanding! He makes an excellent chairman, even when confronted with students.

Professor Wall is frequently called upon to help with the reorganisation of schools or the organisation of educational research. Thus it was not surprising that he should be appointed Dean of the University of London Institute of Education in 1968, an Institute founded many years ago by that distinguished educator, Sir Percy Nunn, whom I had the honour of counting among my friends. There, Professor Wall has been concerned, above all, with the initial and in-service training of nursery, primary and secondary school teachers in Colleges of Education and Universities.

In short, Professor Wall is an educator in the most complete sense of the word. He combines the qualities of professional psychologist and teacher and reconciles a high idealism with the practical abilities of a first-class administrator and negotiator. That is why so many of his friends and admirers have collaborated in producing this book in his honour and that is why I am so pleased and honoured by being asked to contribute the foreword. On their behalf and on mine, I wish to express our gratitude for the tremendous work he has done.

Jean Piaget

Preface

This volume has a dual purpose. First, it is a tribute to Professor W. D. Wall from his colleagues (and some former students) in this country and abroad; it marks their deep appreciation of the man and his work, and it so happens that it also marks his sixtieth birthday. Secondly, this collection of original papers presents an up-to-date picture of research and thinking in the three fields of educational psychology in which Professor Wall has played a major and often innovatory role, namely learning and educational achievement; exceptional children; and adolescence.

The breadth and depth of each of the contributions reflects not only the range of Professor Wall's interests and concerns but also his international outlook and involvement. Moreover, they also indicate the blend of research and action, theory and practice, which has continued to characterise his work. The various chapters of this book pursue further the distinguished lead he has provided in making educational psychology relevant to the development and needs of children and young people in the world of today and tomorrow.

The editors would like to express their deep appreciation to all the contributors for their willingness to spare time from their very busy lives to prepare a paper, and for their ready acceptance of our general suggestions regarding the particular theme on which they might write. We would also like to thank The British Psychological Society for agreeing to receive the royalties and place them in a W. D. Wall Fund.

Mia Kellmer Pringle
Ved P. Varma
London 1973

Contents

The contributors

B. S. Bloom
Professor of Education, University of Chicago, USA

Sir Cyril Burt
Late Fellow of the British Academy; Honorary Fellow, Jesus College, Oxford; Emeritus Professor of Psychology, University of London

M. Chazan
Reader in Education, Department of Education, University College of Swansea

D. M. C. Dale
Senior Lecturer in the Education of Deaf Children, Institute of Education, University of London

L. Gardner
Principal Psychologist, The Spastics Society, London

R. Gulliford
Senior Lecturer in Education, School of Education, University of Birmingham

James Hemming
Writer, Broadcaster, Consultant Educational Psychologist

F. Hotyat
Former President of the Institut Supérieur de Pedagogie, Centre Universitaire de l'État, Mans, Belgium

Torsten Husén
Professor, Department of Educational and Psychological Research, School of Education, University of Sweden

J. A. Leonard
Formerly Reader in Psychology, Department of Psychology, University of Nottingham

K. Lovell
Professor of Educational Psychology, Institute of Education, University of Leeds

J. B. Mays
Eleanor Rathbone Professor of Social Science, University of Liverpool

P. A. Osterrieth
Head of Laboratoire de Psychologie, Université Libre de Bruxelles, Belgium

Jean Piaget
Professor of Experimental Psychology, University of Geneva, Switzerland

Mia Kellmer Pringle
Director, National Children's Bureau, London

G. Robb
Senior Educational Psychologist, Essex Education Committee

J. M. Tanner
Professor of Child Health and Growth, Institute of Child Health, University of London

J. Tizard
Research Professor of Child Development, Institute of Education, University of London

Ved P. Varma
Consultant Psychologist; formerly Educational Psychologist, London Borough of Brent Child Guidance Service

Phillip Williams
Professor of Educational Studies, The Open University

W. D. Wall: an appreciation

The aim of this volume is to trace and illustrate the way in which Bill Wall has influenced, and in many ways changed, the course of research and practice in educational psychology. From earliest manhood, his interests have been catholic, embracing architecture, painting, poetry and literature. His wartime service in the Royal Army Ordnance Corps was concerned with personnel selection and instructor training, and his compassion was aroused by the misery of illiterate soldiers unable to write to their families and girl friends. This led to an interest in the psychology of teaching and learning, and to the decision to read psychology while still a serving soldier. His subsequent career flowed from this step.

Born in 1913, Bill Wall was much influenced during his formative years by three men: his own father—who died when he was seventeen years old—and two of his father's friends. His father did a great deal of voluntary social work and was regarded by his community as a guide and mentor. The friends were gentlemen of leisure and of wide culture. Baynard Tahourdin was interested in British orchids and in neolithic archaeology; Paul Faraday, a grand-nephew of the famous Michael, was an unsuccessful but talented artist, man of letters, and dilettante intellectual. Both shared their interests with him, and Faraday, to use Wall's own words, 'led me into many byways of literature, history and science, archaeology and antiquities; he ruthlessly criticised my style of writing and painting whilst encouraging any effort I might make'.

These interests led him to spend two periods in France, one at the age of thirteen and the other at sixteen; he was mostly on his own—an early indication of his rather solitary and self-sufficient personality. He spent the first time in Paris 'doing the museums, and very thoroughly indeed'. For the second period he went to Provence, where he sketched and studied mediaeval and Renaissance architecture.

Orthodox schooling proved somewhat less enthralling and he was 'an early leaver'. After only one year in the sixth form, he went into an architect's office as a 'general dogsbody pupil', as he describes it. In the evenings he studied at the then Central School of Arts and Crafts, getting certificates in the History of Architecture. Then he returned to school to take the Intermediate B.A. Examination, also managing to get a scholarship for a three-year degree and an exhibition to the Bartlett School of Architecture, University College. Though very much attracted to the latter, he was dissuaded from it, both because he lacked private means and because of the economic depression. So he went instead to the English School of University College, London where he read Honours English, taking French as the subsidiary. Far from being a second best, he deeply enjoyed the course and took a brilliant first-class degree in 1934.

For the next six years he taught English in grammar schools having drifted into teaching as being the occupation most likely to give time to read and write: 'It did both, but particularly it interested me passionately in the interaction with adolescents of all kinds—the more difficult the better.' Thus began his interest in this period of growth which was in fact the subject of his second book The Adolescent Child (Exercises in Comprehension in English, *written while teaching before the war, is now in its 4th edition). He married in 1936 and his first son was born in 1938.*

At the beginning of the Second World War, prior to being called up, and while still teaching, Bill Wall cooperated in the evacuation survey carried out by the Fabian Society and helped to develop an 'index of nutrition'. During the same year he enjoyed another interesting and relevant experience, namely collaborating in the Manpower Survey carried out by Beveridge and Cole. This work took him into factories all over County Durham and Northumberland, where he interviewed both managers and trade unionists.

Army service between 1940 and 1945 provided him with further experiences which eventually decided him to take up the study of psychology. Being given responsibility for the instruction of both army and civilian personnel, he was confronted at first hand with the problems of learning difficulties and of illiteracy among young adults. Characteristically this sparked off not only a theoretical interest in the nature of these problems but also led him to take practical measures to deal with them. He developed three different schemes of day-continuation education for adolescents; and he established the first centre for the remedial education of illiterate men and women. Thus he can be regarded as the 'father of remedial education', yet, sad to say, provision for adult illiterates still remains woefully inadequate. He reported the results of this work in three major and influential papers which were published between 1944 and 1946 in the British Journal of Educational Psychology.

An early paper on selection for courses of instruction and another on problems of illiteracy were passed on (unknown to him) to Professor C. W. Valentine at Birmingham. This led to his meeting not only Valentine but, through him, Professor (later Sir) Cyril Burt, both of whom became close and admired friends. Looking back, Bill Wall feels that it was the influence of those two men, and their generous help and encouragement, which really shaped his career from 1943 onwards. In that year, while still on war service, he became a postgraduate student in the Psychology Department of University College, London, taking the B.Sc. Honours as a qualifying examination in the subsequent year.

On his discharge from the army in 1945, he was invited by Valentine to join the Department and Institute of Education at the University of Birmingham, where he remained for six years. Within three years, he rose from lecturer to reader in education. Altogether, the following six years which he spent in the University, proved to be a very creative and productive period. He revived and became tutor to the diploma course in the Psychology of Childhood. Then he established an entirely new postgraduate Diploma in Educational Psychology which was not only the first post-war university-based training course but also had many innovative features, some of which have remained unique to this day.

An equally unique venture was the Remedial Education Centre, set up in collaboration with Professor (later Sir) Fred Schonell, to study and treat learning difficulties in children of average or above-average ability. Also in collaboration with Professor Schonell, he founded the journal Educational Review *and a series of occasional monographs. Throughout this period, he published numerous papers and articles in this country and abroad, and was much sought after as a speaker. In addition, he was closely associated with the building up of the Institute of Education and with the constituent colleges.*

Four features of his activities deserve special comment because they illustrate how much in advance of his time Wall's thinking was, particularly on issues of crucial practical importance. He stressed the need to consider a child's difficulties 'in the round', looking at the 'whole child' within the familial, school and social setting; and through his work at the Remedial Education Centre illustrated the value of detailed, meticulously assembled case studies in which the physical, social, psychological and educational aspects were all fully taken into account. Also the work of the Centre served as a laboratory experiment in the development of psychological services for schools.

Secondly, he was among the first to attack 'Binet bashing' as the barren activity it is; pointing out how it failed to make use of the long years of training which an educational psychologist has undergone. Thirdly, and linked with the previous point, he attacked the practice of school medical officers with four weeks' training being required to undertake the psychological examination of pupils in need of special educational treatment. Now these views are widely, though still not universally, accepted. At the time they were criticised and attacked.

Fourthly, he believed it to be essential to the raising of educational standards and to the application of research findings in the classroom that teachers should be able to acquire first-hand knowledge of research methodology. To this end, Wall pioneered the idea of research teams, composed of practising teachers who, under his leadership, carried out a wide range of projects, the results of which were subsequently published.

It was during this time, too, that he began to be actively involved in the problems of handicapped children. He was appointed psychological adviser to Carlson House, the first day school in this country for the cerebrally palsied, and in collaboration with Mrs Eleanor Schonell, whose Ph.D. he supervised, he carried out research into their educational problems. Also he established the Research Committee for the Blind, a joint venture with Mike Myers, one of his M.A. students, who subsequently became headmaster of the two pioneer ventures, Condover Hall School and Pathways.

Though the number of his postgraduate students was relatively small, it is to a considerable extent a reflection of his superb teaching ability that practically all of them today occupy distinguished positions in various parts of the world. He was generous, too, in tutoring those who experienced difficulty in obtaining the help they needed from their own university. In 1951, Bill Wall was invited by UNESCO to become the Head of their Education and Child Development Unit within the Department of Education, the headquarters of which were in Paris. By then he had a family of three children, two sons and a daughter, and after a period during which he commuted from England, they went to settle in France.

During the following five years, he established himself as the first British educational and child psychologist to penetrate the international scene. Initially his assignment was far from clear, except that he was to be responsible for the organisation of a European Conference on Education and Mental Health in 1952. It grew into a responsibility for a wide programme concerned with the applications of psychology to the improvement of education. This was achieved through international expert studies of such problems as psychological services; the organisation of nursery school education; failure in school; examinations and other means of guidance; evaluation in education; and aspects of special educational treatment. Also the International Institute for Child Study was set up in Bangkok, Thailand. Formidable indeed, all the more so since very limited finance was available for the execution of such an ambitious programme.

With characteristic willingness to accept a challenge, he decided to try and meet these objectives by means of three strategies. First, he fostered the growth of voluntary organisations—for example the World Organisation for Early Childhood Education (OMEP), the International Federation of Parent-Teacher Associations, and FICE (the International Association of Children's Communities)—and he encouraged them to work with UNESCO. Secondly, he established a number of expert groups, some of which met just once or twice to consider a particular topic, while others with a degree of continuity in their work and membership led to long-term studies, such as the International Evaluation of Educational Achievement.

The third strategy was to develop advisory work at governmental level, thus bringing influence to bear both on policy making and on legislation.

It was during this time that Miss Ursula Gallusser, a Swiss child psychologist, a former assistant to Piaget and founder of the psychological service of the Village Pestalozzi, joined his staff. Their collaboration grew increasingly close and culminated in her helping him to prepare material for what is perhaps to date his major book, Education and Mental Health. Published in 1955, it went into a third edition within three years and has been translated into more than a dozen languages. Other books resulted from his work at that time: Psychological Services for Schools and Failure in School. Yet other publications—Mental Hygiene in the Nursery School, Examinations and Other Means of Evaluation, reports on the Physically and Mentally Handicapped—arose out of expert groups, organised by him in collaboration with WHO and the UN Department of Social Affairs. Miss Gallusser eventually became his second wife and mother of his fourth child.

In 1956 Bill Wall returned to this country to take up his appointment as Director of the National Foundation for Educational Research in England and Wales. During the twelve years of his tenure, he transformed the Foundation from a relatively small body with a modest annual budget of £20,000 and a staff of 20 into a well-known and authoritative organisation, spending some £300,000 a year on research and with a staff of 150. When he came to the Foundation, there was no career structure for their research workers, most of whom were on short-term contract; this he also succeeded in changing.

Under his guidance, the Foundation's Test Agency was put on a proper footing so that it became a going concern. He established an information service, transformed a small bulletin into the journal Educational Research and also initiated a new series of paperback books. Indeed he fought hard to make the Foundation a publishing house in its own right, since he judged correctly that this could be both intellectually and financially a profitable undertaking. This only came to pass quite recently, although his efforts in this direction laid the foundation of what has just now become an independent publisher.

As for the research programme, he considerably widened and deepened the Foundation's range of enquiries. While continuing to mount large national surveys he initiated operational research projects such as the comprehensive schools enquiry, the study of teaching French in primary schools, the work on streaming, and the monitoring of a teacher's day. What had been a trickle of publications when he came to the Foundation turned into a steady stream and eventually became a veritable torrent. Throughout those years, he maintained many of his international contacts and remained much in demand for international conferences, seminars and consultations.

Despite very onerous and unremitting responsibilities (without the long vacations of academic life during which the pace slackens), Bill Wall continued to find time for writing. In addition to numerous papers, he produced three further books, Child of our Times, Adolescents in School and Society and Longitudinal Studies and the Social Sciences.

Then, in 1968, he accepted an invitation to become Dean of the Institute of Education at London University. During the four and a half years in this post he was concerned with general academic policy-making, chairing a great many committees, dealing with reform of examinations, changes in curricula, and the development of the Centre for Advanced Studies and Research, among other matters. It was also his task to organise the Institute's Enquiry into Teacher Training which involved mounting very quickly a complex research programme. His responsibilities during these years also expanded to include training and examining for professions other than teaching, and notably medical education, the training of the police, and university examinations. Outside activities included service on the BBC Committee on the social effects of television; on the working party on unplanned pregnancies set up by the Royal College of Obstetricians; and on the Police Training Council. It was during this period, too, that he began re-writing Education and Mental Health, preparing a completely revised version of two volumes, provisionally entitled Constructive Education.

After shouldering these very heavy administrative duties, he decided to return to what has—since his Birmingham days—been his real love, the teaching of young adults. Thus he began yet another phase of his career on being appointed, in 1972, Head of a large department of Child Development and the Psychology of Education and holder of a professorial chair at the Institute. Meanwhile, his second son has also become a psychologist, taking a brilliant first degree, followed by a doctorate, both at Nottingham University. Now he is doing research in a Medical Research Council unit at Sheffield University. His eldest son is designing and managing hotel gardens in the Bahamas and Florida; while his only daughter has become a teacher of art with a particular interest in adolescents.

Throughout his professional life, Bill Wall has succeeded to an unusual degree in blending scholarship with a severely practical and applied approach. A real sympathy with, and understanding of children—much rarer qualities than is generally supposed—illumine his thoughts, actions, and writings. His theoretical stance has always been eclectic except for a distrust of the psychoanalytic approach. He is a lively, provocative speaker who knows how to make use of the abrasive phrase when the occasion warrants. He has not only remained a disciple of Valentine and Burt but much more than a mere follower in the footsteps of the two men whose thought and teaching he most admired.

Bill Wall has devoted his great abilities and untiring energy to the causes which he has held dear from earliest manhood. He initiated studies into remedial teaching; he has helped to pioneer systematic enquiries into the needs of exceptional children; and he has made the study of adolescence very much his own.

This appreciation comes at the end of his first thirty years as a professional psychologist; on the eve of his sixtieth birthday; and at the beginning of new responsibilities. Yet another turning-point, but the general direction is likely to remain the same!

Mia Kellmer Pringle
1973

Bibliography of W. D. Wall's published work up to 1972

BOOKS

Exercises in Comprehension in English. Cambridge: University Tutorial Press, 1940 (2nd edn 1964).

The Adolescent Child. London: Methuen, 1948 (3rd edn 1956). (Portuguese translation 1969.)

Education and Mental Health. London: Harrap-UNESCO, 1955 (3rd edn 1958). (Trans. *Education et Santé Mentale.* Paris: Bourrelier-UNESCO, 1956; *Erziehung und seilische Gesundheit.* Austria: Edition Vienna, 1958; translated also into Spanish, Italian, Arabic, Polish, etc.)

Psychological Services for Schools. New York: N.Y. University Press, 1956. (Trans. *Die Psychologie im Dienst der Schule.* Hamburg: UNESCO-Institut für Pädagogik, 1956; *La Psychologie au service de l'école.* Paris: Bourrelier, 1958.)

Child of our Times. London: National Children's Homes, 1959.

(With W. C. OLSON and F. J. SCHONELL) *Failure in School.* Hamburg: UNESCO Institute, 1962.

Adolescents in School and Society. Slough: NFER, 1968. (Italian and Portuguese translations pending.)

(With H. L. WILLIAMS) *Longitudinal Studies and the Social Sciences.* London: S.S.R.C. Heinemann, 1970.

(With V. P. VARMA, eds) *Advances in Educational Psychology 1.* London: University of London Press, 1972.

CHAPTERS IN BOOKS

'The Psychology of Basic Educational Techniques.' In C. A. MACE and P. E. VERNON (eds) *Current Trends in British Psychology.* London: Methuen, 1953.

'Problems of Development.' In *Art et Education.* Paris: UNESCO, 1953.

'Teaching Methods—Psychological Studies of the Curriculum and of Classroom Teaching.' *In Univ. of London Inst. of Ed. Studies in Education. No. 7.* London: Evans, 1955.

'Guidance Services in Europe.' In R. KING HALL and J. A. LAUWERYS (eds) *Year Book of Education 1955*. London: Evans.

'Cultural and Educational Problems in Developing Countries.' In M. V. C. JEFFREYS (ed.) *Education in an Age of Technology*. Alva: Cunningham, 1959.

'Curriculum and the Promotion of Mental Health.' In G. Z. F. BEREDAY and J. A. LAUWERYS (eds) *Year Book of Education 1958*. London: Evans.

'Learning to Think.' In W. R. NIBLETT (ed.) *How and Why do we Learn?* London: Faber & Faber, 1965.

'The Role of Education—1. Theory and Policy.' In M. L. KELLMER PRINGLE (ed.) *Investment in Children*. London: Longman, 1965.

Summary in J. DOWNING *et al. The i.t.a. Symposium*. Slough: NFER, 1967.

'The Work of the NFER.' In H. J. BUTCHER (ed.) *Educational Research in Britain 1*. London: University of London Press, 1968.

'From Teaching to Learning?' In E. J. KING (ed.) *The Teacher and the Needs of Society in Evolution*. Oxford: Pergamon, 1970.

RESEARCH PAPERS

'Decay of educational attainments among adolescents after leaving school. A research based on testing of adolescents in two army centres.' *Br. J. educ. Psychol.*, 1944, **14**, 1, 19-34.

'Reading backwardness among men in the army. Part 1.' *Br. J. educ. Psychol.*, 1945, **15**, 1, 28-40.

'Educational interests of a group of young industrial workers.' *Br. J. educ. Psychol.*, 1945, **15**, 3, 127-32.

'Reading backwardness among men in the army. Part 2.' *Br. J. educ. Psychol.*, 1946, **16**, 3, 133-48.

'The opinions of teachers on parent-teacher co-operation.' *Br. J. educ. Psychol.*, 1947, **17**, 2, 97-113.

'Happiness and unhappiness in the childhood and adolescence of a group of women students.' *Br. J. Psychol.*, 1948, **38**, Part 4.

'Newspaper reading interests of adolescents and adults. Part 1.' *Br. J. educ. Psychol.*, 1948, **18**, 26-40.

'Newspaper reading interests of adolescents and adults. Part 2.' *Br. J. educ. Psychol.*, 1948, **18**, 87-104.

(With W. A. SIMSON) 'Effects of cinema attendance on the behaviour of adolescents as seen by their contemporaries.' *Br. J. educ. Psychol.*, 1949, **19**, 1, 53-61.

(With E. M. SMITH) 'Film choices of adolescents.' *Br. J. educ. Psychol.*, 1949, **19**, 2, 121-36.

(With W. A. SIMSON) 'Emotional responses of adolescent groups to certain films. Part 1.' *Br. J. educ. Psychol.*, 1950, **20**, 153-63.

(With W. A. SIMSON) 'Responses of adolescent groups to certain films. Part 2.' *Br. J. educ. Psychol.*, 1951, **21**, 81-8.

(With T. JONES and C. G. HEY) 'A group performance test and scale of intelligence.' *Br. J. educ. Psychol.*, 1952, **22**, 160-72.

(With K. M. MILLER) 'Motivation and countermotivation.' Proceedings of the XIV International Congress of Applied Psychology, Copenhagen, 1961.

(With M. L. KELLMER PRINGLE) 'The clinical significance of standard score discrepancies between intelligence and social competence.' *Human Development*, 1966, **9**, 121-51.

GENERAL PAPERS

'The adolescent and the cinema.' 2 articles. *Educational Review*, 1948-49.

'The backward adult.' 4 articles. *Journal of Army Education*, 1948-49.

(With F. J. SCHONELL) 'The Remedial Education Centre.' *Educational Review*, 1950.

'Illiteracy among the young.' *The Listener*, 29 March 1951.

'Delinquency.' *Educational Review*, 1951.

(With M. L. KELLMER PRINGLE) 'Case study and the techniques of individual diagnosis.' *Educational Review*, 1951.

'L'adolescent et le cinéma.' *Revue de Filmologie*, 1952.

'École et famille en Angleterre.' *École des parents*, No. 10, Oct. 1953.

'Les facteurs sociaux et affectifs dans le retards scolaire.' *Enfance* (Paris: Presses Universitaires de France), 1954.

'Le retard scolaire en Grande-Bretagne.' *Enfance* (Paris: P.U.F.), 1954, **VII**, No. 4.

'Kven skal oppsede dei heimlause barna?' *Norsk Pedagogisk Tidskrift*, 1954, No. 7, 38.

'Les services de psychologie scolaire en Europe.' *Enfance* (Paris: P.U.F.), Jan-Feb 1955.

'Dreaming with eyes wide open.' *Unesco Courier*, No. 1, 1955.

'The educational aspects of delinquency.' *International Review of Education*, 1955, **I**, No. 4. (Trans. 'La escuela y la delincuencia infantil.' *Mater amabilis*, Barcelona.)

'The psychology of the handicapped child in relation to his family.' In *Child Welfare in Relation to the Family*. Geneva: Int. Union for Child Welfare, pp 65-79, 1955. (Trans. 'La psychologie de l'enfant infirme en relation avec sa vie familiale et sociale.' *La Protection de l'Enfance et la Famille*: Quelques Aspects du Probleme. Travaux du congrès mondial 1954 tenu à Zagreb du 30 Août au 4 Septembre, pp 69-83. Union Internationale de Protection de l'Enfance, 16 rue du Mont-Blanc, Geneve, Suisse. 1955.)

'Guidance and Education.' *International Review of Education*, 1956, **II**, No. 3.

'The remedial action of the environment.' *Re-education*, 1956, **10**, Nos. 80-3.

'Le réadaptation des jeunes par le milieu.' *Rééducation*, 1956.

'Perspective de la recherche filmologique.' *Revue de Filmologie*, 1956.

'L'Institut international de psychologie de l'enfant, à Bangkok.' *Chronique de l'Unesco*, Bulletin mensuel, 1956, **II**, 6, 175-9.

'Co-operation between the family and the school.' *Familles dans le Monde*, 1956, **9**, No. 2.

'Psychologie et psychologues.' *Bulletin de Psychologie* (Université de Paris), 1957, **X**, No. 5.

'Beruf und Ausbildung der Psychologen.' *Schweizerische Zeitschrift für Psychologie und ihre Anwendungen*, 1957, **XVI**, No. 4.

'Security, motivation and learning.' *New Era*, 1957, **38**, No. 1.

'The Leicestershire experiment.' *Education*, 1957, **109**, No. 2834.

'The trend of reading ability.' *Education*. 5 July 1957.

'Quelques considerations sur les methodes de la recherche pedagogique.' *Courrier de la Recherche Pedagogique*, No. 7, 1957.

'High intelligence—asset or liability?' *Unesco Courier*, No. 10, 1957.

'Some reflections on education in the developing countries and in Europe.' *School Review*, 1958, Spring issue, pp. 56-69.

'Examinations and their bearing on education.' *International Review of Education*, 1958, **IV**, No. 3, 257-74.

'The wish to learn—research into motivation.' *Educational Research*, 1958, **I**, 1, 32-7.

'Highly intelligent children. Part 1. The psychology of the gifted.' *Educational Research*, 1960, **II**, 2, 101-11.

'Highly intelligent children. Part 2. The education of the gifted.' *Educational Research*, 1960, **II**, 3, 207-17.

'L'enfant d'aujourd'hui pose-t-il de nouvelles tâches à l'école?' *Rencontres*, No. 4, 1960. Nos. 1 & 2, 1961.

'Meeting the deprivations imposed by handicap.' *Special Education*, 1961, **L**, 4, 24-32.

(With K. M. MILLER) 'Educational research in countries other than the United States: The United Kingdom.' *Review of Educational Research*, 1962, **XXXII**, 3, 354-60.

'Resistances, organisation and costs. Part IV of a symposium on educational research to-day.' *Br. J. educ. Psychol.*, 1962, **32**, 224-33.

'Surcharge des programmes.' *Revue d'Hygiène et Médecine Scolaires et Universitaires*, 1963, **XVI**, No. 2 (from a lecture given at a seminar on fatigue in school children, Centre International de l'Enfance, 13-15 December 1962).

'The contribution of Sir Cyril Burt to educational psychology.' *Forward Trends*, Spring 1963.

'Guidance and education.' *Health Visitor*, 1964, **37**, No. 1.

' "Mods" and "rockers" are symptoms of a malaise.' *The Municipal Journal*, 1964, **72**, No. 3712.

'Hotyat, the humanist.' *Au service de l'Education: F. Hotyat.* (F. Nathan, Editors, Paris). Labor. Brussels. 33-40. 1965.

'Aspects of learning.' *Br. J. Med. Ed.* (Studying in Depth Series), 1967, **I**, 2, 82-8.

'The future of educational research.' *Educational Research*, 1968, **10**, No. 3.

'Intellectual and emotional care.' *Nursery Journal*, 1969, **LIX**, 571, 2-11.

'Sir Fred Schonell—an obituary.' *Forward Trends*, 1969, **13**, No. 2.

'Educational research.' *European Teacher*, 1970, **7**, 2, 5-15.

'Research and educational action.' *International Review of Education*, 1970, **XVI**, 4, 484-501.

'Parents' future role in education.' *The Parent Teacher*, No. 28, Autumn 1970.

'School libraries in the 1970s.' *Education Libraries Bulletin*, Supplement 15, 1972.

(With D. S. MAY) 'Teacher training and the role of the teacher.' *London Ed. Review*, 1972, **I**, 1, 42-50.

'Problem children in schools.' *London Ed. Review*, 1973, **2**, 2, 3-21.

PAMPHLETS

Educational Research and the Needs of the Schools. National Association of Inspectors of Schools and Educational Organisers. Annual Conference, Poole, Dorset, 2 October 1959.

(With ANNA FREUD) *Enrichment of Childhood.* Nursery School Association. National Conference, London, 1960.

Procedures for the Allocation of Pupils in Secondary Education. Slough: NFER, 1963.

Guidance in Adolescence. 12th Charles Russell Memorial Lecture. National Association of Boys Clubs, London, 1964.

(With T. HUSÉN) *Educational Research and Policy-Making*. Slough: NFER, 1968.

Part One

Learning and Educational Achievement

F. *Hotyat*

1. How children learn new skills *

Learning is generally defined as a process in which a form of behaviour is modified in a more or less permanent way as a consequence of a series of experiences. Since this chapter is written within the framework set by educational psychology, we will limit the meaning of learning to that permanent modification of learning which results from teaching. To put it another way: the change brought about by a programme of deliberately chosen activities under the supervision of a teacher.

We shall look at the question only from the point of view of education strictly speaking: all the conflicting theories of psychology—associationism, conditioning, Gestalt psychology, problem-solving—can help only in part in understanding the diversity of situations met in the classroom. In any case, the results of psychological experiments are really only hypotheses awaiting verification because the factors which influence learning in the classroom are often quite different from those which operate in the laboratory where the results were obtained.

Types of skills to be learned

These are extremely varied and cannot be classified according to any single criterion.

1. From the point of view of the content of the skill, one can distinguish along the lines of Bloom's taxonomy (1956):
(*a*) Psycho-motor skills, e.g. walking, athletics;
(*b*) Knowledge and techniques, e.g. learning to read, mathematical procedures;
(*c*) Cognitive capacities, e.g. the abilities necessary to comprehend, to analyse, to synthesise, to apply and to evaluate;
(*d*) Attitudes, the complex result of a long development, e.g. critical

* Translated by Mr and Mrs A. W. Hornsey. Mr Hornsey is Senior Lecturer in Modern Languages at the University of London Institute of Education.

spirit, creativity, acceptance or rejection of certain values or certain types of thinking.

2.   From a functional point of view, the following distinction is important because it has implications for method:
(*a*)   The coordination of simultaneous actions, the classic example being the 'knack' of doing something right like planing wood or correctly pronouncing the English 'th' if your native language is French;
(*b*)   The rational and sequential organisation of simple operations like making a telephone call, making a model or solving a compound problem.

Maturation and readiness

Madame Montessori has popularised the notion of the 'psychological moment', being the point in the growth of the child when the capacity to acquire a certain skill has just emerged. This is the right moment to put the new capacity to use, as is shown by the frequency with which the child keeps coming back to his new-found skill; it is clear that he is highly motivated to exercise it.

Specialists in the field of genetic psychology (Piaget 1947) have been able to trace the way in which a new operation develops to its maturity. For example, the cycle often described in Piaget's researches consists of the following steps: a little before the child reaches the threshold of a new skill, he goes through a period when he can be seen to be practising in advance certain operations which will be necessary for the eventual mastery of the skill (this is the case with learning to walk). There follows a succession of growth stages and new levels of mastery. During each growth stage, the learner is required to reorganise himself and he feels as if he is attacking a difficult climb; at each new level of mastery, he exploits the ground he has gained and prepares for the next growing stage.

There has been some discussion of the possible effects of teaching a child a new skill in advance of, or subsequent to, the 'psychological moment'. It is agreed that too long a delay in exploiting a newly acquired capacity could only mar its development. On the other hand, the work of Arnold Gesell and other psychologists has shown that it is hopeless to try and obtain permanent results by advancing the normal time for the training in a new activity. Although experiments in very early teaching have been going on for several years, it is too soon to draw any firm conclusions from them yet. The most important verification of results in this sort of field can only occur when the whole period of the subjects' schooling is over. It is not impossible however to suppose that in some cultural environments conditions of life may accelerate or retard certain aspects of development.

School programmes do not progress along a steady gradient of difficulty; in particular, through the alternating progression of growth stages and levels of mastery, average or weak pupils manage to assimilate new bodies of knowledge with great difficulty. There are, for instance, programmes which involve concepts on an advanced level of abstraction (for example, in mathematics or chemistry) or which demand that the pupil progresses beyond concrete operational thinking to the area of logical thought (as he moves from simple mathematical projection to descriptive geometry). Similar hurdles are met in the practical work associated with training for a particular trade or profession, e.g. in understanding cross-sectional drawings of doors or windows in carpentry, or in appreciating the demands of narrow tolerances in metal work. The teaching method applied in such cases takes a variety of forms and depends on careful grading of difficulty:

(*a*)   Introduction as an *initiation*, that is to say, over a long period in which familiar concrete situations are presented which contain the difficulty in a way which allows it to be easily overcome; for example, the notion of function can be gradually acquired through the longitudinal presentation of weather charts or graphs showing the departure times of the dispatching system in the railways;

(*b*)   *Illustration*; for example, in history, the notion of the passage of time can be illustrated with a succession of historical characters from different epochs as a kind of frieze along the walls of the primary classroom;

(*c*)   By gradual steps, as in the step by step progression from the sand pit to the wall map as a means of presenting geographical data.

Incentives and motivation

To induce children to persevere in their attempts to master learning situations, many means have been tried to replace the purely arbitrary stimulations of the past.

The method of apperceptive introduction put forward by Herbart and his followers was very much in vogue in the nineteenth century: it was the teacher's task to awaken the learner's interest and curiosity about the material to be mastered. This procedure can be effective when the teacher makes the class really 'see' a problem, by recalling for instance the situation which provoked Archimedes' discovery of his principle or by recalling the experiment of Torricelli. But the systematic application of such methods often turns into an artificial game which does not fool the children.

But a child's interests veer and change continually as he grows up and are not always in harmony with long-term educational goals. Hence, teachers work on the principle of linking their curriculum with systems of motivation closely adapted to the environment, levels of attainment and particular interests of their pupils: centres of interest, small- or large-scale projects and practical experiments in the neighbourhood of the school are the most common attempts to apply this principle.

As the level of academic achievement rises, indirect motivation can be relied on more, especially when the pupil can choose a programme of study which reflects his own inclinations. In professional and technical departments, teachers of the general courses can turn to the teachers of the practical material for suggested lines of approach to stimulate interest in their particular discipline. Teachers can also tap the powerful enthusiasm of adolescents for subjects of immediate concern by basing their lessons on current problems and gradually extending them to touch on the abstract, the past and the future.

The pattern of learning

We may now turn to some educational problems related to the clear structuring of the material to be learned, graded progression of tasks, repetition and reinforcement.

Structuring

The aim of this first step is to create a mental plan of the operation to be learned; it involves an effort of comprehension, a mental picture of the component parts and how they are organised to form a whole. Once this task is completed, the pupil already has the ability to perform that operation (be it motor or cognitive) either consciously or subconsciously. Guillaume (1936) has provided us with a good example of this stage of the learning process: dressing a baby, or even just putting his coat on, is difficult for adults; partly because, when very young, the child remains completely passive throughout the operation, and partly because the adult is nervous of harming his fragile limbs. But after lots of dressing sessions, we notice that the job is becoming a little easier: the baby begins to clench his fist in anticipation because he has disliked getting his fingers stuck inside the sleeves every time; at a later stage, he also straightens his elbow, and then stiffens his shoulder. At this point, we can leave him to put his own coat on: the child has learned to dress himself unaided and the actual repetition of the action will eventually make it automatic.

Of course the structuring procedure varies according to the nature of the skill to be mastered:

1.   The mastery of a psycho-motor activity involving the coordination of simultaneous movements can rarely be analysed in words: one does not learn to swim by reading how to do it in a book. The correct mental image of the operation is usually formed and perfected by a process of trial and error on the part of the learner, though the teacher will intervene and control any possible harmful experiments. In order to exercise this control, he has recourse to various means according to the nature of the skill in question: for example, a film of a craftsman performing the particular task may be shown to an apprentice or, in the case of a pupil trying to master the pronunciation of a foreign language, tapes allow the pupil to hear his own voice as well as that of the model. Whatever the skill to be mastered, the teacher should reduce his interventions to a minimum: anticipate major areas of difficulty and deal with them before the learner begins the operation rather than interrupt in the middle of it.

2.   But as the child grows older, the operations to be learned are concerned more and more with the organisation of a series of simple actions towards a desired goal. A large number of operations fall into this category, varying from simple sensori-motor combinations to purely cognitive skills. A few examples will serve to illustrate the different methods used to establish the right 'mental picture'.

(a)   For completely manual operations, very young children are left to meet the challenge and to enjoy overcoming it, unaided, by a process of trial and error, but discreet intervention may be necessary to prevent loss of confidence by the child's choosing very unprofitable paths. Once a child has learnt to read, part of his lessons will take the form of a series of instructions to be followed, just as in everyday life he will have to interpret instructions for the use of household electrical gadgets, new materials, food products or medicines.

(b)   Many techniques involve successive actions which imply the application or condensing of a system of underlying principles, as is the case in arithmetic or algebra. With mature pupils, the structure of the successive operations is established with the help of abstract logical reasoning. With young children, for whom such a procedure would be premature, reference to concrete experience leads to the formation of a model of the desired activity which is, in the first instance, non-verbal; the scientific

B

justification and the translation of the process into a set of rules will come later, when situations have to be faced where empirical, concrete schemata are lacking. Teaching and learning are the relevant response to a problem posed, and the methodology here is thus considerably influenced by the precepts of displacing of Claparède (1930).

(c)   For the memorisation of verbal material, both traditional mnemotechnic procedures and recent experimental research (Le Ny *et al.* 1964) have established the importance of recognising links between the various items to be memorised. Research done by the Gestalt school of psychology has set out to specify the conditions best suited to efficient retention of facts. Recent research undertaken by Mandler (1967), based on the fact that only 5 to 9 items will be committed permanently to memory at one go according to the individual concerned, suggests that the material to be memorised should first be arranged in the hierarchical system of a hologram. For instance, 5 items may be picked out to start with; the next step is to make each of these 5 items the 'father' of a further 5; the same process is then followed for the third generation and it is thus possible to memorise a total of 155 items:

$$5^1 + 5^2 + 5^3 = 155$$

(d)   Depending on the standard of the pupils, the subject and the skills required to cope with the task, part of the initial steps must be left to the pupils when it comes to teaching them how to perform a mental exercise (e.g. tackling a problem or acquiring the habit of grammatical analysis to ensure correct spelling when writing French: to distinguish for example between the unsounded 's' in *allais* and the sounded 't' in *allait*).

Occasionally, the first exercises requiring the manipulation of the particular skill to be taught are given to the pupils without previous preparation: they then discuss one another's efforts in class and gradually a method emerges which is practicable and suited to the level of the class.

However, a teacher using this technique runs the risk of establishing bad habits when the material to be taught requires a rigorous discipline. Because of this danger, in spelling French where analysis of each case is essential, many teachers prefer to give directions at the start and allow the pupils to exercise proportionately more initiative as they reach a higher standard. From nine to ten years upwards, the teacher introduces one or two rules and a few minutes are spent at the beginning of each French lesson on discussing the spelling of a text two or three lines long. Whenever something occurs which the class is not completely sure of, the pupils are asked to look carefully at the sentence, to point out the particular problem and explain it orally. This same practice is followed for dictations a few months later, the children being first warned about a possible difficulty and advised to think carefully before writing. This is repeated when the dictations are corrected, though now it is one of the pupils who has made a mistake who is asked to explain the correction. At the final stage, warnings from the teacher are dispensed with, except in cases of extreme difficulty.

In short, the choice of these procedures is the result of classroom experience; very few questions of this type have been actually solved by objective research.

Training

Most of the problems here can only be answered in relation to the particular skill to be taught. Moreover, procedures are subject to continual modification as the environment and social conditions change and as technological progress makes new aids available. In this short chapter we can only touch on a few of the general problems.

1.   How effective is group work compared with individual work? A lot of research has been done on this aspect of teaching and the general conclusion is that individual work is more fruitful when dealing with simple techniques where there is nothing to be gained from an exchange of views.

But there is general agreement that more advanced intellectual operations benefit from group work. This seems to be because more suggestions are put forward; the quality of the work tends to be set by the level of the most able members of the group; since they will be judged by their peers, the individuals are keen to cooperate and to show up well; ideas proposed are subjected to immediate approval or criticism.

Pupils themselves are quick to suggest the types of work which are best done in groups; for instance, senior pupils at boarding schools said that they often did the following exercises together (Hotyat 1965): Latin translations, problems in physics and geometry, preparation of essays—all of which fit in with the criteria listed in the previous paragraph.

As to the question of the ideal size of a group doing school work, most research points to no more than three or four members; Bales (1952) has shown that in larger groups, members make less contribution, particularly the more passive ones. In addition, the smaller groups knit together better.

2.   R. Nielsen (1951) placed children representing different age-groups in situations that would encourage cooperative activities, in order to study

the genetic evolution of group work. She distinguishes distinct phases of development:

(a)   the unsociable phase from o to 3 years;

(b)   the egocentric or pre-social phase from 3-4 to 7-8 years;

(c)   the phase which marks the awakening of interest in the exploration of social activities from 7-8 to 13-14 years;

(d)   the adult phase of conscious exploration of social relationships.

3.   Amaria, Biran and Leith (1961) have studied the efficacy of group teaching in relation to ability. At the primary stage (ten-year-olds), the highest levels of mean gains are achieved by children with a below-average IQ in unstreamed groups and this remains true even in tests which measure the degree of transfer by examining material not previously taught. The results are less clear at the secondary stage; in particular some pupils were not well integrated in their group.

Repetition and reinforcement

It used to be considered that constant repetition was the basic essential of practice if any real progress was to be achieved. But as a result of a good deal of research, we now know that other factors are also important, notably: active participation of the pupil, reinforcement after each stage of the learning process, adaptation of reward and punishment to the pupil's age, a carefully graded series of sub-goals leading up to the final goal.

The success achieved by programmed learning has confirmed how vitally important it is to divide complicated material into small parts and to offer the learner immediate reinforcement after each part has been completed. These findings have, for example, caused the value of home-work to be queried again because there is dissatisfaction about the time lapse between the work being finished and being returned corrected to the pupil. At primary level, homework is fast disappearing as a teaching procedure, although many parents continue to demand that it should be set. At the secondary stage, the position is quite different. Here homework affords training in self-discipline, though no teacher should be allowed to make excessive demands (Hotyat 1965).

Suitable methods of reinforcement change with the age of the pupils: young children respond best to tangible rewards and direct personal encouragement whereas adolescents, who may well have long-term goals in mind, gain satisfaction from the anonymous and functional approval inherent in making responses which are correct.

Laboratory studies of rates of progress in learning abound. Research has, for example, attempted to explain the frequency with which falling curves on graphs of progress appear when simple tasks are being taught; or to explain the sigmoid lines in which the beginning corresponds to a phase of comprehension and organisation; or to explain the succession of plateaux and steep upward curves on the graphs, the latter resulting from sudden new motivation or more effective methods of working. In the same way, research has gone on over a number of years into the effect of the timing of the repetition of material, particularly in connection with efficient memorisation (Jost's studies in this field date back to 1897).

To what extent has all this research affected the practice of teaching? The idea of self-evaluation, as a better stimulus to progress and leading to an increase in personal responsibility, is gaining ground only slowly. Norms and curves of results are already widely used by athletes, but their performances are susceptible to fairly straightforward measurement. There is much more caution shown on the subject of pupils assessing their own performance in schools. But it is spreading, particularly in subjects where standardised tests of attainment are available. Especially in the field of secondary and higher education, self-instruction goes hand in hand with the willingness to accept such audio-visual aids as the teaching machine, the tape recorder, the language laboratory and closed-circuit television combined with video-recording.

In recent years there has been a revival of interest in overlearning and the periodic relearning of essential skills and areas of knowledge. As has been suggested previously by Krueger (1894), the practice of overlearning at 50 per cent has been confirmed as effective. Thus specialists in oral language teaching using the audio-visual, structural-global method accept the need to extend learning beyond the minimum requirement in the progressive development of their programmes; they therefore envisage the following sequence of steps: comprehension and assimilation, habitualisation, guided structuralisation and automatisation, spontaneous structuralisation (and some would add: saturation) (De Grève and Van Passel 1968).

There has been less reference to the need for periodic diagnostic testing and relearning, perhaps because many of the important skills, such as reading and writing, are constantly in use in daily life. But many subjects are not in constant use and are gradually forgotten. This applies, for example, to some procedures in mathematics, in making measurements, in reading maps, skills that are mastered at primary level. Unless these techniques are taught only when they are needed for immediate use, they must be retained through periodic relearning if they are not simply to atrophy. When some international research work was carried out using children of 13 to 14 years from twelve countries (Foshay *et al.* 1962), it was found that the profile of their standardised marks (around zero mean) of the Belgian sample was depressed on tests of comprehension, probably because, though this type of exercise was practised regularly in the primary schools, it was superseded in the secondary schools by literary analysis alone.

Variability in performance

Studies have been going on for a long time into the factors which underlie the considerable diversity in the results of teaching. The factors are numerous for each different skill being taught and no single one can account completely for the variability.

1.   A part of the differences can be attributed to the attitude of the learner and this is governed partly by his past experience and partly by the tension produced by his wish to perform well (a wish which improves the performance of some and inhibits that of those who are overanxious or lacking in confidence). This factor is so important in the teaching of handicapped children that the teacher's first concern must be the creation of educational situations aimed at restoring the pupils' self-confidence and will to succeed.

With a view to gaining a more accurate knowledge of the concepts of under- and over-achievement, attempts have been made to analyse the concept of perseverance, that is to say the time actually devoted by a pupil to learning a particular skill as compared to the time he should ideally have spent on it to enable him to achieve complete mastery (Carroll 1963). In this connection, several studies have demonstrated the absolute and relative values of levels of aspiration and expectation as factors contributing to the success of teaching (Robaye 1957). In French-speaking countries, teachers using Freinet's methods of individual teaching pay particular attention to helping and training their new pupils to plan their weekly work along lines which will allow a high degree of achievement of the aims incorporated in their plans.

2.   Many studies have attempted to assess the role of the pupils' IQ in the variability of performances achieved in the classroom. Most of the correlations are indeed positive but not high. For example, when comparing all the data from one class—intelligence tests and performances in subject examinations—there is considerable variability in the results of the pupils in the middle range of intelligence, but even at the extremes, there

are weak pupils who nevertheless achieve satisfactory results. These findings are encouraging for the educationist for they suggest the possibility of improvement in the efficacy of the learning process if methods can be developed which take into account all the factors involved in progress.

3.   Criticism has been growing of the use of the normal curve of distribution of marks in refining examination marks. The gaussian curve is not however an irrefutable truth, a gift from heaven: it is simply a picture of the consequences of the random distribution of numerous factors that influence the scores of a sample group of people in an aptitude test, whereas the task in the classroom is to reduce the element of random chance by eliminating conditions which would otherwise reduce the level of performance. Wittrock (1969) advocates a return to methods of evaluation which are based on measurement and assessment of individual progress rather than on the identification of individual differences. Such methods would allow the early diagnosis of factors in the material or human environment which could have hindered the learning process, so that they may be eliminated before the process reaches an advanced stage.

Bloom and his colleagues (1968) have studied, at university level, the factors influencing the poor results in written examinations of those students whose scores did not reach the top grades. They were surprised to discover an attitude which accepted as normal that 30 per cent of any group would have low marks. Bloom's hypothesis is that students with low marks assimilate material slowly; their methods of work may be time-wasting and leave certain points unclear, and there may be a lack of drive if the teaching is not attuned to their type of intelligence or personality. He believes that these handicaps are not insurmountable and lists various methods which might be used to overcome them: work in groups of two or three students who would help one another to come to grips with difficult problems, regular help from a personal tutor, access to programmed material, concrete examples or access to audio-visual systems. At the beginning of the academic year 1965-66, he prepared a strategy which involves the use of these methods and the training of the students to see the examinations not as a competition but as part of their training to reach a high level in their speciality. The questions set in 1966 were as difficult as those set in 1965; while only 20 per cent of the students were awarded A grades before the experiment, 80 per cent and 90 per cent received A in 1966 and 1967 respectively. An improvement in methods and attitudes had led to a clear improvement in performance.

Transfer and generalisation

1.   The consciences of nineteenth-century teachers were not troubled by the problem of the transfer of knowledge and skills: confident of the truth of the psychology of the time, which saw intellectual functions as emanating from autonomous faculties, they regarded the study of the classical languages and occasionally mathematics as privileged subjects, which possessed the virtues of a sort of intellectual philosophers' stone.

Modern analyses have not confirmed this optimistic point of view. Experiments have shown that spontaneous transfer is usually negligible or non-existent. Moreover, the elusive concept of intelligence, seen sometimes as a single unit and sometimes as a multiplicity of features, has not received a clear definition: Dewey's schema indicates the stages but not the functional units involved in the effort of objective adjustment to a new situation; on the other hand, pluralistic conceptions, bordering on Guilford's 'structure of intellect', have been aiming at introducing order into the great diversity of human cognitive activities.

We should not forget that even Guilford's model constitutes only a simple schema and that each of the 120 items, far from having a separate existence of its own, is the synthesis of a large number of activities with aims in common but different content and procedural approaches. For example, exercises in comprehension of the written word have as their common goal the assimilation of the thoughts of another person, but they differ in content and language, in the internal logic of each branch of learning, in the considerable variety of the questions to be considered. Moreover, it is rare for the effort involved in a comprehension exercise to be limited to comprehension pure and simple, for this is constantly being overlaid with the work of analysis, synthesis and critical evaluation.

From the point of view of genetics, the steps and levels in the educational development of skills are seen to ripen at different times according to the matter concerned. What is more, especially in the case of young children, new knowledge and skill have a tendency to be placed into rigid, watertight compartments which make its acquisition sterile. As our pupils think aloud, we can observe this factor if, for example, they are trying to apply their mathematical knowledge to overcome some difficulty. While mature adults would in such cases show extreme mobility in their thinking and apply the content of their thoughts in many different directions, beginners make fewer and fewer hypotheses and end up by falling completely silent as though their thoughts had become completely bogged down. The educational lesson to be drawn from these observations is as follows: teaching leading to the assimilation of a piece of knowledge or a technique is only truly complete when a variety of exercises of these new acquisitions has caused them to be integrated into the totality of previously acquired knowledge or skill.

Such considerations should cause teachers to plan their contribution to the intellectual growth of their pupils according to the following principles:

(*a*) The development of cognitive ability is not the prerogative of any single subject: all branches of study have a contribution to make;

(*b*) As for all learning situations, education should be active: pupils should be confronted with novel situations which they see as obstacles to the fulfilment of their inclinations. They are then provoked to answer these challenges either through individual or cooperative efforts according to the complexity of the challenge;

(*c*) Since the techniques of cognitive activity follow a more diffuse and sophisticated pattern of growth than those associated with motor operations (e.g. the development of reversible thinking), it follows that the same steps will have to be gone over again when dealing with less familiar topics or with higher levels of thought. It will be necessary to draw attention to the common ground between skills with broadly similar aims, to show general principles and avoid rigidly watertight areas of learning so that the pupil, at the right moment, will be ready to accept principles of organisation and generalisation consistent with the growth of efficient intellectual activity.

2.   The social problem of developing flexibility in the use of skills has become particularly important in the field of vocational training because technical change is occurring so rapidly, and changes in the nature of work and in the provision of services are brought about by complete changes in industry. In addition, the narrowly specialised job which a man has to do in the huge factory of today and the increase in automation have given a new meaning to the concept of 'qualification' in the sphere of manual work: less dexterity and initiative are called for and more power of concentration together with a minimum of 'knowledge', and a greater ability to adapt to new work demands.

The industrialised nations are making the effort to find solutions to these problems. In France, Friedmann has proposed a widening of the theoretical and technological training which apprentices receive; in the USSR, a system has been worked out which combines general training with a polytechnic training related to the preoccupations of local industry; in other countries, there are moves to delay the point at which commitment to a given job is necessary by providing multi-disciplinary training programmes based on methods allowing observation and progressive orientation over a wide field during cycles of two to four years. It is difficult to suggest an ideal solution: economic needs are different in different countries; and what is more, those responsible for technical education are torn between two almost irreconcilable requirements: the demands of industry for employees who are immediately fully productive, as against the humane wish to prepare today's pupils to meet in the most satisfactory way possible any eventual needs for complete change in the future.

To what extent are the intellectual aspects of personality gradually moulded by the learning process and by individual emotional responses to successes and failures? Krathwohl, Bloom and Masia (1964), taking as their guideline the internalisations of the influence of education, distinguish the following successive periods, which are further subdivided into smaller stages of progress: the reception of ideas, the active acceptance, and the differentiated valuation of subject matters, modes of thought and methods of work. Over the years, there develops a definite hierarchy of different values as the result of the combined influence of school and the world outside, and this gradually becomes permanent. Out of a mixture of satisfying and dissatisfying experiences, special preferences emerge and dominate until they form stable mental types characterised by certain attitudes and particular ways of thinking. In school life, certain significant events, 'peak learning experiences', can also be decisive moments which may even stimulate awareness of vocation: a personal triumph applauded by the rest of the class, situations of great emotional intensity, or which bring to light an outstanding talent, or a deeply satisfying human relationship with a teacher.

Torsten Husén

2. The purposes of futurologic studies in education

Introduction

The young people we now have in our schools will be entering the most productive, and publicly the most influential, period of their lives in twenty to thirty years, i.e. towards the end of this century. In planning the objectives of the education that the school gives them, and the content of the instruction they are subject to, we must obviously consider that it is not today's society—much less yesterday's—that these youngsters will take charge of, but rather a society which lies only a few paltry (but oh so important) decades ahead of us: we have only to reflect upon the process of change that has swept across this society at an accelerated rate, especially since 1945. Accordingly, contemporary educational planning must allow for the effects it is likely to have on the society—not to mention the world —that we are going to have twenty to thirty years from now. Not even that will suffice, however. Let me take the following illustration. The Swedish *Riksdag* passed legislation on a new system of teacher training in 1967, and the first crop of teachers under the new system emerged in 1969 (Marklund and Söderberg 1967; Husén and Boalt 1968; Marklund 1966, 1968). These teachers are expected to be active professionally for an average thirty-five to forty-five years. They will be teaching young people whose own productive lives will run for about fifty years. This is by way of saying that the teacher-training decisions taken during the 1960s will have repercussions up to the mid-twenty-first century.

The foregoing remarks should suffice to justify futurologic studies in education of the type which seeks to define the consequences of present-day planning and decisions for tomorrow's school. Could it be that the schools of three decades hence will bear little if any resemblance to the time-honoured type we know today? In the present century, at any rate, 'education' and 'school' have increasingly come to be regarded as synonymous concepts. In Sweden, the establishment of a compulsory elementary school was accompanied by the formal abolition of the guild system, within whose institutional framework training for the handicrafts had taken place. The apprenticeship system for training in the trades continued to linger on for some time. But during the course of the past century education has increasingly come to be carried on in the institutional forms that regular schooling has established with grades, teacher-led class instruction, tests, marks and examinations. From time immemorial, moreover, we have learned to regard education as a matter exclusively associated with the years of our youth.

In other words, the basic and applied knowledge and skills needed to make our way in the world are supposed to be acquired early in life. But already at the beginning of this century the free and voluntary adult education programmes sponsored by the various people's movements developed apace, and to a large extent, at least in Scandinavia, these were detached from the institutional school system. The non-formal voluntary system, by means of study circles and evening classes, long focused on giving a basic general education, on imparting certain skills in, for example, the native language and the society-and-nature orientation that the great masses did not receive from the elementary public education, which after all was rather meagre. In other words, no question of training for careers or of imparting saleable skills was involved. But during the past decade we have been witnessing, at least in Sweden, the onsurge of adult education which aims at bread-and-butter goals. Both the traditional programmes of adult education and, to some extent, the vocationally oriented system of adult education, have operated outside the traditional school framework. As regards the voluntary adult education programmes, one can discern a deliberate effort to move away from the traditional forms and towards the goals they serve.

Recent developments in adult education have opened our eyes to the fact that education takes in a great deal more than mere formal schooling in the traditional sense. The young people attending school today belong to the generation that has been exposed to television from pre-school years and that will be exposed, as transmission time increases, just as much to what comes out of the magical cathode ray tube as to what comes out of a teacher at his classroom desk. A moment's reflection tells us that the school's sphere of influence has also diminished in this respect. In our changing society, education is in process of becoming a lifelong concern for the great majority of people, and thus more than a matter to which one dedicates the years of childhood and youth. In that connection the school as an institution—and under forms that are changing drastically—will answer for only certain limited educational functions.

These sketchy indications should suffice to provide a general background to my principal topic, namely the tasks and methods of futurologic studies and the visions of education that may reasonably be contemplated for the coming turn of the century.

Three cardinal purposes for futurology

What are the cardinal purposes in education that can be imagined for futurology? As far as I can see, three lines of development suggest themselves.

1. Research can be confined to identifying the future consequences of contemporary planning and policy decisions relating to school organisation, construction, curricula, teaching aids and teacher training. The layout given to a new school plant implies certain definite notions as to how work will be carried on in the projected building for many decades to come. A structure full with bearing walls, and divided up into classrooms of a certain size, presupposes that these rooms will have a specified number of pupils—regarded as normal for so-called class instruction in today's situation—who are going to imbibe wisdom that is mainly imparted by specially trained teachers. Planning of this kind more or less rules out certain alternatives where the school's work-practices are concerned, alternatives based on a common assumption that practices will vary and that pupils will become more active. In any event and at the very least, such planning has the effect of making these alternatives less likely to materialise.

The example just cited illustrates how important it is to clarify the long-range implications of today's school decisions. It also illustrates a vital thesis: futurologists do not aspire—or should not aspire—to explain what is *supposed* to happen but what *can* happen. In his book *Dialog i det fria* (Dialogue in the Open), the Swedish writer Sven Fagerberg has a section he calls 'The Soothsayers', especially inspired by an issue about the year 2000 that the American periodical *Daedalus*, put out in the summer of 1967 (see Bell 1967). This issue was given over to presenting the results of deliberations made by a committee appointed by the US National Academy of Science. Fagerberg has this to say: 'Forecasts have . . . a great importance; they compel us to analyse the here and now and to try to understand what is happening at this moment. But they can never tell us what is going to happen.' In this way investigation into the future can also help to create that future.

As long as the investigator sticks to analysing the import and consequences of contemporary planning and policy decisions, he stands on pretty solid ground and does not have to rely too much on what he sees in the crystal ball—or whatever metaphor one wishes to use to characterise the doings of futurologists. But his task immediately becomes more difficult if he takes a step further and extrapolates the statistical trends that are now observable. And he will be tackling a really formidable task if he goes yet one more step to identify those general development patterns and value trends that will dominate society a quarter-century hence. I shall have something more to say about these riskier ventures presently. But first some more viewpoints about the task of making clear the nature of the ultimate commitment that follows from decisions already taken or implemented.

I assume that all parties endorse the rational principle—by paying lip service, if nothing else—that educational planning, as well as social planning in general, in our changeable society ought to aim at maximum flexibility, the object being to keep open as many acceptable future alternatives as possible. That is a demand which ought to be imposed on those responsible for planning physical facilities and building-design guiding school construction. Or to put this principle the other way round, contemporary planning should rule out as few alternatives as possible. This means that the futurologist ought to study present-day policy decision-making from two angles.

First, do today's planning and political decisions harmonise with the general objectives of public policy that have been adopted *for the long run*? Second, what future alternatives have been excised by today's actions? When the Swedish authorities decided, a few decades ago, to go in radically for centralising schools in urban areas and shutting down the majority of the small rural schools, they were motivated by the prospect of certain administrative benefits, and perhaps economic ones as well: since large-scale educational operation would be more advantageous than continuing with the little red schoolhouse, the latter ought to be closed down. However, the transportation of young people to large urban schools which followed from the closures combined with the abandonment of farms to generate a vast depopulation of the countryside. In a recent study, Dr Sixten Marklund (1969) has shown that small schools offering middle-department courses (i.e. grades 4 to 6) do not perform worse than the large schools, indicating that the pure educational advantages of doing away with all the many small rural schools at the lower and middle levels have been of dubious value. On top of that, the social and economic impact on sparsely populated areas has been highly negative.

Politicians are easily tempted to look for short-term solutions to current problems—which is perhaps understandable considering that they are reminded of their mortality at fairly brief intervals, i.e. at the regularly recurring elections. Hence they readily go astray when confronted with situations where they have to choose between that which imperils themselves in the short run and that which imperils the voters, that is, society, in the long run.

The administrators, especially if they work in a strongly bureaucratic setting, risk (for partially different reasons) losing sight not only of the future but of the basic meaning of the tasks they have in hand at the moment. Current worries, the day-to-day routine, often assume overwhelming proportions, or are perceived to be so overwhelming that no time is left for thinking in terms of the 'long pull'. Now it happens to be the very essence of bureaucracy not only to build empires but also to become so engrossed in the formal and technical perfection of a present preoccupation that questioning the real meaning of what one is doing seldom, if ever, comes to mind. A brilliant, and illuminating, document on this point is to be found in *Grisjakten* (The Pig Hunt), the book written by P. C. Jersild. Secretary Siljeberg is so absorbed with the task his boss in the Ministry has assigned to him—to exterminate all pigs in Sweden as efficiently as possible (starting with the experimental district of the island of Gothland)—that he never stops to ask what purpose all this technical perfection is really supposed to serve.

There is something else which impedes the bureaucratic-political establishment from enquiring into the future consequences of its present actions. During the past five or six years we have seen how protests— voiced not least by today's youth—have become increasingly clamorous against the imputed penchant of authorities to plan and decide over the head of the common man (Keniston 1960, 1968). It is contended, not without reason, that an inner circle of technicians and experts, political experts included, steamroller decisions on city planning, road building, school construction and water impounding which fly in the face of what a growing grass-roots opinion perceives to be desirable long-range objectives. One example, now very much the object of controversy, is the extent to which private automobiles should be allowed to circulate freely in downtown areas. A great deal of prestige readily tends to hang on questions of this kind. That which was planned a long time ago, when the conditions were different, builds up such powerful convictions and momentum among the bureaucrats that it rolls on with juggernaut force. Experts and persons in authority who have long worked on and sweated over the issues thereby feel they have become privy to a higher insight, and not seldom they put on a stiff and even supercilious tone towards the protesters. In other words, they 'know better'.

2.   The futurologist can try to determine certain trends expressed in numerical terms, such as school enrolments, development of costs and use of teaching aids, and then extrapolate these trends, i.e. find out in which direction the curves are pointing. This kind of peering into the future, which amounts to drawing upon demographic data to compute the need for school plants and their sizes, has become routine nowadays in both the local and central school planning that is pursued in most quarters. Yet it was not more than a few decades ago that no one in Scandinavia even seemed to think it possible to predict with great accuracy the number of children that would be starting school six or seven years after a certain cohort was born!

Even so, attempts to extrapolate trend curves can have their parlous sides. An example is the estimate of the supply of and demand for special-subject teachers that was made by the 1955 Commission of Enquiry into the Swedish Universities. When the Commission published its special report in 1958 (Government Printing Office, Stockholm), it went on record as saying that secondary school teachers would already be in surplus by the early 1960s, and that the surplus would grow as the decade progressed. The analyses were based on the reported number of secondary school leavers having completed a *gymnasium* program and passed the *studentexamen*, together with the number of matriculants and degree takers at the faculties of arts and sciences up to the mid-1950s. It could be established that the number of leavers from the pre-university school by and large had increased linearly from 1940 to 1955. The assumption was that this would continue till the mid-1960s, at which point the curve would level off, since the increase could not very well be expected to go on as in the past. Further, it was assumed that first-year enrolments in the arts and sciences faculties would not mount substantially. Lastly, the experiences gained from the pilot programme with the nine-year comprehensive school were drawn upon for that proportion of pupils in the upper department (grades 7 to 9) who had made so-called academic options, which was largely identifiable with the percentage of an age-group who had elected to study two foreign languages.

It did not take more than a few years for the actual course of events to confute all these assumptions. The curve for secondary school leavers turned out to increase not linearly but exponentially, that is, at a geometric rate. Not only that, but the subsequent course of events has been described as an 'educational explosion', and rightly so. By the mid-1960s, when the incidence of *studentexamen* was supposed to have levelled off, the acceleration was greater than ever. Far from stagnating, new admissions to the arts and science faculties increased sharply. The number of pupils with so-called academic choices grew apace, especially after the basic school reform of 1962, so that the proportion of pupils making such choices rose to more than two-thirds from about one-third during the 1950s. With the introduction of a universal basic school in 1962, followed by reforms of secondary education in 1964, the educational opportunities were expanded far beyond the prospects envisioned in 1958, and all the earlier forecasts were shattered in the bargain. The predicted surplus of Swedish and modern language teachers in the early 1960s never eventuated. As for the liberal arts graduates, the much-talked-about surplus turned out to be a hampering shortage, which for a time even exceeded the shortage of mathematics and science teachers in certain parts of the country (Government Printing Office, Stockholm 1964).

I have not picked out this example in order to appear wise after the event, but because I feel a generous helping of imagination is called for when one tries to extrapolate development trends. In this particular case the acceleration tendencies which already existed ought to have given cause to think about the role of education both as investment and consumption, and hence about its attractiveness as well. If such reflections had been allowed to govern, the forecasts could have been corrected. It should also have been possible to predict the short-range effects of broadened educational opportunities.

3.   Social and political values are legitimate objects of research for the futurologist. For example, he can study how pluralistic and monolithic societies respectively function in educational terms. However, the futurologist cannot avoid being drawn into the debate about *what kind of future society* is being sought. In entering this debate he can indirectly help to create values and gain their wider adoption. The appearance of tomorrow's society does not follow in any clear-cut and mechanical way from the scientific and technological potentials we have today, and probably not from the ones at our command tomorrow, either. The crux is *if* and *how* we intend to use these potentials. That is determined by the social preferences, i.e. by the prevailing values. Medical science can give us formulas on leading a way of life that will keep us in good shape physically and mentally. But none the less we put ourselves in situations, both on and off the job, that induce stress and break us down physically and mentally. We allow the waste products of technology to spoil our environment to the stage where it poses health hazards not only for coming generations but also for ourselves.

Will the values that fix priorities and preferences look essentially different two or three decades from now? Will science and technology be more greatly harnessed towards creating a better and healthier environment? And what about notions as to what constitutes the 'good' life, the life worth living? The Protestant ethic (*pace* Max Weber), under which everyone was supposed to stick to his last, and which suffused the life-ideal of a large part of my generation in the Western world (and in the socialistic countries, too, for that matter) may be superseded by another ethic. As long as the 'sweat-it-out' ethic dominates, the awarding of marks on the basis of individual performances in competition will continue to dominate in our schools. The curriculum developers can then talk as piously as they want about group work, cooperation, consideration and social maturity.

Many signs suggest that here, as in so many other areas, the revolt of youth is touching off what Nietzsche called a 'reappraisal of all values' (Keniston 1960, 1968). Thus we have a growing, younger generation who oppose the toiling philosophy of their elders and who no longer want to give top priority to traditional status-promoting achievements in school and the job world. Obviously, such a reappraisal cannot help but strongly influence the school's assessment of the progress its pupils are making.

Hence one of the cardinal tasks for futurology will be to venture predictions about how priorities are going to look in another few decades. What will then be considered essential and inessential? What will one be living for? All of us have personal experiences of how the value accents can shift in a relatively short time. My own generation was not confronted with the problems that relate to the atomic bomb and the developing countries. We rested, if not securely then ingenuously, in the assurance that the Western way of life was superior and our technical civilisation unbeatable. There was no talk of technology being able to harm us in any way; it could only make life richer, better and elevate us to higher and higher standards of living.

I do not propose here to elaborate on how one undertakes to find out about tomorrow's value priorities. If we look at what has happened to change social and political values during the past century, we often detect certain advance signals of what is in store where needs and values are concerned. Such a study will disclose that events constantly thrust up avant-gardists, whose ideas and reactions portend the coming shape of dominant values. These signals that point ahead to the future are to be found among writers, artists and intellectuals, but even more so among articulate young people (US Office of Education 1967).

These young people will take over the society of tomorrow. By investigating what they hold to be questions of vital importance, we can arrive at a broader understanding not only of what they accord top priority as young people, but also of what they may be expected to consider most essential in their adult years. The Swedish National Board of Education recently published an attitude survey whose main purpose was to provide source data for instruction in religion (1969). A questionnaire administered to 1,300 pupils in grade 9 showed that racial problems, international problems and questions of human dignity headed the list of philosophical and ethical topics which concerned pupils at the age of sixteen.

The American investigators who concern themselves with educational policy research have made extremely interesting attempts to map out how vital questions are perceived by more articulate and 'deviant' youth, respectively (US Office of Education 1967). A group of high school students, all of them engaged in putting out 'underground' school newspapers, were invited to a conference, where they gave uninhibited expression to their views of the older generation and the existing society, and portrayed the kind of society they would like to have in the future. Another study included the 'hippies' of San Francisco. A third tied in to an ongoing international study in twenty-five countries which seeks to elucidate the value orientations, attitudes and political opinions of university undergraduates.

When I read the analysis of the taped proceedings from the conference attended by the young high school editors, I could not escape the reflection that young people now seem to be reacting in the same way more or less universally. After all, these are individuals who experience the world and its problems more directly and tangibly, not least through the medium of television, than earlier generations, and for whom there exist quite different means than in the past for the common sharing of experience.

According to these youngsters, the school is out of touch with the important things that are happening in the world and is also trying to protect the pupils against unpleasant realities. They consider themselves 'manipulated', with the school acting as a propaganda machine. One of them said: 'The school system has become an efficient factory in which we are the raw material, who under the pressure of the marking system are turned into automatons and conformists for sale to the highest bidders in the business world.' Another student said: 'What I want more than anything else in the school is interaction between ideas and feelings, and not just neutral, grey knowledge. I want us to get accustomed to people trying to convince us about things.'

I should like to comment briefly on both these quotations, since I picked them out in order to illustrate a favourite idea of mine. The day cannot be far off when we stop adhering to the illusion that textbooks or teaching aids in general are supposed to present 'objective' knowledge

(Swedish National Board of Education 1965). Efforts in that direction make the books so neuter and dull that they cannot possibly stimulate the motivation of pupils. The latter-day debate in Sweden, for instance, about the tacit value assumptions in the textbooks have shown us that we must try another approach. Quite simply, this means that pupils must be put in touch with the debate and clash of opinions in the larger society outside the school; in other words, that the school systematically expose its pupils to these views and train them in their discussion. We shall be living in a society where intentions are becoming more important than opinions.

Futurology, not least that concerned with development trends under alternative 2 above, confronts this crucial question: What trends shall be selected for extrapolation? Some of these trends will be decisively influenced by the policy that is based on future assessments of priorities. Other trends will probably remain more stable. It therefore becomes essential to design 'alternative futures', all according to the congeries of assumptions one makes (Helmer *et al.* 1966).

As for the type of society represented by the industrial countries, it is likely that several of these trends will be reinforced in the future. Just how they will develop mathematically, i.e. linearly or exponentially, will depend *inter alia* on the future's value preferences.

We cannot devise sensible future alternatives unless two fundamental conditions are in hand: (1) we regard education as an integrated system, which means we do not confine ourselves to the school-type sub-systems in the conventional sense; and (2) we view the educational system in its social, economic and political context. What this boils down to is an attempt to design 'comprehensive' future alternatives (Ziegler and Marien 1969).

The factors which characterise the educational system as such are here called endogenous, whereas those influences which derive from the total social context are called exogenous. Accordingly, efforts to design alternative futures must embrace certain assumptions (more or less correlated with one another) concerning both kinds of factors, on the one hand assumptions about the society at large and on the other about the educational system as such.

Assumptions about the society at large

1.   Economic growth will offer opportunities for increased consumption in different respects (better material standard, more leisure, more education and culture).

2. The process of change will accelerate in essential respects, e.g. concerning the manufacture of goods and the provision of services.

3. Greater international exposure is to be expected by virtue of mass media and travels.

4. An accelerating flow of information will have to be coped with both on the production side (scientific research) and on the distribution side (mass media, computer technology).

5. Gainful employment as a means of obtaining life's necessities will become increasingly unimportant. An overabundance of goods and services in the highly industrialised countries will be available to the masses.

6. Increased influence for experts, with a tendency towards meritocracy.

7. Increased pluralism, at least for a transitional period, as regards life outlooks and values.

8. It will be increasingly difficult to maintain a balance between the ecological system and technology (owing to pollution and ravages of nature).

These assumptions obviously present varying degrees of plausibility. The first four appear to intercorrelate highly and their current manifestations are so patent that they should be considered very plausible. By contrast, the four last assumptions are more debatable, one reason being that contemporary values will supposedly carry over by and large to the future, e.g. that education will continue to be a strong status-promoting factor, or that technological advances which make for greater benefits now are bought at the price of tomorrow's devastation. To my mind, the most debatable assumption is the one about increased pluralism.

General assumptions about the educational system

Now, what assumptions can we make about the future educational system? Before going into details, I should like to single out what ought to be regarded as the most important overlapping conditions for tomorrow's learning society, where it will become increasingly urgent to work out 'systems solutions' and not merely short-ranging partial solutions (Coombs 1968). Three such conditions make it particularly acute to formulate systems solutions, namely (1) the enrolment explosion, the increased proportions of more and more cohorts who are going in for full-time education; (2) the knowledge explosion, which aggravates the problem of processing, storing and communicating information; and (3) the need to individualise instruction, that is, to enable every individual to learn at the pace and with the breadth and depth that suits him best, in short the demand for greater specificity in the process of imparting knowledge and skills. Individualisation in our schools will soon become a necessity, not a luxury as heretofore.

What can be specifically assumed about the future educational system that looks more or less plausible?

1.   Education is going to be a lifelong process. The type of school associated with youth will not provide the fare on which one can subsist for all time.

2.   Education will not have clearly defined 'cut-offs' as in the past, beginning with an entrance examination and ending with a near-dramatic climax, such as a secondary school examination or a university degree. It will become more of a continuous process, both as regards its effluxion over time and its involvement in the other functions of life.

3.   Education will take on a more informal character as it becomes accessible to more and more individuals. In addition to 'learning centres', facilities will be provided for learning at home and at the workplace, e.g. by the installation of terminals.

4.   Formal education of the type that used to take place in conventional school plants will, as it becomes accessible to more and more individuals, also become more meaningful and relevant in terms of its applications.

5.   To an ever increasing extent, the educational system will become dependent on large supporting organisations or supporting systems. Agencies of this kind, whether they be public or private, are needed to produce systems of teaching aids, systems of information processing, and multi-media instructional materials. The information systems arrived at will consist of carefully tried-and-tested storage and retrieval components. One of the problems involved will be to create 'compatibility' between medium and receiver.

For me it stood out as fairly self-evident more than ten years ago that the basic school of the future would have to concentrate on inculcating certain fundamental learning skills. It would have to impart skills and knowledge for two purposes: to train for general citizenship and to qualify the young for the initial training needed for certain occupations. Further, it would have to prepare the young for changing careers, for instance by providing a basic repertoire of skills as well as attitudes of flexibility and a taste for more, a motivation for going on with education.

In the light of these remarks, the following objectives strike me as paramount. Some of them may be regarded as controversial because they proceed from values which also form part and parcel of political judgments.

1.   It will be increasingly important for democracy to create the broadest possible frame of reference for knowledge, skills and attitudes. The production and uses of information will become more and more specialised. This will readily lead to rule by specialists and experts, which brings formalism and alienation in its train. At the same time that scientific research and high-level education become increasingly important to society, the merits attached to them increase concomitantly. We seem to be headed towards a meritocracy. Among other things, a common frame of reference means making initial provision for a common liberal schooling to the greatest extent, with vocationally oriented specialisation to follow much later. The development of communications skills should be so greatly emphasised that the maximum number of citizens will be enabled to speak the same language and hence understand one another.

2.   Basic schooling ought to be of the kind that lays the groundwork for re-educability, for instance by providing what was referred to above as an adequate basic repertoire of skills and the ability to assimilate further knowledge.

3.   The school ought to instil receptivity to change, in other words a flexible attitude conducive to a willingness to go ahead both with general education and vocational training. It should get across a realisation that the whole of life will be one long continuation school.

4.   The school must prepare its pupils to live in a society of pluralistic values. Among other things, this means developing individual ability to pick and choose on the basis of certain criteria of authenticity.

5.   Schooling for internationalism and the defeat of present-day educational provincialism is necessary if the world is going to survive.

6.   It will be necessary to build up skills to deal with the ever more torrential flow of information unless we are to be swept away by it. Among these skills are computer language and technology.

7.   Schooling for a life where gainful employment and recreation (in the old sense) will become less and less important, and where 'work' will increasingly take on the character of self-realisation.

8.   Schooling for comprehension of the importance of maintaining the ecological system and technology in balance (involving the whole complex of problems which relate to such things as pollution of air, water and soil, and the wanton exploitation of natural resources).

9.   Schooling in the ability to live as an independent individual, without necessarily having to rely on support in some primary group such as the family.

As I see it, a crucial aspect will be the extent to which education is going to function as a social mobility factor. Will it become increasingly important as a determinant of status (to judge from current tendencies)? Must we anticipate that the educational system, as regards its school-type sub-systems, will remain pretty much institutionalised? If so, the outlook is for greater bureaucratisation in that the system will be run by an establishment of highly educated bureaucrats.

Specific assumptions about education

1.   General education and vocational training will be more and more interwoven, simply because it will not be possible to predict what specific vocational attainments will be needed in the future. Paradoxically, general education (in the form of a 'basic repertoire' of fundamental skills and knowledge) will be the best kind of vocational training. Basic schooling will constitute the foundation for re-educability.
2.   Basic schooling will aim to accommodate the broadest possible common frame of reference of knowledge, skills and attitudes to cope with an era of ever increasing specialisation.
3.   Skills (above all those which help in the assimilation of knowledge) will acquire greater importance at the expense of specific pieces of information. It will be impossible to uphold the traditional encyclopedic ideal of education.
4.   Instruction will become more and more individualised (for instance as more technical resources are brought into play). Teachers will be 'replaceable' by technical aids to a limited extent only, since the central element of pedagogical activity is the personal contact between teacher and pupil. The teacher's duties will be to plan, support and evaluate the course of progress for the individual pupil.
5.   The educative role in a wide sense of the school (as an institution) will decline in importance as increased leisure confers greater influence on the family and the peer groups. Mass media will extend their influence, and television especially so by virtue of lengthened transmission times and an increased number of channels.
6.   Education in the formal schooling sense tends to become more expensive. Since more and more young people (and adults) are studying, while annual costs per pupil are rising concurrently, it appears that the margin set by the overall allocation of resources will soon become so narrow that far-reaching rationalisations in order to achieve a more efficient utilisation of resources will have to be put into effect. These may

be expected to alter fundamental aspects of the school as an institution. That is likely to have radical repercussions on the erection of school buildings, since their design inevitably proceeds from assumptions about the uses of these buildings for several decades to come.

Now it may be asked: Isn't everything that is supposed to happen happening anyway, regardless of our hopes for the future and our efforts to enlist the help of research towards imbuing an air of rationality to the actual development process? Can futurology help to create the future? It might seem as though many technicians and politicians are acting—or failing to act—after the principle of 'après moi le déluge'. Fagerberg has very aptly affixed the label of 'No-motion Messiah' to this mentality. I trust I am not indulging in lax quasi-philosophising when I say that the hallmark of contemporary man is his conviction that he can choose and shape his own future. The traditional run of humanity naturally sees itself as caught up in an unpremeditated and fated historical process, and considers its sole purpose on earth to continue, repeat and reproduce the life that earlier generations have lived. In spite of all, contemporary man is inspired by the optimistic conviction that he holds the future in his hands (US National Science Board 1969). In spite of all, he entertains the hope that he will be able to write the 'scenario' for his own life and for the lives of his descendants. Indeed, he goes as far as to hope that he will be able to stage the drama of life in accordance with the scenario's directions.

B. S. Bloom

3. Affective consequences of school achievement

For students in the United States, school attendance is a dominant feature in their lives for a ten- to sixteen-year period. During this period, the student devotes at least a forty-hour week to school attendance, home-work, and school-related activities (for nine months out of the year). Thus, annually, the typical student spends about 1,500 hours on school and related activities. The student who completes secondary school has devoted almost 20,000 hours to school and related activities. It is the way in which the student and the school use this tremendous amount of time that determines school achievement and the affective consequences of such achievement.

During this long period of time, in some of the most impressionable stages of the individual's development, the student is being taught at least two courses of study or curricula. One is the *explicit* curriculum of the school, while the other is a curriculum which is *implicit* in the interactions of persons within the school.

Most visible is the *explicit* curriculum the student is expected to learn. This curriculum includes the reading, mathematics, science, literature, social studies, and other school subjects he is taught. This curriculum may be of great importance to the learner because of the competence he develops, the interests and attitudes he acquires, and the career opportunities which are made available to those who learn it well. Undoubtedly, it may include important as well as trivial content. It may be taught well or it may be taught poorly. It may be meaningful to some students and it may seem meaningless and a waste of time to other students. Some of it may be remembered and used repeatedly by the learners while some of it may be forgotten quickly and discarded. The explicit curriculum is visible, it is documented in many ways, and most of the resources and personnel of the schools are dedicated to the students' learning of this curriculum.

The second curriculum is not so clearly visible. This is the *implicit* curriculum which is taught and learned differently by each student. This is the curriculum which teaches each student who he is in relation to others.

It may also teach each person his place in the world of people, of ideas and of activities. While the student may learn this curriculum more slowly than the other, it is likely that he will not be able to forget it as easily as he can forget the details of history, the rules of grammar or the specifics of any subject of study in the explicit curriculum.

While there are many ways of viewing the implicit curriculum, we will confine ourselves in this chapter to those aspects of this curriculum which are most clearly related to the effects of the judgmental processes in the school. It is because of the pervasive use of relative judgments about students in the school that some aspects of the implicit curriculum manifest themselves and can be studied quite directly. Other aspects of the implicit curriculum may be examined only through case studies of individuals or by more deep seated and complex psychological and anthropological methods of study.

In the many hours of school attendance and school work pointed up in the opening paragraph, there are few hours in which the student is not judged (relative to others) by his teachers, peers, family and others. Likewise, there are few school hours in which the student is not *judging himself* against the standards set by himself, by the teacher, or by peers and his family. Nowhere else in his career as a worker, as a member of a family, as a citizen, or as a person engaging in leisure-time activities will he be judged so frequently by others and, it is possible, judged by himself. In most of these post-school activities, the individual is expected to meet some minimal standards of competence or behaviour—if he does so, he is usually not judged in more detailed terms. For example, the majority of workers are expected to meet some minimal standard of work—usually relatively low—and are only rarely judged relative to others.

In school, the likelihood is that each student will be judged many times each day in terms of his adequacy relative to others in his class, group or school. No matter how well he does, if others do better he must come to know it and to place himself accordingly. No matter how poorly he does, if others do less well, he also comes to know it. Obviously, these relative judgments arise because almost all of the student's school learning is as a member of a group—probably of the order of twenty-five to thirty-five members. Also, these judgments are made so frequently because the schools have for so long stressed competition as a primary motivational technique. Only rarely are the judgments in school based on some criterion of adequate work or learning independent of relative performance among the students. Relative rather than absolute norms are the bases for most judgments (Bormuth 1970; Glaser and Nitko 1970; Popham and Husek 1969).

Furthermore, because of the consistency of the learning tasks from one year to another, and because of the sequential nature of many of the tasks in a subject or field, the student who moves from one task to the next tends to remain in much the same relative position to other students (providing he remains with the same group of students or with representatives of much the same sample of students) from one year to the next. The increasing stability of marks and test performance are well documented in the longitudinal research summarised by Bloom (1964), Hicklin (1962) and Payne (1963).

We are accustomed to the notion that courses and instruction in school are divided into subjects and time-periods such as an academic year or term. However, we believe it possible to understand affective consequences of school achievement more clearly if we consider the learning task as the basic unit. If we conceive of the typical learning task as requiring about six to eight hours of instruction or learning activity on the part of a student, we may then see that, in an academic year, a student may encounter about two hundred separable learning tasks. And, over a ten-year period of school, he may encounter of the order of two thousand separable learning tasks.

However, in the student's perception, there are really not that many separable learning tasks—that is, each one is not completely isolated from every other one in his view—nor are they so isolated in the teacher's view. The student comes to perceive the learning tasks in a subject or course of study as all having somewhat the same characteristics.

The curriculum and textbook makers and the teacher attempt to organise learning tasks by subjects or fields of content and then arrange the learning tasks in a sequential or logical order. Thus, in arithmetic, at the third grade level, there may be about twenty-five learning tasks arranged in a sequence that someone believes appropriate from a logical, instructional or learning point of view. Similarly, reading, language arts, science, social studies, etc., are also composed of learning tasks arranged in some order.

In a subject, then, the student encounters the first learning task in a series of such tasks. He is instructed as to what to do, he is provided with instructional material, he is expected to make the appropriate efforts, and he is judged by the teacher on how well he succeeded in this learning task. Typically the student may be given some quantitative index by the teacher such as a mark or grade on his achievement over the learning task. Frequently he may be given some qualitative judgment or appraisal by the teacher on his work over the task. In addition, the student may judge his own success on the task by inferring whether the teacher approves or disapproves of him and his work on the task. The student may also infer how well he accomplished the task by the degree of confidence he has in the work he did, the questions he answered, or the procedures he used in responding to the task. However he comes to know it, the student has a rough idea of his accomplishment of the task.

Interest

If the student secures evidence that he did the first task superbly, he is likely to approach the next task in the series with a bit more enthusiasm and confidence. If he secures evidence that he did the first task very badly, he is likely to approach the next task in the series with somewhat less enthusiasm than he approached the first task.

And so the student progresses from task to task. For each task, he secures some simple judgment about the adequacy of his performance—from the teacher, from himself, or both. For the most part, these judgments on each task are not made public and a student may entertain the delusion that he is doing better or worse than he really is.

At various stages in a series of tasks, the grades or marks are partly made public—at least to the parents. It is here that the student may have difficulty in reconciling the report of his marks with his own more private impressions of the adequacy of his performance on each of the tasks in the subject, especially if the mark is lower than he expected. At this point, he may believe the teacher was in error; that the test or other evidence on which the mark was based was not valid or fair; or that the teacher was unfair and/or doesn't like him. Since his reported marks are more public, they are likely to have a somewhat greater effect on the student than the more private day-to-day judgments about the adequacy of performance on each of the learning tasks in the series. And marks at the end of the term or year are likely to have an even greater effect than marks given at various stages during the term. In general, the more public and official the judgments (or marks) the greater the effect they are likely to have on the student's perception of his adequacy in the subject.

Over a long series of learning tasks of a particular type, the student comes to secure many judgments of his own performance and capability with this class of learning tasks. With some variations from task to task, and with many corrections imposed on his private judgments by the more public appraisals of his performance, he comes to see himself as highly capable with this type of task, moderate in capability, or low in capability. Since he is likely to get one or more years of a particular type of task—and probably of the order of twenty-five tasks of a particular type in a year—

sooner or later he is forced to accept some judgment about his capability with this group of learning tasks.

If the same type of learning task (e.g. arithmetic, reading, or social studies, etc.) is used for four to six years the student may have experiences with the order of 100 to 150 learning tasks of a particular type. Because of the similarity in the type of learning task; because of the sequential nature of many of these learning tasks; and because of the student's gradual structuring of his aspirations, approach to the tasks, and his views of the task, there is likely to be a high relationship between the adequacy-inadequacy of his performance over several years or terms. That is, the student gradually acquires a consistent performance as the tasks begin to accumulate in larger numbers.

As these performances and the student's perceptions of them accumulate and become more consistent, his motivations for the next tasks in the series take on a stable quality. If his performance has been adequate, he approaches the next task with confidence and assurance that he can do it well—and he may even develop a desire for more such tasks. They are easy to do, they can be learned, and they may even be likeable tasks because they can be mastered, solved, learned or overcome. If his performance has not been adequate over a number of tasks of a particular type, the student comes to believe in his inadequacy with respect to this type of learning. He approaches the next task in the series with marked reluctance. He expects the worst and is prepared for it. If it is painful enough, the task is avoided, approached with little enthusiasm and, if anything, marked dislike. Where the student is convinced of his inadequacy, he finds no great energy to accomplish the next task, has little patience or perseverance when he encounters difficulties, and takes little care and thoroughness in accomplishing the task (White 1959; Atkinson and Feather 1966).

Interest in a subject or category of learning tasks may be defined behaviourally in terms of whether or not the individual would voluntarily engage in additional learning tasks of this type—if free to make such a choice. Interest may also be defined more subjectively in terms of the individual's liking, enthusiasm, positive view, preference and desire. Here we are taking the position that the student's subjective feelings about a subject or set of learning tasks are influenced by his perceptions of his adequacy or inadequacy with such tasks. In turn, his perceptions of adequacy or inadequacy are based on his previous history with such tasks and especially the previous judgments about his learning of such tasks.

Studies on the relation between achievement and interest measures have been reported for various school subjects (Neale 1969; Husén 1967;

Anttonen 1969; Baraheni 1962; Frandsen and Sessions 1953; Wyman 1924). In general, the relations are between $+0.20$ and $+0.50$, suggesting statistically, at least, that the relationships are most clear for students at the extremes on achievement (or interest).

In summary, each of the tasks in a series of learning tasks comes to take on a special meaning for the student which is related to his sense of adequacy in accomplishing previous tasks in the series. The student's confidence in himself with respect to the type of task is enhanced or reduced by his performance over the previous tasks. Eventually, the student's prophecy for the next task in the series, based on his previous perceptions of success or failure, becomes fulfilled. Under extreme conditions, we can imagine individual students who resist accepting adequacy or inadequacy as their lot with this type of task, but even they cannot hold out forever.

We believe this general result will be found in each subject or type of learning experience. An accumulation of experience with learning tasks perceived to be similar or in the same category of tasks (as perceived by the student) gradually becomes stabilised for the student and he comes to view the next task in the series with disinterest, interest, or something in between.

This assumes that the definition of adequacy or inadequacy is based on the local situation—the school the student attends, the teachers' marking schemes, and the student's performances relative to other students in the same class. It is likely that, for some few students, their perceptions of adequacy or inadequacy are based on a sibling-like rivalry with a few other students in the school or class or with an actual sibling. Under these conditions, for a student to be slightly below his rival may be catastrophic, while to be slightly above his rival may appear to him to be success. However, these are individual cases. For the most part, adequacy or inadequacy for most students is defined in terms of their standing in the upper or lower portion of the local distribution of marks.

Thus interest in a subject is largely a perceptual phenomena based on the way in which students classify learning tasks and based on the judgments they make of the adequacy of their performance relative to the other students in the school or class they attend. What we are stating here has consequences for further efforts at learning the particular subject or type of learning tasks. Indications of inadequacy over a series of learning tasks are effective in foreclosing further motivation for this type of task. Such indications have important effects on career choice, choice of educational specialisation, and even on the avocational use of a school subject or area of learning (Husén 1967, 1969).

Success (or adequacy) in a school subject opens it up for further consideration and use. Failure (or inadequacy) in a school subject effectively closes this subject for further consideration. The system of grading and instruction operates to open doors for some students while effectively closing doors for other students—and this system is independent of success or failure in any absolute sense. It is dependent on local definitions of success or failure relative to other students in the class or school.

We are thus postulating a high degree of relationship between clear indications of adequacy or inadequacy in learning a particular type of learning task and interest or disinterest in that type of learning task. Given freedom to continue learning more tasks in the series, a high proportion of those who perceive themselves as inadequate over the previous learning tasks in the series will avoid further learning tasks of this type; while of those who perceive themselves as highly adequate a high proportion will choose to learn more tasks of this type. However, with increasing age and maturity, the choices of those who perceive themselves as adequate will be based on meaningfulness of the task and its relevance to their overall desires and plans for the future. Such students have many more possibilities open to them and they will increasingly make decisions on other criteria than school success.

In summary, clear indications of adequacy or inadequacy in learning are likely to have causal effects on interest or disinterest in a subject.

Attitudes

So far, we have been discussing a series of learning tasks which the student perceives as members of a single category. Here we considered the effect of a stabilising picture of success or adequacy and failure or inadequacy on the interest or disinterest the student develops for this type of task and his willingness to voluntarily engage in more learning tasks of the same or related type (as perceived by the student).

If we turn to other learning tasks which the student is getting at the same time as the tasks in the series previously considered, we can also ask about the effect of evidence of adequacy or inadequacy. Thus, in a school year, the student may study as many as five school subjects and may encounter as many as 200 learning tasks. As he encounters each of these tasks, he has a sense of adequacy or inadequacy. These impressions are corroborated or altered by marks assigned by teachers at various marking periods. As these various indices accumulate, over many learning tasks and over several years, the student begins to generalise about his adequacy or inadequacy in school learning tasks. If his experiences are positive, that is, the results are generally adequate, he comes to have a positive attitude toward school and school learning. If the results are generally negative and his learning is regarded as inadequate by the student, his teacher and his parents, he comes to have a negative attitude toward school and school learning.

By attitude we mean a general disposition to regard something in a positive or negative way. We are here treating attitudes as more general than interests. If the student develops a negative (or positive) attitude toward school it may include the subjects, the teachers and staff, and even the whole idea of school and school learning.

We believe that different amounts of failure (or success) may be needed for different students to develop this negative or positive attitude toward school. However, we believe that this is only a matter of degree, and that all individuals who accumulate experiences of failure (or success) to some point (which varies from individual to individual) will develop negative or positive attitudes toward school.

Many studies have been done on the relation between school achievement and attitudes toward school. Some examples of such studies are those by Flemming (1925), Khan (1969), Kurtz and Swenson (1951), Michael, Baker and Jones (1964), and Russell (1969). Especially for students who are at the extremes on school achievement, there is a relation between positive and negative attitudes and indications of adequacy or inadequacy in school achievement. It is evident in some of these studies that relatively strong attitudes have been developed in many students by the end of the elementary period of schooling.

Here the degree of certainty of attitude formation is likely to be much greater for the negative attitudes and repeated evidence of inadequacy than it is for the effects of repeated evidence of adequacy. While indications of success in school are likely to result in positive attitudes toward it, other variables may enter in to determine whether the school and school learning is viewed as positive and favourable (e.g. values of parents, peer group attitudes, meaningfulness of schooling for the individual's career aspirations, etc.).

However, the attitude toward school and school learning is much more generalised than the interest in a specific subject or type of learning task. Interest is specific and while it generalises to a class of learning tasks, it need not extend beyond the members of the category. Attitude generalises to the whole institution of the school, to most of the school subjects, to the staff of the school, and even to the students who attend the school. In

c

effect, repeated evidence of inadequacy in school makes the entire institution the source of the individual's sense of inadequacy and he must avoid the institution or find some way of reducing the amount of pain it gives to him. This he does by efforts of retreating, attacking, or minimising its effects on him. Such negative attitudes, if developed fully enough, may have consequences for all later efforts to do school learning or learning which is in any way related to schools.

Self-concept

In both interests and attitudes, the object of the affect is *outside* the individual. The student develops an interest in something or he develops a disinterest in something. He develops a positive attitude toward school and school learning or he develops a negative attitude toward school and school learning. While there is a difference in generality between interests and attitudes, as we have defined them, in both the object of the affect is external to the individual.

If this process of adequate or inadequate appraisals with regard to learning tasks is generalised over a large number of tasks over a number of years, eventually the object of appraisal for the student becomes shifted from the subjects or the school to the *self*.

For the individual to work and study in an environment in which the majority of learning tasks over a period of years are accompanied by self-appraisals and external appraisals of himself as adequate, is to develop in the individual a general sense of adequacy—at least in connection with school activities. Similarly, if most of the encounters with learning tasks are accompanied by appraisals of inadequacy, the individual is likely to develop a deep sense of inadequacy—at least in connection with school activities.

While we recognise that some individuals may need more successful-unsuccessful experiences before they come to accept a particular view of themselves, we believe this is only a matter of degree. Given a sufficient number of unsuccessful experiences, almost everyone must eventually succumb to an acceptance of a self-view which is negative or inadequate. Similarly for the successful encounters with learning experience—given enough of them, one must eventually come to a view of oneself as positive or adequate.

We do not believe that a few successful or unsuccessful experiences have a major effect on the self-concept—in fact, it is possible that occasional unsuccessful experiences which can be turned by the individual into successful experiences may be of special significance in strengthening the individual's self-image. However, it is the frequency and consistency of adequacy or inadequacy over a period of years which has its major effects on self-concept.

We do not know what level of objective success or failure will be interpreted by the individual as success or failure. But, in general, we believe that to be in the top third or top quarter of his class group (grades of A and B) over a number of years in a variety of school subjects is likely to be interpreted by the student as adequate or as success. Also, to be in the bottom third or quarter of his class group (grades of D and F) over a number of years must leave the individual with a negative self-view—at least in the academic area.

Torshen (1969) has summarised the studies showing relationships between self-concept and school achievement. While the relation with *total* self-concept and school achievement is of the order of + 0·25, the correlation between *academic* self-concept and school achievement is about + 0·50. It is evident in these studies that the academic self-concept is relatively clearly defined by the end of the primary school period. These correlations indicate that, for the students at the extremes (upper and lower thirds) on academic achievement, the relations with academic self-concept are very strong, with little overlap in academic self-concept between these extreme groups.

It is probable that occasional individuals may take some comfort in the fact that a few members of their class are in even worse academic shape— but this is probably of little comfort over a long period of time. So too, some individuals may be depressed that a few members of their class are slightly higher than they are, but again we believe that to be in the top third or quarter of their class will eventually be interpreted in a positive way.

It is the middle third or half of the students who may be least affected by the school insofar as self-concept may be concerned. They are given enough positive evidence of their adequacy to balance the negative evidence, or at least they can take some comfort that they are more adequate than a sizeable proportion of their peers. Undoubtedly, they must turn to other areas of activity and to other aspects of themselves to find more positive signs of their worth and adequacy.

In taking these views, we are assuming that each individual seeks desperately for some positive signs of his own adequacy and worth. If these indications are denied in one area, the individual must seek other areas in which he can find such indications.

In the work of Sears (1963) in measuring self-concept, there are twelve areas in which an individual may appraise himself. Some of these may be clearly classified as *academic* self-concept, such as learning, school subjects, work habits and relations with the teacher. Others, which may be classified as *non-academic* self-concept, have to do with self-appraisals with regard to athletics, relations with peers, relations with others, and appearance.

There is a low relationship between these two large categories of self-concept (about $+0.35$) indicating that individuals who are high on one may or may not be high on the other. Some individuals who are low in academic self-concept may be high in non-academic self-concept and vice versa. It is likely that individuals who are low in both are in great difficulty and this may be true for up to half of the students who are low in academic self-concept.

It is possible for some individuals who are low in academic self-concept to get considerable comfort from a positive non-academic self-concept. However, the academic self-concept is important in its own right as determining whether or not the individual will voluntarily engage in academic learning when he is free to do so or not, as he pleases. Also, a low academic self-concept increases the probability that an individual will have a generally negative self-concept.

We believe that the individual who is denied positive reassurance of his worth in school is impelled to seek such positive reassurance wherever he can find it. If society offers him opportunities for work which is satisfying and rewarding financially as well as otherwise, the individual can find positive indications of self-worth here. However, in a highly developed society like the US, negative indications of school achievement (including school drop-outs) are likely to provide serious barriers against securing skilled or higher occupational employment. Some individuals must turn to less socially approved areas (gangs, illicit activities, etc.) to find the rewards and self-approval denied them in school and school-related activities.

In summary, successful experiences in school are no guarantee of a generally positive self-concept, but they increase the probabilities that such will be the case. In contrast, unsuccessful experiences in school guarantee that the individual will develop a negative academic self-concept and increase the probabilities that he will have a generally negative self-concept. But the individual strives desperately to secure some assurance of his self-worth and if he is denied it in one area he will search for it elsewhere. The likelihood of his finding it is considerably decreased by consistent lack of success in the school.

Mental health

An individual develops a positive self-regard and a strong ego by continual evidence of his adequacy—especially in early childhood and in the periods of latency (ages 6 to 11) and adolescence. Since the school period (ages 6 to 18) occupies these latter two periods, we regard continual evidence of success or failure in the school as having major effects on the individual's mental health.

While mental health and self-concept cannot be sharply distinguished, we may think of mental health as concerned more directly with ego development, with reduction in general anxiety, and with the ability to take stress and frustration with a minimum of debilitating effect.

There is considerable empirical support for relating the individual's perception of his adequacy in school learning to the development of related interests, attitudes and self-concept. When we turn to mental health, we must be more speculative because of the difficulties in defining mental health, because of the difficulties in measuring it, and because of the limited research which directly relates adequacy in school learning to mental health. Some support for these speculations may be drawn from a longitudinal study by Stringer and Glidewell (1967) which related the academic progress of elementary school pupils to indications of mental illness. A more recent study by Torshen (1969) of the relation between teachers' grades, self-concepts and indications of mental health gives some further support to these ideas. However, the crucial empirical test of these hypotheses has not been done (at least to the writer's satisfaction).

If the school environment provides the individual with evidence of his adequacy over a number of years, especially in the first few years of school supported by consistent success over the next four or five years, we believe that this provides a type of immunisation against mental illness for an indefinite period of time. Such an individual should be able to surmount crises and periods of great stress without suffering too much. His own sense of adequacy and his personal and technical skills (some learned in school) should enable him to use realistic methods in surmounting these crisis situations.

It is not likely that all students in the upper fourth or third of their classes in school achievement should secure this ego strengthening from adequacy in school learning. However, we believe this should be true for about two-thirds of students in the upper third of their classes (i.e. over 20 per cent of students). We are not quite sure why the other third should lack this immunisation. Probably some of these are compulsive students who achieve school success at great personal cost. Perhaps, also, some of these are highly competitive students who make school grades and competition with others more central than the learning represented by these grades. Perhaps, also, some of these are overly docile students who lose independence by conforming overly much to the demands of adults (parents, teachers, etc.) without developing their own personal goals.

At the other extreme are the bottom third of the students who have been given consistent evidence of their inadequacy in the school learning environment over a period of five to ten years. Such students rarely secure any positive reinforcement in the classroom and are unlikely to secure positive rewards from teachers or parents. We would expect such students to be infected with emotional difficulties arising from the rarity with which they can secure any sense of adequacy in the school environment—and especially in the classroom. There must be an increasing spiral in which some difficulty in learning at one point becomes exaggerated at a later point, gradually producing a sense that there is nothing one can do right in such a situation.

From this, we would expect that about two-thirds of the students in the bottom third of their classes (about 20 per cent of students) over a period of years should exhibit symptoms of acute distress and alienation from the world of school and adults. Again, we can only speculate about how and why some students can escape from the infection likely to result from a deep sense of inadequacy in school. Some students must be able to secure a strong and positive sense of adequacy in their work, with their peers, from their parents, etc., to compensate for the effects of the school. Others may find it possible to reject the school experiences as irrelevant to their own goals or they may regard the judgments of the school as unfair and thus escape from the effect of what would otherwise be negative experiences and judgments.

For students in both the upper and the lower extremes, we would expect the effects to be most pronounced when the parents are most interested and concerned about the educational achievement of their children. When the parents' educational aspirations for their children are high, they will reward achievement and punish lack of achievement. Under such conditions, the reward and punishment system of the school is paralleled by the reward and punishment system of the home—for such children the affective consequences of school achievement should be far greater than when the home has a different basis for reward and punishment than does the school.

We would also expect that the effects of failure in the cognitive learnings in the school would be minimised when the school includes many types of learning and activity which have relatively low relations to the cognitive learning (i.e. athletics, social activity, art, music, vocational instruction, etc.). Under such conditions, it is likely that a high proportion of students can experience some degree of success in some school-related activities and thus escape from a complete sense of failure in connection with the school.

The speculations and hypotheses on the preceding pages may be derived from such work as White (1959) on competence motivation, Erikson (1963) on stages in development, and Bower (1962) in his review of research on mental health in education. In spite of the speculative nature of this section of the chapter, the suggestive research already done, the theoretical work of child development specialists, and the experiences of psychiatric and psychological workers all give indications in the direction spelled out in this section of the chapter. The extreme importance of this area for the individual and the society make it important that these speculations and hypotheses be the subject of more definitive research.

Part Two

The Needs of Exceptional Children

J. Tizard

4. The epidemiology of handicapping conditions of educational concern

'Family and school are the two main social environments in which a school child lives; it should be recognised even more widely than it is at present that when a child has special psychological needs and problems, these involve an interaction in him of influences of both family and school, even though his difficulties may show themselves in only one setting or the other. The first concern of psychologists in education services is to contribute to the resolution of these problems.' (Summerfield Report 1968.)

Much of the work of the educational psychologist is concerned with the assessment and treatment of individual children. Assessment requires the psychologist to have a knowledge of developmental and educational norms, and of the social context in which these norms are valid. Treatment is the complement of assessment; it may involve many activities, but like assessment, it necessarily implies the existence of services. To provide developmental norms, and to estimate service needs, epidemiological knowledge is required—this includes the study of the incidence (or inception rate), the prevalence, and the prognosis, of handicapping conditions.

In 1964 and 1965, members of the Child Development Department of the University of London Institute of Education, in collaboration with colleagues from the Institute of Psychiatry, the School Health Service, and the Local Authority, carried out a series of studies in a single Authority to determine the prevalence of handicapping conditions of educational concern among children of primary school age. The exercises were collaborative, involving teachers, parents and children as well as the County Education Officer, the Medical Officer of Health, and their staffs who participated in the planning of the studies and in the field work. The research was carried out on complete age-groups of children living on the Isle of Wight, an island of approximately 147 square miles, some four miles off the south coast of England. The main objective was to give a comprehensive picture of 'handicap' in a total population of children who lived in a defined geographical area and who were in the middle years of their schooling.

A full report on this research has been published (Rutter, Tizard and Whitmore 1970; Rutter, Graham and Yule 1970). This chapter summarises the main conclusions and considers some of their implications.

Planning the surveys

The surveys had their origin in a request by Dr Peter Henderson, Principal Medical Officer of the Department of Education and Science, to collaborate in a study which the Department was planning of the medical and educational problems of slow-learning children. These problems could not however be studied simply by examining children who had been 'ascertained' as educationally subnormal, since the numbers of children so ascertained vary according to the facilities available for treating them. It was therefore decided to undertake a survey of a representative sample of children of primary school age, and to carry out subsequent surveys as the children grew older.

At the outset there was a choice of strategy. We could have sampled widely to get an overall picture of conditions in the country as a whole: this was done in the Scottish Mental Surveys (Maxwell 1953, 1961); the National Survey of Health and Development (Douglas 1964); and the National Child Development Study (Pringle, Butler and Davie 1966; Davie, Butler and Goldstein 1972). Alternatively, we could have carried out a more intensive study of a single area (cf. Spence *et al.* 1964; Birch *et al.* 1970). A third possibility was to sample from a number of areas, as Lewis (1929) did in his survey of the prevalence of mental deficiency in England and Wales.

We chose the second strategy, partly because we were interested in exploring the service implications of our findings, which required us to have a knowledge of local conditions, and partly because in a local survey it is easier to arrange for children and their families to be seen by the same relatively small team of trained investigators, using standard methods. The Isle of Wight was particularly suitable for such an enquiry because it resembles England as a whole in its social composition, and because it is reasonably representative of non-metropolitan areas in other parts of the country. The population (a little short of 100,000 with about 1,200 children in each age-group) was sufficiently large to provide an adequate number of children with fairly common handicaps which were our main concern, and as an island it had the great merit for the epidemiologist of having well-defined boundaries. We were particularly fortunate in selecting an area in which we were able to obtain most generous cooperation from all departments in the Local Authority, the teachers, the children and the parents.

Initially two surveys were undertaken. The first, in 1964, explored the prevalence of low intelligence and of educational backwardness among children of junior school age; the second, in 1965, explored the prevalence of maladjustment or psychiatric disorder, and of physical and neurological handicap in the same cohort of children. In both surveys the population studied comprised all children born between 1 September 1953 and 31 August 1955 whose homes were on the Isle of Wight (N = 2,199). The children were thus aged nine or ten years at the time of the first survey.

A subsequent survey of the prevalence of reading backwardness among these children was undertaken in 1966 when they were in the first and second years of secondary schooling; and in 1968 and 1969, surveys of psychiatric disorder and of educational backwardness were again carried out on the children as they neared the end of the final year of compulsory schooling. This latter study was undertaken by Rutter, Graham, Rigley and Yule and is in process of analysis.

In each of the surveys a two-stage strategy was employed. First, all children in the age-groups were screened by means of group tests, parent and teacher questionnaires, and by examination of medical and school records, to pick out those who appeared to be likely to suffer from the particular handicaps which we were studying. Then in the second stage all of these children, together with a control group of 160 children randomly selected from the population under study, were seen individually by educational psychologists and by doctors, and their parents were interviewed by social scientists. Each year more than 20 per cent of the population of that age were seen individually on several occasions, and their parents were interviewed. To enable the field work to be done in a few weeks, extra staff were taken on. They comprised psychologists, psychiatrists and social scientists, most of whom had had their postgraduate training at the Institute of Psychiatry.

The definition of handicap

The handicaps investigated were (a) subnormality of intelligence; (b) backwardness in reading, which was used as an index of general educational backwardness; (c) maladjustment or psychiatric disorder; and (d) physical handicap and neurological handicap. No systematic studies were undertaken to assess the prevalence of social handicaps—that is, of handicaps arising from poor material or social conditions which might reasonably be thought to retard a child's physical, mental or educational development. We did enquire into the social circumstances in which both the handicapped children and the randomly selected control group of children lived, and so we were able to assess the relative frequency of poor or unsatisfactory home circumstances among the handicapped as compared with the control children. But the research was focused primarily on the children, and not on their social circumstances.

The numbers of children described as handicapped are, obviously, a function of the manner in which the word *handicapped* is defined. In the Isle of Wight surveys great attention was paid to definition. Backwardness in intelligence or intellectual subnormality was defined psychometrically: a child was deemed intellectually backward if his IQ was more than two standard deviations below the mean of his age-group (the control group) on a shortened form of the wisc. Reading backwardness was similarly defined: a child was backward in reading if his score on the Accuracy or Comprehension Scales of the *Neale Analysis of Reading* test was more than twenty-eight months below that of the average child of his age (This was, roughly, a score 2 standard deviations below the mean: see Yule 1967).

Neither psychiatric disorder nor physical handicap could be so unambiguously and easily defined by means of well-validated, standardised tests. For these conditions we had to fall back on judgments. Two factors were taken into account: chronicity and severity. The survey was concerned with chronic conditions and therefore only conditions which had persisted for more than a year were included in our numbers. Severity we related to the degree of impairment of functions shown in the child's everyday life, and graded the disability as slight, moderate or severe. These terms were denotatively defined in terms of things which the child was regularly unable to do, or problems or difficulties in personal life or social behaviour. They were further objectified by the use of illustrative examples. For both psychiatric and physical handicaps an inter-rater agreement approaching 90 per cent was achieved between two examiners rating a number of cases independently in terms of severity, and the reliability of the judgments was equally good at all points on the scale.

The prevalence of handicapping conditions

The observed prevalence of each of these four types of handicap is given in table 1, the data being expressed as age-specific rates per 1,000 children. As may be seen from the bottom row of the table, 2·64 per cent (26·4 per thousand children) were diagnosed as intellectually backward, 7·89 per cent as backward in reading, 5·38 per cent as suffering from a psychiatric disorder (of moderate or severe intensity) and 5·52 per cent as physically handicapped. These rates accord closely with those which have been obtained by other workers, though strict comparisons cannot be made, since different investigators have used different criteria in making their assessments.

TABLE I   *Prevalence of four handicapping conditions among nine- to eleven-year-old children. Age-specific rates per 1,000 children, based on Isle of Wight population surveys* (N = 2,199).

	Intellectual retardation	Educational backwardness	Psychiatric disorder	Physical handicap	Rate per 1,000 *
One handicap only	2·7	44·7	34·2	39·2	120·8
Two handicaps					
Intellectual +	—	12·3	0·5	0·9 ⎫	
Educational +	12·3	—	10·0	3·2 ⎬ 30·5	
Psychiatric +	0·5	10·0	—	3·7 ⎪	
Physical +	0·9	3·2	3·7	— ⎭	
Three handicaps					
Intell + Educ + Psychiat	1·8	1·8	1·8	— ⎫	
Intell + Educ + Physical	4·6	4·6	—	4·6 ⎬	
Intell + Psychiat + Physical	1·4	—	1·4	1·4 ⎪ 7·8	
Educ + Psychiat + Physical	—	—	—	— ⎭	
All four handicaps	2·3	2·3	2·3	2·3	2·3
Total with each handicap*	26·4	78·9	53·8	55·2	161·4

* Computed

In our study we attempted not only to assess the reliability of our judgments (by having some children seen more than once by different examiners who had no knowledge of what other clinicians had diagnosed); we also investigated the extent to which our screening and sampling procedures might have led us to 'miss' cases of handicap. The 1966 survey of reading attainments gave us a check on the 1964 estimates of reading backwardness: few additional backward readers were identified in 1966, and *all* those identified in 1964 continued to be backward two years later. A check to determine the number with psychiatric disorder who might not have been selected through the screening procedures (i.e. the number of 'false negatives') indicated that as many as 20 per cent might have been missed. The true prevalence rate for psychiatric disorder might thus be as high as $\frac{5}{4}$ times the observed figure, namely 6·8 per cent.

We endeavoured to arrive at a complete coverage of the physically handicapped by using as many sources of information as possible. We scrutinised all school health record cards and hospital records; checked on all children seen by speech therapists or audiologists, or referred for any special examination by school doctors; we enquired about all children referred to the local paediatrician, and used teacher questionnaires and parent questionnaires as additional sources of information. A special search was made to discover the names of all children not in ordinary schools (e.g. in hospital schools, special schools or training centres, or children who were exempt from schooling).

We had a further check on the adequacy of our case finding of children with physical handicaps in that during the 1964 educational survey 450 children had been given a special medical examination, and parents had been asked to complete health questionnaires on them. As so many sources of information were drawn upon, it seems unlikely that many children with moderate or severe handicaps can have been missed from our total figures, though we discovered after the survey had been completed that there were a few additional asthmatic children (mainly with disorders which the information at our disposal suggested were only of slight severity) who had not been notified to us.

The rates in table 1 include children with mild physical handicaps as well as those whose disabilities were moderate or severe. Thus in this category some of the children whose lives were least affected by their disability were included. A small number of asthmatic attacks during the preceding year, or a visible skin lesion was sufficient for inclusion in this group. Of the 121 physically handicapped children identified in the course of the survey, about a third (42) had only mild handicaps, while in a further 19 cases, of whom 17 were asthmatic children, we had no information about severity. The remaining 60 children were, however, moderately or severely handicapped, as were all children in the other three categories.

Numbers of handicapped

Information about the prevalence of handicapping *conditions* gives us some indication of service needs. Of much more interest however from the point of view of the educational authorities is the number of *children* involved and the proportions of these who have more than one handicap. These data are also given in table 1 as rates per thousand children aged nine to eleven. As the table shows, 161·4 per thousand children, or one in six of the total population of children in the age-group, are handicapped in the sense in which the term is used here. Three-quarters of them (120·9 per thousand) have only a single handicap of educational concern, but 30·5 per thousand have two handicaps, 7·8 have three and 2·3 per thousand have four or more handicaps.

The significance of the overlap between handicaps can be seen more clearly if the data are set out according to the proportions of children with each type of handicap who have additional handicaps. Table 2 presents the findings. More than four-fifths of the intellectually backward have in

TABLE 2   *Percentage of children with intellectual, educational, psychiatric or physical handicaps who have additional handicaps.*

	Intellectual retardation	Educational backwardness	Psychiatric disorder	Physical handicap	% with different numbers of handicaps
One handicap only	10·3	56·6	63·6	71·1	75·0
Two handicaps					
Intellectual +	—	15·6	0·8	1·7	
Educational +	46·6	—	18·7	5·8	18·8
Psychiatric +	1·7	12·7	—	6·6	
Physical +	3·4	4·0	6·8	—	
Three handicaps					
Intell + Educ + Psychiat	6·9	2·3	3·4	—	
Intell + Educ + Physical	17·2	5·8	—	8·3	4·8
Intell + Psychiat + Physical	5·2	—	2·5	2·4	
Educ + Psychiat + Physical	—	—	—	—	
Four handicaps					
Intell + Educ + Psychiat + Physical	8·6	2·9	4·2	4·1	1·4
Total number of cases	58	173	118	121	354

addition an educational handicap (46·6 + 6·9 + 17·2 + 5·2 + 8·6 = 84·5%); 22·4 per cent also have a psychiatric handicap; 34·4 per cent also have a physical handicap. Among the educationally backward the proportion with additional disability is less, but it still amounts to more than two-fifths of the total (43·4%). Nearly two-fifths of the children with psychiatric disorders had other disabilities as well, 26·3 per cent being educationally backward. In many respects the physically handicapped children were the least affected by additional disabilities, less than a third of them having another handicap.

It has been mentioned that the physically handicapped children included those with mild handicaps as well as those with moderate and severe ones. The reason was that all of these children require to be seen by school doctors at regular intervals in order that their condition might be reviewed. However, to include them among the numbers of children whose handicaps were of *educational* concern is perhaps unwarranted, and the data have therefore been re-analysed, children with mild physical handicaps and those on whom we had no information regarding severity being excluded. The revised figures are presented in table 3. In this table, in which only children with moderate or severe physical handicaps are

TABLE 3   *Prevalence of four handicapping conditions of educational concern and of moderate or severe intensity. Age-specific rates per 1,000 children in a population of 2,199 children aged nine to eleven years, Isle of Wight.*

	Intellectual retardation	Educational backwardness	Psychiatric disorder	Physical handicap	Ratio per 1,000
One handicap only	3·6	46·4	36·4	16·9	103·3
Two handicaps					
Intellectual +	—	12·7	0·5	0·5	
Educational +	12·7	—	10·0	1·4	26·5
Psychiatric +	0·5	10·0	—	1·4	
Physical +	0·5	1·4	1·4	—	
Three handicaps					
Intell + Educ + Psychiat	2·3	2·3	2·3	—	
Intell + Educ + Physical	4·1	4·1	—	4·1	
Intell + Psychiat + Physical	1·4	—	1·4	1·4	7·8
Educ + Psychiat + Physical	—	—	—	—	
All four handicaps	1·8	1·8	1·8	1·8	1·8
Total with each handicap*	26·4	78·7	53·7	27·3	138·9

* Computed

included, 13·89 per cent of children are seen to be affected by one or more of the four types of handicap being investigated. 10·33 per cent of the population has a single handicap of moderate or severe intensity, while 3·61 per cent have multiple disabilities.

It must be stressed that all of these children were indeed handicapped in an ordinary everyday sense of the word. The intellectually backward suffered from the problems that affect nearly all children of low intelligence. A few were in special schools, and a few others in special classes, while the great majority were making very poor progress in ordinary classes. (Only nine children, with IQs of less than 50, were not at school, being under the care of the mental subnormality services.)

The backward readers were, at best, on the borderline of illiteracy.

Furthermore, their reading difficulties, as shown by our follow-up enquiries, were remarkably persistent, so that not only did they fail to benefit fully from their schooling but it seems likely that most of them would be limited in the life they could lead after leaving school. About half of these children were intellectually backward, but the other half were of normal intelligence. We were surprised to find, when we retested these children in 1966, that the progress of the intelligent children was no better than that of the educationally backward: none of them in fact 'caught up' in reading during the two-year interval between the surveys.

The children with psychiatric disorder were also very much handicapped in their everyday life. Maladjustment may mean suffering in the shape of anxiety or unhappiness or it may mean conflict between society and the child, bringing trouble to both. Some of the neurotic children were unable to do what they wanted because of incapacitating fears, many lay awake at night worrying, and distress was a frequent experience for all. For the child with a conduct disorder, conflict and discord at home and at school were characteristic, but many were also miserable, fearful or worried as well. Perhaps most striking of all was the high proportion of children with all types of psychiatric disorder who had serious difficulties in their relationships with people; for example, half were said not to be much liked by other children.

The physically handicapped whose disabilities were rated as being moderate or severe all presented significant problems of educational concern. They were frequently absent from school through illness, or restricted in physical activities or often both. Of the twenty children in the total sample with neurological disorders affecting the central nervous system, seventeen were moderately or severely handicapped, and for at least half of these handicap meant an inability to lead an ordinary life, and partial or even total dependence on others for feeding, dressing or getting around.

Implications

A survey such as this has obvious implications for educational planners and for classroom teachers, as well as for educational psychologists. The outstanding finding is that handicaps of moderate or severe intensity and of long duration, are exceedingly common in the ordinary school population. No system of special schooling can cope with the numbers involved, nor indeed would it be desirable that one child in every six or seven should go to a special school or be educated in a special class. Most responsibility for special educational treatment will therefore continue to fall—and rightly fall—on the ordinary class teacher.

Our findings, it is true, refer only to children in the later years of primary schooling. There is however abundant evidence that the prevalence of handicapping conditions in children in other age-groups is at least as high. Moore (1966) reports, in a longitudinal study of difficulties in adjusting to primary school, that 'about 80 per cent of children were found to experience difficulties in the infants school, of which nearly one half were of moderate or marked severity. The number of difficulties decreased in the junior school, but a substantial number of children still showed more than mild disturbances.' Pringle, Butler and Davie (1966) report that 'more than 5 per cent of children were already receiving special educational help in infant classes and there was a further 8 per cent who, it was considered, would benefit from such help', and no one can believe that adolescence and secondary schooling mark an end to educational backwardness, behaviour disorders and neurosis, to poor intelligence or to chronic physical handicaps.

All of this should be of practical concern to educational administration, to teacher training and to classroom practice as well as to educational psychology. A primary task for an education authority, though not necessarily one which comes first in time, is to assess the total size of the problems for which services are required. Our own survey was designed to do this, and we were able to engage a professional team to carry out the fieldwork. However, even a rough-and-ready survey may be better than none at all. Taken in conjunction with other normative data it will give an approximate idea of the numbers in an educational authority thought to require some form of special educational treatment.

We have, like most epidemiologists, expressed our findings in age-specific rates per thousand children. It is however important to translate these into actual numbers of children in a given Authority to appreciate their significance for educational planning. When this is done it immediately becomes apparent that most children with handicaps of backwardness in intelligence, educational backwardness, psychiatric disorder and the common forms of physical handicap must be coped with in the ordinary school situation. However, for rare and severe disabilities such as childhood autism, cerebral palsy, severe subnormality of intelligence, sensory handicaps, clear choices present themselves. Children can either be educated in highly specialised schools or units (and in the case of rare disabilities this will often entail boarding provision being made for children who live too far away from the facilities to make use of them otherwise). Alternatively we can associate special units with ordinary schools, as is being increasingly done in the units established for partially hearing children. A third possibility is to set up a 'comprehensive' special school for children who suffer from a variety of disabilities. In such a school there could be specialised units, if the special educational needs of the children warranted these. Whatever the administrative solution adopted, decisions about the number of places to be made available will still have to be made.

'Early recognition of handicaps is important.' There is in fact little definitive evidence as to the value of early diagnosis and treatment in preventing or mitigating later handicaps. Longitudinal epidemiological studies of the effects of early treatment on common handicaps have not as yet been undertaken. Until such research is done it will not be possible to say which treatments are effective, and which are not, or to carry out serious investigations designed to improve methods of treatment for specific conditions. However, experience suggests that whenever treatment is seriously undertaken it is likely to have *some* beneficial effects in modifying or eliminating secondary handicaps. And even if treatment does not succeed in curing a child's condition, our welfare and medical services still have the responsibility for helping him and his family to cope with it.

In the Isle of Wight studies we made enquiries about the circumstances in which the children lived. These revealed, as other investigations by ourselves and others (e.g. Rutter 1966; Tizard and Grad 1961; Ingram *et al.* 1962; Miller, Court *et al.* 1960), a two-way interaction between the child and his handicaps on the one hand, and the family of which he was a member on the other. In some cases family circumstances had exacerbated or even caused the child's disabilities; in other cases the handicaps of the child exacerbated or even caused family problems. How to cope with these is in large part the province of the personal social services, a review of which forms the subject-matter of the Seebohm Committee Report. The implications for an Educational Authority and for individual teachers are again obvious.

All of these matters raise questions about the role of the school psychologist in an educational setting. What should be his training—and what should be his job? How much time should he spend in child guidance and how much in teacher guidance? How much in parent guidance? What is the value of the traditional child guidance clinic with its traditional staffing? Are there alternative ways of using our scarce resources which offer more benefits to children and their families? How far, with limited resources, can we take cognisance of the large number of handicapped children whose needs are at present never even 'ascertained'? Does the existing diversity of psychological services provide us with opportunities for comparative evaluation of the merits and shortcomings of alternative ways of organising a psychological service?

The new developments in educational psychology must be related to these questions, for without appraisal and reappraisal of our strategy tactical advances are likely to be limited.

Acknowledgments

The investigations summarised in this chapter were planned and written up by a survey team consisting of Dr Michael Rutter, of the Institute of Psychiatry, Dr Kingsley Whitmore, Department of Education and Science, Dr Philip Graham, Hospital for Sick Children, London, Mr Leslie Rigley and Mr William Yule, University of London Institute of Education, and the writer. Colleagues from the Isle of Wight Health, Education and Welfare Departments, and teachers, parents and children on the Island collaborated fully in the research.

Grants for the work were given by the Nuffield Foundation, the Medical Research Council, the Department of Education and Science, the American Association for the Aid of Crippled Children and the Social Science Research Council.

5. The treatment of maladjusted pupils: research and experiment 1960-69

Introduction

During the past decade there has been a growing emphasis on the importance of the early detection of signs of maladjustment in children and of giving greater attention to the psychological development of young children (Summerfield Report 1968), in the hope that the modification of adverse influences at this stage will improve mental health later on. However, additional evidence on the considerable size of the problem of maladjustment in childhood and adolescence, which has come from the findings of epidemiological studies such as those of Pringle *et al.* (1966) and Rutter and Graham (1966), has ensured that the immediate need for an expansion of treatment services is in no danger of being overlooked. Gradually, knowledge about the incidence, nature and aetiology of childhood disturbance is being accumulated, to provide a firmer basis for prevention and treatment (see reviews by Chazan 1963, 1968; and Thouless 1969). Particularly valuable is the attempt by the World Health Organisation (Rutter *et al.* 1969) to provide a commonly agreed classification of psychiatric disorders in childhood, which is greatly needed for the systematic study of such disorders.

This chapter presents a review of research and experiment, mainly that carried out in Great Britain, in the treatment of maladjusted children during the 1960s. The complexity of the problems involved and the variety of relevant publications make it impossible, within a restricted space, to review developments comprehensively, but it is perhaps useful to look back over a limited period of time and to highlight what seem to be the main trends of significance. Recent American publications are reviewed by Morse and Dyer (1963), Balow (1966), and Glavin and Quay (1969), in the *Review of Educational Research*, but, as most of the innovative experiments have originated in the USA, some mention of work carried out there will be made below.

The treatment of maladjusted children usually involves a variety of measures used in combination. These include clinical procedures with parents and child, education in special schools or classes, and, in some cases, a permanent or temporary removal from the family to a hostel, Home, or other placement. A large number of emotionally disturbed children remain in the ordinary school, where, as Kounin *et al.* (1966) have shown, teachers with the appropriate skills can contribute to their management and to the modification of their behaviour, but the present review will be confined to a consideration of clinical procedures and special educational treatment for maladjusted children.

Clinical techniques

The number of children treated at child guidance clinics trebled between 1950 and 1969 (DES 1971). In 1950, 22,000 children were treated; in 1969 the number was 66,000 in nearly 400 clinics. Just under one per cent of the school population attended a child guidance clinic in 1969, this figure masking large regional variations. More children are treated, for example, in South-east or South-west England than in North-west England or Wales (Univ. London Institute of Education 1973). The expansion of child guidance facilities took place in spite of the continued shortage of psychiatrists, psychologists and social workers, highlighted in both the Summerfield and Seebohm Reports in 1968. At the same time, there was a rapid development of school psychological services in most parts of the country, working closely with child guidance clinics and ensuring that the educational needs of maladjusted children would receive attention. The clinical facilities are still, however, unable to meet the demands on them, and in particular those for psychotic children and severely disturbed adolescent boys and girls are seriously inadequate.

The techniques of treating the adult mentally ill in which the greatest advances have been made, such as pharmacological and electric shock treatment, are not for the most part appropriate for children, and, on the whole, child guidance clinics in this country have continued to work along the same broad lines for the past four decades. It is true that they have become more eclectic in their approach, and that there has been an increasing disinclination on the part of therapists working with children to use methods based wholly on psychoanalytic theories, but few new approaches have been reported. The multi-disciplinary team approach to diagnosis and treatment has been maintained, although the roles of the main members of the team—psychiatrist, psychologist and social worker— have overlapped a good deal. This blurring of distinctive functions has occurred sometimes because of the team's desire to be flexible, sometimes as a result of a failure to define roles clearly, and sometimes because clinics have not been fully staffed, so that the traditional distribution of work could not be sustained.

Treatment at a child guidance clinic normally involves work with the parents of the child referred as well as direct therapy with the child. In a small proportion of cases, drugs may be used (Grant 1962), for example with hyperactive children (Werry *et al.* 1966), but this aspect of treatment will not be discussed here.

Throughout its history, the child guidance clinic has always put great stress on the fact that the child is a member of a family unit and that treatment must involve the parents and possibly other members of the family if it is to be effective. Work with parents includes the giving of advice on handling the child, supportive therapy, or even prolonged and intensive treatment. There has been a close examination of the dynamics of family casework, in particular the function and use of relationship (Association of Psychiatric Social Workers 1963); and family group therapy, based on the work in America by Nathan Ackerman (1958), has been developed as a procedure whereby all the members of the family are treated together. Wolff (1969), while agreeing that psychotherapy involving parents and child together can be very useful at times, does not consider this approach to be appropriate in every case: the parents do not always need treatment, and even when children's deviant behaviour is clearly related to disturbed family relationships, family group therapy may not be suitable.

As far as direct therapy with the child is concerned, most child guidance clinics have continued to use individual psychotherapy as their main approach to the treatment of emotional disturbance. As Clyne (1966) states, the term *psychotherapy* is used very loosely and the techniques employed may include persuasion, suggestion, counselling, listening and interpretation. Psychotherapy may be carried out in the play or interview situation, individually or in small groups. Group methods have not been used widely here, rather surprisingly seeing that they offer a number of advantages over individual treatment. For example, the social setting of the group is natural and nearer to the actual life of the child outside; there is not so much emphasis on the child as a 'patient', thus lessening the danger of his suffering from excessive attention; group play is more enjoyable to the child, providing scope for hilarity and harmless aggression; and group treatment is more economic in time, space and staff—not an unimportant argument in view of the costliness of child guidance. Foulkes and Anthony (1965) discuss a variety of group psychotherapeutic methods based on psychoanalytic principles, stressing the importance of verbal expression of feelings but recommending the use of play and activity to encourage verbalisation in younger children. The 'small table' technique for children aged four to six years, the 'small room' technique for children aged five to twelve, and the 'small circle' technique for adolescent groups are described in their book. Some of these techniques are based on those used by Slavson (1943) and, together with other group approaches (Mhas 1970), seem worthy of further development. It must, of course, be recognised that group therapy is never a complete substitute for individual treatment and that there are certain types of disturbed children who cannot fit into a group, and who would neither benefit from group treatment nor contribute to the development of the group.

Although accumulated experience and feedback has doubtless refined and improved psychotherapeutic skills in general, it is difficult to know exactly what is taking place during psychotherapy and therefore difficult to evaluate it. The scientifically minded have tended to turn to behaviour therapy techniques as offering more precise ways of treating disturbance and as being based on a sounder foundation of psychological theory. 'Behaviour therapy' covers a large variety of techniques aimed at modifying maladaptive behaviour, but essentially the term relates to approaches based on experimental psychology and especially learning theory since Pavlov; for a comprehensive account of the principles and practice of behaviour therapy see Eysenck and Rachman (1965), and Meyer and Chesser (1970). Eysenck and Rachman included in their book a discussion of the application of behaviour therapy techniques to the treatment of maladjustment in childhood, but on the whole these techniques have not been enthusiastically adopted by child guidance clinics in this country, and they have been used only to a limited extent with children. Nevertheless, during the 1960s there have been an increasing number of reports of experimental work involving behaviour therapy, with both parents and children.

For example, the need for a systematic approach to parent-child therapy is underlined by Wahler *et al.* (1965), who point out that investigations into the value of techniques of parent-child psychotherapy have not been sufficiently controlled, in that they have not permitted the assessment of variables which serve to maintain children's deviant behaviour, nor have they analysed with precision those variables responsible for changing deviant behaviour. Wahler's own pilot study with the mothers of three children suggests that, at least within the confines of an experimental setting, it is possible to specify the variables functioning to maintain deviant behaviour in children and then to eliminate these variables systematically with the aim of modifying the children's behaviour. Patterson *et al.* (1967)

describe a set of procedures designed to alter the schedules of reinforcement used by the parents of a six-year-old boy and to modify the child's responses of negativism and extreme withdrawal, and Engeln *et al.* (1968) report on a systematic programme of therapy carried out with a family unit, involving the mother, father and older brother of an aggressive six-year-old boy. The programme involved systematic reinforcement of certain responses made by the child in the clinic playroom; concurrent training of the mother in the clinic in the relevant principles and in reinforcement and extinction techniques; establishing in the home a programme of systematic reinforcement of the boy and his older brother; and establishing cooperation between the boys in the playroom by making reinforcement for both boys contingent on cooperative behaviour. Experiments such as these, although carried out on small samples, point the way to greater precision in both diagnosis and treatment, and have implications for the handling of maladjusted children in educational settings as well as in the clinic situation.

A number of experiments have been carried out using techniques such as desensitisation, conditioned inhibition, negative practice and operant conditioning. Walton (1961) reports on the use of negative practice and conditioned inhibition methods with an eleven-year-old boy suffering from severe tics. Sloane *et al.* (1967) give an account of a field study involving the treatment of a highly aggressive nursery school boy with excessive fantasy play through the giving or withdrawal of positive social reinforcement contingent upon certain behaviour. McKerracher (1967) reports on his attempt to treat a highly anxious enuretic boy of eleven, of average intelligence but backward in reading, by an operant conditioning technique employing both reward and avoidance conditioning. Gittelman (1965), drawing on the techniques of psychodrama and certain learning theory concepts, describes a method involving the use of role-playing or behavioural rehearsal, whereby various instigatory situations are played out by the child and in the case of group therapy by various members of the group. He found that it was particularly useful to elicit from the child various situations which had provoked him to aggression or defiance in the past, and then to present these situations, through acting, to him. Initially the milder situations are presented, and when the child develops tolerance for these, the more stimulating situations are constructed. Fischer (1968) has reviewed experiments on the application of operant conditioning techniques to the treatment of psychotic children. He concludes that while too much should not be expected from operant conditioning methods used with psychotic children, they facilitate the description of abnormal behaviour and are proving useful when directly applied to therapeutic problems. In particular, these methods suggest an approach to therapy which can integrate the efforts of the different professional disciplines involved.

Eysenck and Rachman (1965) recommend further experimentation with operant methods in the clinic situation, since they can be used to generate and/or sustain stable behaviour patterns. They list the advantages of operant methods as permitting, when required, non-verbal operations, strict control of variables, quantification of operations, exclusion of 'clinician variables' and single-case studies. They do, however, need special equipment and experimental rooms, and may be time-consuming. Eysenck and Rachman feel that both operant conditioning and the more familiar methods of behaviour therapy are likely to make a significant contribution to child psychology in the future.

There are few studies evaluating the results of child guidance treatment, and no studies have been carried out in this country comparable to those of Levitt (1957, 1963) and Robins (1966) in the USA. Levitt, on the basis of an examination of the evidence on the effects of psychotherapy on the children, has concluded that there is still no sound basis for contending that psychotherapy facilitates recovery from emotional illness in children. He showed that about two-thirds of children treated are rated as 'improved' when treatment ends, but the same proportion of untreated children with emotional and behaviour problems show improvement after a period of time. He tentatively concludes that children referred for anti-social behaviour are most resistant to treatment, and that children with identifiable behavioural symptoms like enuresis and school phobia respond best. Robins (1966) in a thirty-year follow-up of 524 child guidance clinic patients, compared with a control group of 100 'normal' children, found that the anti-social children were more often psychiatrically ill later on than the controls, but the neurotic children resembled the controls as adults. As Glavin and Quay (1969) observe, the normal group were much brighter than the clinical sample and were selected on the basis that they had not shown up problems in school, but this investigation was more rigorously conducted than other follow-up studies have been.

In this country, Wolff (1961) followed up forty-three pre-school children (24 boys, 19 girls) with ages ranging from 2 years 3 months to 4 years 11 months, three to six years after their first visit to the Maudsley Hospital, where they were referred mainly for phobic symptoms, habit disorders, and aggressive behaviour. Fifteen boys and five girls were assessed as moderately or severely disturbed at the time of follow-up, but only four children were receiving psychiatric treatment at the time. The outcome was worse for the boys than for the girls, and children did less well when coming from broken homes and families where there was open marital disharmony, and when the parents had themselves been treated for psychiatric disorders in the past. Warren (1965) made a follow-up study of 157 adolescent in-patients six or more years after they had been discharged from a London hospital adolescent unit, partly through psychiatric inter-views, partly through social worker contact with a near relative, and partly through questionnaires or other reports. He found that about one-third of the group with neurotic disorders and about one-quarter of the mixed neurotic and conduct disorders had serious further illness; nearly all those with psychotic disorders had such further disturbance, but there was little amongst the conduct disorders. This sample was a very specialised one, but the follow-up study reported is a welcome attempt to discover the relationship between particular types of disturbance in adolescence and those shown later on.

Shepherd *et al.* (1966) compared a group of fifty children aged five to fifteen attending child guidance clinics in Buckinghamshire and a control group of children matched for age, sex and behaviour but not attending clinics. They found that 63 per cent of the clinic cases had improved over two years, but 61 per cent of the matched children had also improved. Maclay (1967) carried out a questionnaire follow-up of children treated at a London hospital child guidance clinic ten to fifteen years previously. 424 questionnaires were sent to parents, of whom 70·6 per cent replied. Of the 299 respondents, 67·9 per cent had no further difficulties, 32·1 per cent having had further psychiatric and/or social problems. The children who had had good relationships with their peers did well. Poor prognostic features were membership of a large family, discharge to a residential school or in-patient unit and an estimate of 'no change' or 'worse' on discharge. Children with psychosomatic disorders did well and those with psychosis and/or organic conditions did badly. No details are given of the kinds of treatment given, and little is said about the distribution of types of disturbance in the total sample, but Maclay's findings are of considerable interest in as much as traditional treatment approaches have emphasised adult-child relationships rather than peer relations. Her findings support the need for group methods of treatment.

In addition to these general follow-up studies, a number of reports have been made on the outcome of the treatment of specific types of emotional or behaviour disorder. During the decade under review, there has been a particular interest in school refusal (Clyne 1966), learning difficulties closely linked with emotional blockage (see symposium with papers by Chazan, Williams and Yule 1969) and childhood autism (Wing 1966; Rutter and Lockyer 1967; Rutter *et al.* 1967; Lockyer and Rutter

1969), and our knowledge of the nature and aetiology of these conditions has been greatly increased. It must be concluded, however, that our knowledge of the efficacy of methods used in the clinical treatment of maladjusted children is still very scanty.

Special educational treatment

Glavin and Quay (1969) comment on the increased tendency in recent years toward educational intervention in the case of children with behaviour disorders, and this has been a marked trend in this country. In January 1960, 1,426 boys and 316 girls were in special schools of some kind on account of maladjustment; by January 1970, there were 4,993 maladjusted boys and 1,300 girls in special schools in addition to 2,961 in independent schools and 2,854 receiving education otherwise than at schools, i.e. having home tuition, tuition whilst in hospitals, or tuition in special classes and units not forming part of a special school (DES 1971). The number of maintained boarding schools for maladjusted pupils rose during the period from twenty-four to fifty-three (in addition to eighteen non-maintained boarding schools), but the most rapid development was in the provision of day schools for maladjusted pupils, the number of which increased from five to thirty-nine. In spite of the increased provision, waiting-lists remained long: in January 1970, 263 pupils were awaiting admission to day schools, and 1,486 to residential schools.

Alongside with the expansion of day school provision for maladjusted children, smaller day units or special classes have been established by a number of local education authorities, in some cases on the grounds that such units are preferable to day schools which are difficult to run. A day school needs to be of a reasonable size to be viable, but it is hardly desirable to place a large number of disturbed children together in the same building. The special day units or classes may be attached to a child guidance clinic or to an ordinary school, or be completely independent. They have the advantages of enabling children who cannot easily settle down in the ordinary school to remain at home while receiving attention, either on a part-time or full-time basis in accordance with individual need, from teachers specialising in the education of maladjusted children. The work of a number of day units is described in *Therapeutic Education* (June 1967), and Bartlett (1970) has surveyed the work of eleven units in England and Wales. She found that the majority of the children in these units were school refusal cases or presented educational problems, and that the units were able to contain and help withdrawn and anxious children rather than those who presented aggressive, hyperactive or psychotic symptoms. Over half the pupils were in the secondary school age-group, with boys outnumbering girls. Most of the units described their approach as being 'informal' rather than 'formal' and 'permissive' rather than 'authoritarian', but all structured their programme to some extent and tried to adapt their methods to individual needs. On the whole the teachers in these units enjoyed their work, although it was often frustrating and improvement in the children was not easily apparent. Overall, 62 per cent of the children who had attended the units were reported to have been treated successfully or to have improved appreciably, and many of the school refusal cases were returned to school.

In recent years, behaviour modification techniques have proved useful in the USA in classes and schools for emotionally disturbed children. As Hewett (1967) writes, this approach, rather than seeing the emotionally disturbed child as a victim of psychic conflicts, cerebral dysfunction or merely scholastic deficits, concentrates on bringing the overt behaviour of the child in line with standards required for learning. Such standards may include the development of an adequate attention span; orderly response in the classroom; the ability to follow directions; tolerance for limits of time, space and activity; accurate exploration of the environment; and appreciation for social approval and avoidance of disapproval. The basic goals of the behaviour modification model for educational programmes are promoting successful development of these standards as well as self-care and intellectual skills through the assignment of carefully graded tasks in a learning environment which provides both rewards and structure for the child in accord with principles of learning theory. Hewett describes, in his article (1967), the physical environment provided by the engineered classroom as well as the hierarchy of educational tasks to be mastered and the planning of interventions to achieve the aims of the programme. Other relevant publications include those by Ullman and Krasner (1965), Valett (1966), Whelan (1966), Whelan and Haring (1966) and Dupont (1969), all of whom discuss comprehensively the relevance of behaviour modification techniques for teachers of emotionally disturbed children.

Haring and Phillips (1962) also advance the thesis that emotionally maladjusted children need a structured environment—a selected and regulated set of experiences—in order to assume responsibility, to learn more effectively and to move towards normality in living. They consider that previous efforts to help the emotionally disturbed, such as those described by Bettelheim (1950, 1955), have, in following a permissive policy, not put enough stress on programmed educational methods. Lewis (1967) discusses the value of a bold short-term programme for disturbed children in Nashville and Durham, USA, designed to provide an intensive re-educational experience for them in a period of crisis, and based on the around-the-clock work of two teacher-counsellors, who are responsible for each group of eight children. These teacher-counsellors live and work with the children, assisted by a number of aides, and place a heavy emphasis on formal school work, adapted to the needs of each child. An improvement rate of 75 to 87 per cent is reported, and it is claimed that the programme involves less time and expense than is usual in the rehabilitation of disturbed children.

In this country, although the contribution which can be made by the teacher and the school to the treatment of maladjusted children is increasingly recognised, relatively little is known about the actual methods used in special schools and classes, and little systematic research has been conducted on the value of special educational treatment for maladjusted pupils. Most of the published reports on schools for maladjusted children have concerned independent rather than local authority schools, and while valuable in themselves, are not based on an objective evaluation of the work carried out. Lenhoff (1960) has produced a clear and well-written account of the daily life of boys at a residential school for 35 to 40 boys, aged ten to sixteen, of good intelligence. At this school, treatment methods lay stress on relaxation from the tensions of the home situation and other pressures, learning from the group in a small community, and forming satisfactory relationships; group discussions are considered valuable. The book does not contain a statistical evaluation of the work done nor any figures of 'cures' or 'improvements'.

Shields (1962), discussing work at an experimental residential school for maladjusted boys under the old London County Council, stresses the need for understanding the intra-psychic processes which led to failure in the initial home situation and for an awareness by the staff of the unconscious motives and fantasies which impel a child towards actions which are socially unacceptable. Of 216 boys admitted and discharged over an eleven-year period, 181 (84 per cent) made a reasonably normal readjustment to life outside the school, at home or at work. Shields recommends that residential schools should be schools, not residential clinics, and that they should reproduce a good home situation as far as possible; but they should not rely on too rigid and systematic an approach, nor *only* on love, patience and tolerance.

Shaw (1965) gives an account of his school for the educational and psychological treatment of maladjusted boys of very high intelligence, founded in 1934. Treatment methods include 'radical psychoanalysis' in about half the cases, the others mostly responding to 'a genial guidance within a confidential interview' and accepting advice blended with cautious criticism and friendship. The atmosphere of the school is fairly permissive, with no corporal punishment or compulsory games. A school court deals with personal disputes, and there are committees dealing with such matters as food and hygiene, sports and library. Pupils tend to stay five or six years to complete their academic careers; about half the pupils pass academic examinations to the extent of qualifying for the professions. 67 per cent of the intake are said to be 'radically and permanently cured', and 21 per cent to be 'improved'. An appendix by Holland demonstrates how important satisfaction derived from educational progress may be in treating maladjusted pupils.

Balbernie (1966) shows what had happened to thirty-two ex-pupils of a residential school for maladjusted pupils by the age of eighteen; they had been admitted to the school at the average age of twelve years six months. Six of the thirty-two were then in Borstal, one was at a detention centre, two were in mental hospitals with a poor prognosis, and three others were showing very clear evidence of deterioration in adjustment, i.e. twelve of the sample were in serious difficulties. There were four more very doubtful cases, and only five out of the thirty-two boys found adequate support and security within their own homes after they left residential care. Balbernie concludes that existing residential facilities for adolescents do not meet the needs of the especially difficult cases. It is also clear that a proper aftercare service is essential if residential schools are to be worthwhile.

The accounts of schools for maladjusted children mentioned above do not give a picture of what is being done in such schools generally. The Child Psychiatry Section of the Royal Medico-Psychological Association (1966) sent a questionnaire to fifteen day and forty-seven residential schools for maladjusted pupils in the official list, and obtained replies from two-thirds of the sample. It was found that very few of the teachers had any sort of special training and that few of the schools had regular visits from psychiatrists or psychotherapists. Although most of the children rapidly improved in behaviour, the average stay at special schools was four years. Aftercare was uneven, and parental visits were regular only in one-half of the residential schools. The relationships between the child and the outside community were unsatisfactory and inadequate, and there was great difficulty in finding jobs for school leavers. Therapy took a very poor second place to ordinary educational processes, and very little was done to help inadequately trained staff with the psychological problems they met from day to day. The Report concluded that a large number of children are sent to these schools not directly for any special benefit, but to remove them from an unsatisfactory environment; the psychodynamics of the

D

special school community were only dimly seen and narrowly appreciated. Further research, of the kind initiated by Williams (1961), Petrie (1962) and Roe (1965), is needed into what happens in a therapeutic setting for children.

Williams (1961), examining which criteria tend to be associated with recovery in children treated in residential special schools, found that improved educational attainments and attitudes were positively and significantly correlated with recovery. While other criteria, such as increased toleration of frustration, were also associated with recovery, Williams observes that the objectivity with which educational progress can be assessed, coupled with the high incidence of educational retardation among maladjusted children, makes this finding of particular importance. Petrie examined factors related to progress in the readjustment of twenty-three children at a special boarding school for maladjusted children, finding an improvement in parental attitudes to be a particularly important factor. Roe assessed the progress in behaviour and attitude of 140 maladjusted pupils in ILEA special schools and classes over a period of up to eighteen months, and emphasises the difficulties which special schools have in coping with some of the pupils sent to them. She suggests that not enough work is done in depth in special schools and that there is a need for a better understanding of the reactions and feelings of maladjusted pupils and their parents. That progress is being made in understanding therapeutic factors in group living, in achieving insight into the needs of children living in residential establishments, and in the training of staff for work in these establishments, is suggested in the collection of papers edited by Tod (1968).

Summary and conclusions

Many parents and children seen at child guidance clinics will readily testify to the value, at least in the short run, of current approaches to the treatment of maladjusted children, in terms of the mitigation of anxiety at times of stress. Teachers, too, faced with an intolerable burden presented by a severely disturbed child, have often found the clinical and special services available to them of great assistance. However, it is difficult to disagree with the conclusion reached by Arbuckle, in his overview of counselling and psychotherapy (1967), that astonishingly little evidence about the results of psychotherapy has been amassed during over half a century of work. In general, a successful outcome is reported in about two-thirds of cases treated, but it is rarely possible to discover exactly what factors have been responsible for any improvement and it cannot be said with conviction that such improvement is directly attributable to the treatment provided.

Behaviour therapy is seen by some to be among the most promising newer developments in treatment and indeed to be 'the most exciting and challenging technique on the current scene' (Bergin 1967). Even if the research reports of behaviour therapists are often open to criticism (Breger and McGaugh 1965), it is to be hoped that considerable resources will be available for the testing out and extension of a variety of behaviour therapy techniques in this country. It is interesting to speculate why so little experimentation has been carried out in British child guidance clinics, and there are probably several factors combining to retard progress in this direction. As compared with the USA, very limited financial resources have been available for research and experimental work by clinical workers, who in any case are usually too hard pressed by the day-to-day demands on their services to find time for anything else. In Britain, too, the educational psychologist, who is the member of the team most likely, by interest and training, to initiate research, has not been so concerned with 'therapy' in the clinical sense as his American counterpart—nor indeed as concerned with therapy as the clinical psychologist in the hospital service in this country. Furthermore, most child guidance clinics are controlled by local education authorities and have only tenuous links with universities, where there are greater opportunities for research.

Other promising developments include the encouraging of community interest and participation in the prevention and treatment of maladjustment—with the emphasis on what can be done by focusing attention on young children at risk and the early years at school (Caplan 1961; Schiff and Kellam 1967; Newton and Brown 1967)—and the growth of counselling in schools. The latter development (see Lytton and Craft 1969; NAMH Report 1970; Jones 1970) is to be welcomed as likely to contribute both to the prevention and treatment of emotional disturbance, particularly during adolescence, as well as to the spread of knowledge among teachers about ways of dealing with behaviour problems in school. However, the part which the school counsellor ought to play in treating incipient or well-established maladjustment is not yet precisely established, and before this question is resolved, there is likely to be a great deal of conflict between the role of the school counsellor and that of the educational psychologist. As Gray and Noble (1968) state in a penetrating analysis of the increasing overlap of the functions of these two professional groups, the point has been reached in the USA where the functions described as appropriate for each of the groups overlap almost completely with the other. The situation is somewhat different in this country, where the school counsellor is not primarily concerned with maladjusted children, though he is in a good position to provide help and support while a child is awaiting treatment, to liaise with treatment agencies and ensure that recommendations about the handling of the child in school are implemented, and also to provide some measure of aftercare when treatment ceases. There is, however, certainly a need here for the reappraisal of the roles of all professional groups working to help maladjusted children, so that training may be more effective and treatment services may operate as economically as possible.

This survey has clearly shown the need for the evaluation of specific forms of treatment and their effects on different types of disturbed behaviour. Present-day treatment procedures, whether in the clinic or the school setting, tend to be carried out without an adequate theoretical basis and often without well-defined goals. Nevertheless, it is important, as Fenichel (1966) emphasises, not to lose sight of the need of the child for his own personal prescription of treatment, training or education 'based on a psycho-educational assessment of his unique patterns of behaviour and levels of functioning'.

Acknowledgment

The writer would like to thank his colleague Mr Douglas Hamblin for helpful comments on this paper.

R. Gulliford

6. Advances in remedial education

What is remedial education?

A recent report of the National Association for Remedial Education (NARE) defined remedial education as 'those special measures used to meet the educational needs of children with learning difficulties in special classes within the ordinary schools; in special remedial centres which pupils attend on a part-time basis; in groups withdrawn from their ordinary school classes for special teaching by a remedial teacher who may be a member of the school staff or a visiting peripatetic remedial teacher. It also includes the work of specialist advisory teachers who may guide and support other teachers or schools. So defined, remedial education is that part of special education concerned with children with learning difficulties which is provided outside the special schools' (Brennan 1971).

This wide definition was no doubt framed with a view to providing a broad base for a career structure for remedial teachers, but it does so by making an unreal division between those who teach educationally backward children in special schools and those who do not. Moreover, it puts the stamp of approval on the tendency to use the word *remedial* for the teaching of any pupils who are slow to learn. Many slow learners, however, do not need remedial education so much as an education which is specially planned to take account of their learning characteristics and future needs. There is also the danger that *remedial* in this context will be interpreted too narrowly in terms of teaching in basic educational skills (this happens) rather than considering the contribution of a wide range of curriculum content to the full development of the slower developing pupils. As the DES Education Survey 15 (1971) says: 'Uncertainty of aims, objectives and methods for "slow learners" was immediately apparent in many—indeed the majority—of the schools visited. Indeed the commonly used term "remedial" may itself be indicative of a fundamental confusion. If the word is to be taken literally then it suggests that the retardation of slow learners is something to be "remedied": that if they are given appropriate treatment—usually interpreted as additional lessons in the three Rs—then their backwardness will be overcome and they will take their place among the more able.' This broadening of the word *remedial* has happened because it is a useful euphemism (more acceptable than *special*) and also because the nature of true remedial teaching has not been sufficiently well developed nor clearly defined. The need now is to develop this special expertise and practice.

The NARE definition contrasts with a more restricted meaning which has often been assumed in practice and experiment during the last twenty years. It is expressed in Sampson's (1969) operational definition adopted prior to a survey of remedial practices: 'Remedial education is any teaching given individually or in small groups to help children in the ordinary schools who are failing in particular subjects, this service being provided by teachers additional to basic staff who work either in special centres or on a visiting peripatetic basis.' Sampson adds that special educational treatment in special schools and classes was specifically excluded. In a similar vein, Gulliford (1971) suggested that 'Remedial education tends to be part-time, relatively short-term and limited to specific objectives such as remedying failures or difficulty in learning certain school subjects, especially in basic educational skills. It is teaching which is additional to normal schooling rather than an alternative form of education.'

This concept of remedial education has usually been associated with the idea of *retardation* or *under-functioning* and, while there are problems in defining retardation, it can be argued that there is still a case for distinguishing teaching which attempts to remedy failure in particular basic educational skills from the broader educational programme for children who for various reasons are slow learners. Since the latter is needed for 10 to 15 per cent of the school population (and in some schools for as many as 60 per cent), it should be regarded as an integral part of normal education, and one that many, if not most, teachers should have some knowledge of and competence in. The more specialised skills of the remedial teacher could be developed and used on behalf of children whose problems seem to call for more expert help. In reporting her survey of remedial teaching, Sampson (1969) expressed the view that 'provision should be parsimonious in the sense that it should be the smallest that will do the defined job'. The problem, of course, is to define the job. In a symposium on remedial education, Lytton (1968) remarked that 'to be effective such help must employ specialised techniques and should be given in small groups, preferably by trained teachers', while Phillips (1968), in the same symposium, diagnoses the malaise in remedial education by saying that remedial teachers 'lack the full complement of tools for a difficult specialisation'.

The problem is, what is this specialisation? How can we define the job? It is interesting and useful to take a retrospective glance at the origins of the idea of remedial education. A distinction between pupils whose backwardness is associated with limited ability and those who are backward for other reasons was frequently made in the 1930s by investigators such as Lewis (1931) and Burt (1937). Brief reference to the idea can be found in the *Handbook of Suggestions for Teachers* (1932) and more fully in the Ministry of Education pamphlet *The Education of Backward Children* (1937). The needs of intelligent but retarded children were given emphasis in the writings of Schonell (1942), and since he may be regarded as one of the major influences in the development in the UK of remedial as distinct from special school or class teaching, it is not surprising that the first remedial services in the late 1940s and early 1950s tended to stress work with children of average ability who were retarded. Schonell himself concluded from various sources of evidence that in classes of backward children 30 to 40 per cent were likely to be pupils of average intelligence. He estimated that 4 to 6 per cent of all pupils were to be considered retarded, which accords quite well with the findings of the Isle of Wight study (Rutter *et al.* 1970) in which the prevalence rate for specific reading retardation was 3·7 per cent, retardation being calculated by a multiple regression analysis using the three variables age, intelligence and reading. The concept of retardation as a criterion for selecting children for remedial teaching took some hard blows in the 1950s. Changing concepts of the nature and development of intelligence (Vernon 1958) undermined belief in the stability of measures of intelligence; the relationship between attainment and intelligence test scores as expressed in achievement quotients or ratios were subjected to serious criticism on statistical grounds (Crane 1959; Phillips 1958) and, finally, evaluations of the results of remedial reading raised the question whether the progress of intelligent retarded children was significantly different from that of dull children.

When this reaction from the concept of retardation as a means of selecting pupils for remedial attention was at its height in the 1950s, it was suggested that there were no valid grounds for picking out retarded children for the benefit of remedial teaching; all backward children could do with it. This view partly reflected the then recent rediscovery of the importance of adverse environmental factors in limiting intellectual development which now finds clearer expression in the idea of positive discrimination in educational priority areas and in the moves to develop compensatory education.

Distinguishing between compensatory and remedial education is important for the future development of remedial education. Many remedial teachers might at present be more correctly described as engaged in compensatory education; their efforts are often concentrated in the poorer areas of towns. Where children arrive at school age poorly equipped with the readiness skills for school learning, it is not surprising that so many have barely made a start in reading by the age of seven. What is required is not just remedial teaching but a change in methods and expectations in primary schools so that the teaching of reading is an accepted and well-organised aspect of junior school teaching.

Several surveys have provided data relating to the need for this. Both Pringle *et al.* (1966) and Morris (1966) showed that about 40 per cent of seven-year-olds had insufficient mastery of the skills of reading to make progress without further help. Morris also showed how few teachers of first-year juniors were equipped by training and experience for helping them. Clark's (1970) survey in a Scottish county showed that 15 per cent of seven-year-olds had not advanced beyond the earliest stages of learning to read, a proportion which was reduced by one-half the following year. By age nine, only 1 per cent of the sample were found to be two or more years backward in reading. While this delayed progress can partly be attributed to environmental factors and to factors in the child (for example, a speech difficulty was a common one), it is also necessary to consider, as Clark does, whether changes in primary school methods may be having some influence in bringing about a later growth of mechanical reading skill. If so, the implications for training teachers and for organising special help should be assessed and made clear to teachers. (She does not of course make a plea for a return to more formal and earlier instruction in reading and recognises that there are some educational objectives much more important than early high standards on a mechanical test.)

In other words, the large problem of children making slow progress in 'basic' skills is one which requires a reassessment of basic teaching in schools rather than being a matter for remedial teachers. It is unlikely that there would be enough remedial teachers in any case to deal with the 7 or 8 per cent who are still backward at age eight. What then should remedial teachers do? Wait until the hard core of backward readers emerge at age nine onwards? To do this would reverse the trend for remedial teachers to be engaged in advisory and survey work early in the junior school and would also run counter to the tendency for remedial teachers to see the need for identifying children with learning problems in the infant school and for preventive work at that stage.

If it were possible to predict at age five or six those children who were likely to have learning problems later, it would provide the remedial teacher with one clear priority. De Hirsch and Jansky (1966) developed a small battery of tests (including visual perception, oral language and visuo-motor performance) as a predictive index of future progress. A research team, in an extension of the Isle of Wight project, has been following up 440 children from the age of starting school and relating results on a battery of visuo-motor tests, language tests and a neurological examination to subsequent progress. The difficulty with these early screening procedures is that ensuring the certain identification of failures requires the selection of a large group of children which will include a large number of false positives. A procedure more modest in intention, based on teachers' observations, might, however, have value in alerting infant teachers to children at risk of subsequent educational failure.

To summarise the discussion so far, it has been suggested that remedial education should be concerned with a narrower field than suggested in the NARE definition, that it is teaching which is additional to the normal curriculum experiences provided, that the large problem of slow learners requires a reassessment of normal schooling and of the training and guidance of teachers, and that the traditional concern of remedial teachers with pupils who are specifically retarded should continue to be at the centre of their work—though this does not mean an exclusive concern. This central problem can now be viewed in the light of much recent discussion of the concept *specific learning disabilities*. A definition which has received considerable support is that by Bateman (1965): children who have specific learning disabilities are those who (1) manifest an education-ally significant discrepancy between their estimated intellectual potential and actual level of performance (2) related to basic disorders in the learning process (3) which may or may not be accompanied by demonstrable central nervous system dysfunction and (4) which are not secondary to generalised mental retardation, educational or cultural deprivation, severe emotional disturbance or sensory loss.

The important feature of this definition for our purpose is that it refers to disorders in the learning process and it suggests that the essential skill of the remedial teacher is the assessment and teaching of children with such disorders. This is not to say that he should necessarily be limited to children who unequivocally come within the scope of that definition—it is impossible to make clear-cut distinctions in practice. But it *is* saying that he is not primarily a teacher of that mixed group of children we label slow learners, nor primarily a specialist in compensatory or in therapeutic education. If this point of view were accepted, it would focus attention on the need to develop this essential expertise. Administratively, a clearer conception of the nature of the remedial teacher's specialisation would raise more acutely the question of what other steps need to be taken to provide adequately for educationally backward children. There are obvious implications for the training and qualification of remedial teachers. These are all issues which merit rigorous examination from a professional as well as an educational point of view.

The assessment of learning failure

One of the requirements, therefore, for the satisfactory development of remedial teaching is good diagnostic assessment. There are, of course, inspiring teachers who are remarkably successful in developing a relationship with pupils and providing just the right kinds of experience and learning at the right time, yet they may have given little thought to the kinds of issue raised below. In proposing an outline for assessment (and therefore identifying areas of teaching), one is not suggesting a completely different style and approach. Rather one would hope that with a clearer conception of the task the good teacher might be even more effective— particularly with those severe learning disabilities which are so often resistant to treatment.

Nor is it being suggested that every failing pupil needs to be 'put through' a battery of tests. What is needed is a framework for diagnostic assessment (and therefore for remedial teaching) which, as well as indicating those psychological functions and educational skills for which suitable tests are available, would also indicate the probably larger area in which the teacher or psychologist must rely on his own or the class teacher's observations or must adopt experimental approaches like those described by Bartlett and Shapiro (1956).

One requirement is to formulate the strategy of diagnostic assessment. Wedell (1970) has outlined a sequential strategy for the educational psychologist which could be adapted for the remedial teacher. It consists of four successive stages. The first covers the whole range of possible causes of the child's learning difficulty *at the level of a screening investigation* in order to identify areas that seem to have relevance to the problem. This screening investigation involves observation of behaviour, case history information, an abbreviated intelligence test and assessments of educational attainment. Stage 2 evaluates these findings and formulates hypotheses which are tested more thoroughly at Stage 3. The aim in Stage 3 is to examine the areas where the child fails, in order to analyse the component functions of educational and cognitive skills and this implies 'a knowledge of the relevant hierarchies of skills'—about which unfortunately, as Wedell says, we have large areas of ignorance. At this stage, information would also be sought about concept development, sensori-motor skills, laterality, social adjustment and case history information. Stage 3 contains forty-four items. All this might be done by means of a combination of testing, observation and experimental teaching. Stage 4 is one of diagnostic formulation leading to various choices of action.

This is not necessarily a more time-consuming process than the average remedial teacher can undertake. The important thing is having the steps of the plan in mind rather than working meticulously through it. Moreover, the area of greatest interest to the teacher is the analysis of the components of educational skills and cognitive skills which lead directly into teaching. The assessment of these skills has until now been dominated by conventional norm-referenced tests, apart from some use of diagnostic tests. In the absence of a standardised test, teachers have tended to feel uneasy and have certainly placed too low a value on their own experienced observation. (In fact some of the most important features of remedial teaching depend on the teacher's awareness that the child is ready for the next stage of learning.)

As Ward (1970) has pointed out, norm-referenced tests have been constructed to distinguish between good and poor performance, whereas in remedial education we know performance is poor. We need to know just what skills are lacking. While norm-referenced tests are not without value for this purpose (e.g. the analysis of errors on a reading test; the comparison of measures of rate, accuracy and comprehension on a test of continuous reading such as the *Neale Analysis of Reading*), the concept of criterion-referenced tests has much to offer in remedial and special education.

The current situation with regard to the assessment of primary school mathematics illustrates this very clearly. A common request of teachers is for an up-to-date mathematics test, since the tests which became widely known in remedial work (e.g. those of Schonell) are seen to be unsuitable in the light of the great changes in the understanding of early mathematical concepts and in the primary schools' mathematics curriculum. Yet both these developments provide sufficient information for itemising and sequencing concepts and skills in at least the earlier stages of mathematics from which criterion-referenced tests could be drawn. In mathematics failure, it is not difficult to pursue what Wedell refers to as 'the analysis of component functions . . . until the psychologist reaches the level where the child succeeds'.

It might reasonably be argued that in reading the component skills are less clearly established—or can be less certainly sequenced. The situation may well be that the processes of learning to read have been obfuscated by fashions and controversies in the teaching of reading; the focus has been on so-called methods of teaching reading rather than the routes by which children learn. In fact a sequence of stages or phases is well known (e.g. word recognition skills, phrase reading and fluency, higher-order skills) and there is information relevant to the analysis of some of the sub-skills. Thus Robert and Lunzer (1968) itemise thirteen part-skills roughly in the order of acquisition. Merritt (1969) has outlined primary, intermediate and higher-order skills, drawing attention, for example, to the phonemic, grammatical and word sequences which are often-overlooked elements in recognition skills at the intermediate level. A considerable number of books, teaching materials and diagnostic tests chart progress in learning phonics; Cordts (1965) offers a very thorough discussion of the whole topic. Presland (1970) has outlined steps in the analysis of handwriting skills with indications for appropriate remedial work.

The analysis of the components of basic educational skills is a priority for remedial teachers since it is basic to skilled remedial teaching. But there is a further requirement: a more comprehensive view of the cognitive functions involved in learning failure. The lack of this is illustrated by the tendency to equate learning disability with perceptual problems and the rather uncritical enthusiasm with which perceptual programmes are taken up and applied, often with flimsy evidence of the need for them. Johnson and Myklebust (1967) find the need to make the same point in relation to their concept of psychoneurological learning disability: *to provide training only in terms of perceptual disturbances is to assume that this involvement is a universal consequence of dysfunctions in the brain.* The sources of learning failure may be found in many different cognitive processes and the situation is complicated by the interacting effects—the fact that a dysfunction interferes with other processes. Following Johnson and Myklebust's account of cognitive processes in which deficits may occur, we have the following outline. (There are of course other ways of conceptualising the problem, e.g. Bannatyne 1971.)

Sensation refers to the basic information received through the senses; the importance of checking for sensory defects is well known.

Perception is the first stage of cognitive processing of information received from the environment. It is important to give adequate consideration to auditory and kinaesthetic as well as visual perception and to notice that many learning tasks involve the integration of information from several sensory channels and from motor behaviour.

Imagery is a rather neglected area of cognitive functioning, consideration of which may have something to offer the study of those children who appear to have poor retention. It may also be a factor in explaining those children who seem to respond to teaching methods emphasising particular modalities. Johnson and Myklebust believe that weakness in imagery is involved in non-verbal disabilities—children for example who cannot recall non-verbal aspects of everyday experience in response to such questions as 'How did it sound? What did it look like?' Such failures are probably commoner than we realise and may well be overlooked through being thought to be trivial by-products of other failure characteristics.

Symbolisation refers to the ability to represent experience. The many facets of language are the major manifestation of symbolic functions which concerns remedial teachers, but non-verbal symbolisation must not be over-looked. Indeed, it is noteworthy that some retarded children manifestly have difficulty with non-verbal symbols such as the clock face, facial expressions, drawings and other representations. In language itself, it is useful to distinguish *inner language* from *receptive* and *expressive* aspects of language. In practice, we tend to judge children's language development primarily from observations of their expressive language and secondarily from evidence of their comprehension of the spoken word. *Inner language* is the language by which the child thinks and associates experience with meaning. The distinction becomes clearer if we consider a deaf child who in spite of receptive and expressive difficulties may still be making progress in thinking as a result of the growth of inner language.

Recent work in psycholinguistics offers, of course, many concepts of value to the remedial teacher wishing to assess language. The pervasive influence of language in many aspects of learning basic educational skills is further supported by the findings of Ingram (1960), Clark (1970), and Rutter *et al.* (1970) about the incidence of speech and language problems in retarded children.

A further step in the hierarchy of learning processes is *conceptualisation*. It is interesting to observe that traditionally we see mathematics failure largely in terms of failure in the acquisition of concepts, whereas some of the severe problems of failure may well be due to weakness further down the hierarchy—problems in perception, imagery and symbolisation. In reading, however, the reverse tends to be the case. Perception tends to be stressed (sometimes even in older, backward readers) whereas less attention is given to the many ways in which language processes may be impeding learning. Likewise the role of conceptualisation is neglected. Reid (1966) has shown that infants often lack concepts for such terms as 'word', 'letter', 'reading'. Can we assume that all readers can easily acquire the concept of *word family* and can engage in the processes of classification involved in phonics instruction?

To this scheme of levels of cognitive functioning it is necessary to add that deficits may occur (1) on either the receptive or the expressive side (input-output). Thus failure to copy a letter may be due to faulty attention and perception rather than the perceptual-motor processes of executing it. Alternatively the child may perceive and recognise the shape adequately but have a marked inability to coordinate the necessary visuo-motor performance. (2) There may be relative strength and weakness in different modalities (e.g. visual, auditory)—or the problem may be in the integration of information from several sensory channels. (3) The weakness may be in the associative thinking processes which organise and give meaning to experience. These processes are difficult to assess but are worth having in mind when we meet children who 'know' letters and sounds but cannot easily combine them into spoken words and are slow to relate them to their meaning. Likewise one meets children who 'read' quite well but are strangely slow to grasp meaning. Two further points must be made: that weaknesses in particular functions are commonly compensated for to a greater or lesser degree; that the degree to which compensation has occurred or will occur is influenced by many variable factors such as the child's emotional state, his management and care at home and the kind of teaching he has received. It is also important to bear age and developmental maturity levels in mind.

All these considerations make the assessment of learning failure a complex and difficult business and, in the state of present knowledge, often rather speculative. The remedial teacher might be forgiven for thinking that in the circumstances a straightforward attack on the educational problem is the best and least time-consuming thing. Yet the quest for a more searching analysis of failures in basic educational skills and, where necessary, the examination of weaknesses in cognitive processes is surely desirable in view of the frequency of children with severe learning disabilities (cf. the pressure for recognising a group labelled dyslexic) as well as the evidence that, in general, children who are retarded at the junior school stage continue to lag behind their fellows (Morris 1966).

This point of view would be endorsed by Frostig (1968) who, while admitting the inadequacy of available tests, describes a test battery in use at the Marianne Frostig Centre for Educational Therapy. 'It is more advantageous to make mistakes than to do nothing when ground has to be broken' and, as she says, the advantage of the battery of tests she uses is that they provide the psychologist and teacher with a rationale for exploring further.

The three basic tests she uses are the Wechsler Intelligence Scale for Children (wisc), the Illinois Test of Psycholinguistic Abilities (itpa) and the Frostig Tests of Visual Perception—plus the Wepman Test for assessing auditory perception of speech sounds and a survey of motor abilities where necessary. The itpa may be viewed as a prototype for tests of specific functions which like the early Binet tests will be further developed and no doubt superseded. It includes tests of the three *processes* previously referred to—reception, association, expression—and tests of different *channels* in these processes—auditory and visual reception and association, verbal and manual expression. The sub-tests are categorised into the *representational* level—the complex mediating processes of utilising symbols which carry meaning—and the *automatic* level, which includes communication behaviour requiring less voluntary but highly organised and integrated patterns (e.g. visual and auditory closure, speed of perception, sequencing). The Frostig tests consist of five sub-tests: eye-motor coordination, figure-ground, form constancy, position in space and spatial relation. Both the Frostig tests and the itpa assess specifically a range of functions undeniably important in acquiring basic educational skills and for each sub-test it is possible to prescribe the kind of remediation required (Frostig 1968; Kirk and Kirk 1971). The wisc is considered useful as a check on evidence obtained from the other tests and for its indications of performance in conceptual and reasoning processes.

A basic pattern such as this can be supplemented by information from other tests and observations relevant to the area of weakness. To take a few examples, suspected weakness in visual association compared with auditory association could be explored by observing performance on the Raven's *Progressive Matrices* or other tests involving reasoning processes with graphic materials and on sub-tests of similarities and differences and verbal absurdities involving reasoning with auditorily presented material. Weakness in auditory sequential memory can be observed in the repetition of digits, isolated words or sentences, or the not-infrequent evidence among remedial cases of failure to learn (or late age of learning) the alphabet, counting, nursery rhymes or addresses. In the area of language, the former lack of tests has been made good to some extent by such scales as the Reynell (1969). Studies such as those by Graham (1970) in the repetition, comprehension and production of sentences suggest methods of exploring language competence. Recent work in psycholinguistics sharpens observation of language in use in informal situations. The wide range of tests and assessment techniques which might have a place are discussed in a number of recent publications (e.g. Mittler 1970).

The important thing, of course, is not the administration of tests but the generation of hypotheses about the learning difficulty. Are any tests relevant to the questions being asked? What observations would be relevant? Would a short period of teaching along specific lines test the hypothesis? An example of the application of an experimental method is Bartlett and Shapiro's (1956) account of the investigation of the learning disability of a nine-year-old boy who showed severe psychiatric disturbance and, even when this improved, a severe learning disability. By means of a succession of small experiments the authors were able to conclude that the pupil had good retention once something was learnt, that an emphasis on visual cues and avoidance of kinaesthetic clues was needed. A weakness in forming associations within and across certain sensory modalities was identified and it was considered that the learning of associations needed to be with small units of information.

Unfortunately, in remedial teaching one is faced with a number of dilemmas; we should recognise them even if we cannot resolve them. We have our educational goals in view; the kind of exploration just described can seem detour behaviour apparently taking us away from the goal or at least wasting time en route. Moreover, we have seen children make good progress without much in the way of preliminary diagnosis; it is tempting to follow well-worn paths until we meet an obstacle. More serious is the fact that experiment may be felt by the teacher and the pupil to be making a doubtful contribution to teaching; in Bartlett and Shapiro's account we find that at one stage the boy wanted to get directly on with reading. Some kinds of enquiry could certainly conflict with a teacher's conceptions of motivating remedial activity. The final dilemma is that the remedial teacher or psychologist could go on endlessly applying tests and making observations to the neglect of teaching; and ample time is a luxury not often found in remedial work. The solution is, as has been suggested, to work from hypotheses and to regard diagnosis as continuing through teaching.

To return to the question referred to earlier: What is remedial teaching? It is suggested that one of its essential features is that it is based on diagnostic assessment which is undertaken within some such framework as has been sketched out here. While these ideas can advantageously be in the minds of teachers of slow learners, it is not absolutely essential to them. It *is* essential that such teachers should be well informed about curriculum developments that will enrich the slow learners' education and should know what modifications in scope and presentation are required.

Just as we turn to the teacher of the deaf for very specialised knowledge and skills about educating the deaf, so in cases of learning disability we should be able to turn to the remedial teacher for a particular expertise and not find that he has turned into a reading consultant, a special education adviser, play therapist or educational technologist—though if he is something of all these as well as being a specialised remedial teacher so much the better.

Methods of remedial teaching

Little information has been gathered about the methods employed by remedial teachers. One of the few recent sources of information is a survey by Sampson (1969) in which 675 remedial teachers reported on their practice and opinions. Asked for their views about methods and materials, they stressed that the approach is entirely dependent on the needs of the child and that a variety of materials, books and methods should be available. The needs of the child appeared however to be assessed rather vaguely in terms of his reading level, his response to word-whole, phonic or mixed approaches and his needs for motivation. Sampson reported that on average only two preliminary assessments were made and that often both of these were on short, word-reading tests. She also suggested that the teachers' identification of preferred books and materials frequently raised doubts as to the individualised character of the methods.

Sampson summarised her enquiry with a composite picture of the typical situation revealed. It portrays the remedial child of today as an urban working-class boy; aged about eight. He is dullish but probably in the normal range. Following reading tests (most likely Burt or Schonell's word recognition tests) he joins a group of five or six children for two or three lessons a week. He has become discouraged by his previous failure but he still wants to learn. The teacher of this group is a part-timer, trained and with ordinary classroom experience. In the relaxed atmosphere of the small group he enjoys her individual attention. She engineers his work so that he experiences early and easy success. She gives him praise and encouragement for the smallest progress. He enjoys word games and friendly competition within the group. He finds interesting books around, among which the Ladybird Keyword series is likely to be included. He may win tangible rewards now and then and almost certainly finds satisfaction in completing his own graph of progress.

A composite picture does not of course do justice to those remedial teachers who are more specialised than this. Sampson quotes teachers who have experimented with programmed learning, who use teaching machines and audio-visual aids and give considerable attention to linguistic approaches, to the use of tape-recorded materials. The typical remedial service is well informed on the range of published materials available; apart from reading schemes, workbooks, reading kits, reading laboratories, and taped materials are widely used. But it would be a fair assessment that the essentials of remedial teaching have not changed much during the last twenty-five years. Sampson's findings seem to reflect the principles laid down by Schonell in 1942: (*a*) individual attention; (*b*) correct attitude by teacher; (*c*) use of materials related to the dominant interests and motives of the child; (*d*) selection of method best suited to the child's difficulties; and (*e*) short, continuous lessons of a systematic kind. Schonell prefaced these principles by stating the need for 'detailed information from a thorough diagnosis . . . the types of errors, the nature of past instruction in reading and the direction of past interests, educational and non-educational'.

The principles of remedial teaching may be re-stated in the light of current thinking in the following way:

1.   The need for adequate diagnosis (as discussed in the previous section).
2.   A plan of remedial action which includes the following aspects:
(*a*)   teaching which is organised to take account of the pupil's strengths and weaknesses in educational skills;
(*b*)   measures for remediating weak cognitive functions where necessary;
(*c*)   particular regard to pupil motivation;
(*d*)   any therapeutic measures which may be needed to alleviate emotional and social difficulties;
(*e*)   liaison, where desirable, with the child's home;
(*f*)   cooperation with the child's school.
3.   The provision of continued supervision and appropiate teaching after remedial teaching has been discontinued.

The first principle has already been discussed but it is worth underlining at this point that *diagnostic assessment* continues through the process of remedial teaching. It is a common situation to have to begin remedial teaching with many questions unresolved. The success or failure of particular methods, the learning characteristics of the pupil, new information about the child's attitudes or environmental pressures on him and many other observations and findings require a continuous process of modifying and checking one's hypotheses. Whereas there are some children with whom teaching can proceed in a normal progression from the point of failure, there are others whose difficulties may require periods of experimental teaching to explore the problem further (see Cotterell 1972).

The basic requirement for *planning the teaching programme* is a thorough understanding of the progressions in learning educational skills, the nature of the sub-skills and their interdependence at different stages. Without this understanding, teaching is liable to degenerate into a series of expedients for tackling the learning problem in piecemeal ways, often with their motivational value as the main consideration. An important example of this is provided by the elementary conceptions held about the teaching of phonics. It is easy enough to decide that a child's understanding is inadequate and to put him on to such activities as the Stott Programmed Reading Kit. Not surprisingly this is sometimes not as effective as hoped, because the function of phonics in the process of reading may be viewed naively as a 'key for unlocking new words' and mainly a 'phonetic' process. The nature of phonics as a means of becoming aware of regularities (and irregularities) in the spelling patterns of words which represent regularities in speech sounds, and the deployment of this awareness *in combination* with meaning, grammatical and other context clues in sentences, may be neglected. Likewise it is not uncommon that, having decided a child needs help with phonics, the teacher prompts him to attempt a phonic examination of words which are beyond the level he has reached. It is indeed difficult in view of the relatively uncontrolled appearance of phonic elements in typical reading books to ensure the transfer of learning from phonic exercises and games to actual reading. It is not superfluous to point out that phonic work is sometimes undertaken without first ensuring that phonic readiness is present.

Another example is provided by the suggestion of Schonfield (1956) that there is a plateau in reading progress at about reading ages $7\frac{1}{2}$ to $8\frac{1}{2}$. This may or may not be substantiated, but it prompts consideration of the factors involved in reading progress and therefore of the nature of remedial work at this stage. It may be that progress in accuracy of word recognition and in fluency in continuous reading is insufficiently supported by vocabulary and general linguistic development, by experience and conceptual development, by more advanced phonic and structural analysis skills or simply by insufficient practice in independent reading (the backward reader is often reluctant to read even when he has sufficient skill to do so). Awareness of these possibilities offers a basis for remedial teaching more satisfactory than simply searching for the next interesting reading book the child can tackle at this level.

Unfortunately, the processes and sequences of learning and the examination of the different skills to be learnt and integrated at different stages have been neglected in favour of controversies about different approaches (e.g. i.t.a., Colour Story reading, Reading in Colour) and the unreal dichotomy between word whole and phonic methods.

For a long time, recommended methods of teaching spelling have remained much the same in essentials, and in spite of more sophisticated concepts about the cognitive processes involved (compared, for example, with Schonell's (1942) account), it is still difficult to prescribe with confidence more specific teaching procedures on behalf of those children who display a severe spelling disability—sometimes in spite of reasonable reading levels. As Peters (1967) has shown, different reading approaches (word-whole, phonic, i.t.a.) tend to result in different types of spelling failure. The examination of spelling errors is not very fruitful because of the difficulty of classifying them and also because of the different cognitive routes from which they derive.

There has recently been a revived interest in handwriting, partly because of its involvement in reading and spelling skills but largely because of the greater awareness of specific perceptual-motor difficulties. Wedell (1968) provides a useful analysis of the latter skills and Presland (1970) outlines a basis for assessment and for remedial teaching. Brenner's (1968) survey in Cambridge revealed a 3 per cent incidence of marked perceptual-motor difficulties in primary school children and it is significant that many of these would not come to the attention of remedial teachers because their reading attainments may not be very retarded. But apart from these, it is a common observation that backward readers have confused knowledge about the best ways of forming and joining letters. The workbooks and teachers' guides of Inglis and Connell (1964) and the suggestions of Frostig provide an ample basis for remedial teaching.

Compared with other educational skills, remedial teaching in mathematics is a neglected area. In particular, failure in mathematics appears not to have been studied and reported upon in the light of changes in the mathematics curriculum and the increased insight into the learning and teaching of mathematics. The account by Schonell (1957), while not without value, is not relevant to the present situation. From one point of view this is not serious in that, with cases of moderate failure, the mathematics curriculum itself offers the means of tracking down the points of failure and selecting relevant remedial work. But there appears to have been little examination of the question whether a curriculum which puts greater demands on thinking rather than rote learning, on guided experience than on direct instruction, reveals learning difficulties due to visuo-spatial, auditory-perceptual or language difficulties. Also, psychologists and remedial teachers meet occasional children who have a marked specific inability in mathematics comparable to the severe reading disabilities which some like to label dyslexia. Apart from a chapter in Johnson and Myklebust (1967) there has been little discussion of this very interesting and virgin field.

One of the clear advances has been in the development of measures for *remediating weak cognitive functions*. How effective they are is another matter, and it would seem important for remedial teachers not to assume that something which has been published is 'the answer'. It needs evaluating in the light of several criteria: (1) its relevance to the pupil(s) in question as revealed by diagnostic assessment; (2) its place in the hierarchy of cognitive skills outlined earlier (what processes is it relevant to? how important are they? what processes are being ignored?); (3) how do the materials fit into a coherent view of (remedial) education? For example, some materials which have been produced are trivial and unedifying compared with the rich educational diet children might be having in their own primary classroom. Frequently, the opportunities for special training are available in the play and activity and the creative work (nature or environmental study) going on in the classroom and it would be sensible to enlist the teachers' help in emphasising the desired activities. Many of the activities suggested in language programmes might be more profitably incorporated into project activities which are highly motivating as well as broadly educational.

However, there is obviously a place for periods of specific remedial instruction based on, say, the Frostig, Tansley (1967) and other perceptual programmes, or on one of the various language programmes or on aspects of remediation suggested by the Illinois Test of Psycholinguistic Abilities (Kirk and Kirk 1971). In the case of many troublesome symptoms such as non-verbal disabilities and distractibility there is little to fall back on, although again Johnson and Myklebust (1967) have some insightful comments to make.

As Sampson's survey showed, *motivational* aspects are very much a concern of remedial teachers. The range of concepts about motivation upon which the remedial teacher can draw is now very much wider. Whereas at one time it was a question of finding materials and activities which will 'interest' the retarded child, the remedial teacher can consider the possibilities suggested by behaviour modification techniques, the place of programmed learning and educational technology as well as more traditional approaches. Hewett's (1964) hierarchy of task levels seems particularly useful in providing a framework for assessing levels of emotional maturity for undertaking learning tasks. While the normal learner (and, one hopes, the learning failure after remedial treatment) is able to function at the achievement level or the mastery level, children with learning difficulties may only be motivated within relationships with the group or the teacher, or through interests and activities at the exploratory level. Not infrequently we have a child who is at the Order task level at which short tasks, easily achievable, are required. At this level, simple remedial games or the use of apparatus such as the Stillitron or teaching machines may be appropriate. At the lower levels (the Acceptance task and Primary task levels), the remedial teacher will be functioning more on therapeutic lines or exploring the possibilities of behaviour modification. The problem, unfortunately, is not just one for the remedial teaching situation but of generalising to the wider school and life situation (hence the items 2e and 3 in the list of principles).

Therapeutic measures

Much is made at the present time of prescriptions and programmes for teaching and while, as has been suggested, these are very much needed, it is always the case that the implications of learning failure for personality development and social interaction have to be given considerable attention. Failure in basic educational skills can have a damaging effect on self-concepts, on relationships with parents, siblings and other children. While with some children effective remedial measures have a relieving effect on the total situation, in others the remedial teacher has to function as a therapist. In a play session, Peter reveals in conversation his anxiety that there is something wrong with his brain; John comes home from school in tears because he could not read the questions nor write the answers in the end of term exams; Paul shows a general disinterest in hobbies, school and out-of-school life because of his reaction to failure and his parents' anxieties; Garry has no friends perhaps because of compensatory assertiveness and boasting. The very best remedial programmes are liable to be negated by failure to tackle this aspect of the failing individual.

Evidence in support of this point of view is given by the report of Lawrence (1971) in an experiment in which four groups of twelve children aged 8½ with reading ages of about 6½ were given either remedial reading plus counselling, counselling alone, remedial teaching or no special treatment. The greater gains were made by the group which only received counselling, followed by the remedial reading plus counselling group. No explanation is offered why remedial reading *and* counselling should not have had the greatest effect! There are of course other reports on similar lines; for example, those showing a similar effect from non-directive play therapy. But much surely depends on the appropriate selection of cases.

Caspari (1973 and in press) discusses educational therapy as it has been developed over the last fifteen years in the Department for Children and Parents of the Tavistock Clinic, London. This approach attaches great importance to a child's feelings and emotional needs and reactions. Of course, it does not exclude other aetiological factors in learning difficulties. It merely assumes that amongst the variety of causes, emotional conflicts may be significant.

Cooperation with the child's home

When the Remedial Education Centre was set up by Schonell at Birmingham University in 1948, a psychiatric social worker was appointed whose work not only contributed at the assessment stage but in continuing parent guidance. When the present writer set up remedial groups with three remedial teachers in six secondary schools in Bolton in 1949, a social worker visited each home to ensure cooperation and to assess the home situation—in relation to the learning problem. Sampson's (1969) survey indicates that home visits are regarded as 'essential' by many remedial teachers 'to find out more about the child' or 'to explain the system and method of teaching'. Some teachers can call upon the assistance of psychiatric social workers.

One would surmise, however, that this aspect suffers from the shortage of teachers' time and the limited social worker resources available. It is worth stating the principle, in common with other areas of handicap, that social work and parent guidance seems an essential ingredient of the remedial programme, difficult though it may be to organise in practice. The increasing trend to increase the scope of home-school relationships in schools should go some way to meet the need.

Cooperation with and within the school

Here again we are scarcely talking about an advance, since Miss Davidson who organised remedial teaching in Edinburgh schools in the 1940s appointed and trained remedial teachers to work as members of the staff within the school. In many places at present we have a two-tiered system, in which part-time or untrained remedial teachers give extra help in schools and trained peripatetic remedial teachers work in areas. Where this occurs there is the opportunity for profitable cooperation between remedial teachers and between them and the class teacher. Otherwise, there can be the problem of the child who receives good remedial help several times a week and returns to a class where the teaching is disastrously inappropriate even when attitudes to the problem are positive. Suffice it to say that there should be some concordance of teaching aims, methods and attitudes, which in view of remedial teachers' work-loads is not always easy to attain.

Finally, there is the need for *continued supervision* of remedial cases after discharge. Much has been made in evaluating the effects of remedial education of the fact that progress sags (not surprisingly) after discontinuation of remedial education. This is a fault of education in the ordinary classes rather than simply something to be laid at the remedial teacher's door. However, it is undeniably a principle to be followed that discharge reports should indicate as specifically as possible the requirements for assisting the child to make further progress and it should also be ensured that the child's progress is observed and supervised.

We should also at this point mention the need for further education of children with learning problems. This is very much a concern in the whole field of special education; schools for the physically handicapped, the partially sighted and even the educationally subnormal have managed to organise further education for their pupils, and one wonders whether colleges of further education should not have a member of staff with particular responsibility in this area. A number of towns have for a long time organised classes in elementary English (or some such euphemism) for young adults (and even grandparents) who feel the need for extra help in literary skills.

Conclusion

In the development of special education, there has been a gradual differentiation of the handicaps and the special methods needed, e.g. the partially sighted from the blind; the maladjusted; the speech- and language-disordered; the autistic. Once particular problems have been explored and the specialisation established, there has been a contrary trend (obvious at the present time) to emphasise the common elements, the similarities rather than the differences in children's special needs.

There has been a similar trend to distinguish kinds of educational failure—below-average intellectual development, environmental handicaps, maladjustment and specific learning disabilities. Some progress has been made towards specifying the aims, organisation and methods required for each, but, if the analogy with special education is valid, the stage is still one of differentiation.

This chapter has suggested that while the remedial teacher has much to offer the whole field of learning failure, the area in which he should ensure the growth of his particular knowledge and skills is in that of learning disabilities. There is now a considerable amount of research and theoretical discussion about learning problems; some diagnostic procedures and instruments are available and some resources for the planning of teaching and remediation. Further advances in exploring remedial teaching in this sense will not only benefit children with severe difficulties but will contribute to the general field of teaching children who have failed to learn.

7. Brain-damaged children: psychological and educational implications

Introduction

The vast body of literature on brain damage, mostly on adults, over the past 100 years—Sigmund Freud showed an early interest, writing on aphasia and cerebral palsy in 1891—is fast becoming equalled by a similar body of literature on children, stemming from: (*a*) child neurologists concerned with aetiology; (*b*) psychologists concerned with behavioural studies and the educational implications; and (*c*) multi-disciplinary teams trying to bridge the gap between our knowledge of brain and behaviour. Most of the adult studies are concerned with the location, extent and types of lesions and their effects on mental functioning in cases where the lesions are relatively circumscribed, such as those caused by a clear-cut head injury or a selective leucotomy, in a brain that had reached a normal adult status and been subject to more or less ordinary environmental experience, prior to the injury. A brief summary of the complexities in this field has been provided by Moyra Williams (1970).

The application of such concepts of brain damage to children is a more recent and even more complex field, the greater complexity being due to two main factors: (1) in most cases the injuries appear to have been present around the time of birth and are usually widespread rather than circumscribed, and (2) the effects of these on the child's interaction with his environment are usually dramatic, so much so that we cannot assume normal environmental influences. Confusion abounds but excitement is high.

The most-quoted pioneers in this field are Strauss and Werner, who in the late thirties crystallised many of the hunches that were intriguing neurologists, psychologists and educators around that time, and like most pioneers they gloriously overstated their case. Their attempts to classify retarded children into two main groups, the endogenous (familial, genetic) on the one hand and the exogenous (brain injury, such as through birth trauma) on the other, have not been substantiated in spite of the efforts of dozens of enthusiastic followers, one of whom as recently as 1964 described Strauss' work as 'the breakthrough that had been coming since Hippocrates *circa* 300 B.C.' (Crawford 1964). Strauss' exogenous group were alleged to show certain behavioural characteristics largely concerned with 'disinhibition' such as hyperactivity, distractibility, perceptual and behavioural difficulties that could not be explained by generalised low intelligence or by environmentally caused emotional disturbance or social deprivation or peripheral sensori-motor handicap. The explanation instead was along neurological lines, to the effect that the higher nervous system had suffered some kind of chemical or structural insult, either around the time of birth, or subsequently in cases of encephalitis or meningitis. He rather rashly asserted (Strauss and Lehtinen 1947, page 20). 'All brain lesions wherever localised are followed by a similar kind of disordered behaviour . . .', but subsequent research has demonstrated that (1) the evidence for any definite pattern of behavioural characteristics is tenuous, and (2) although some children show some characteristics, the link with neurological data is even more tenuous.

These statements will be elaborated later and meanwhile we must hasten to add that although Strauss and his co-workers oversimplified the problems, possibly because they extrapolated too readily from adult studies, using tests and scales that were not very reliable, we are indebted to him for focusing our attention on many gaps in our knowledge of child development, particularly in respect of children whose poor development was formerly thought to be due to some mysterious factor called 'simple mental defect'. His theories of disinhibition and over-excitation bear many resemblances to current ideas that 'hyperarousal' in lower brain structures may account for many kinds of disordered behaviour (Hutt 1964, 1970).

Other sources of the increasing interest in child brain damage in the thirties came from workers who were studying children who showed unequivocal signs of brain damage, such as cerebral palsy. A classic example is Elizabeth Lord's (1930) study of sixty-seven such children in which important questions were raised about the intellectual, perceptual, and motor handicaps and their cumulative effect on subsequent development, which in turn raised equally important questions about the processes by which normal children learn. Before proceeding with a review of recent work in these fields, we should ask by what criteria we should consider a child to be brain-damaged.

Who is brain-damaged?

There is at present no consensus of opinion concerning the criteria by which a child should be designated as brain-damaged (except in frank cases such as cerebral palsy, hydrocephalic and epileptic children) and the very term 'brain damage' has been consistently under fire in recent years on the grounds of over-use and misuse. It implies the existence of lesions, due to some damaging agent, as a causal explanation of certain behaviour, the evidence for which is simply lacking in the majority of cases to whom the term has been applied. Bax and MacKeith (1963) edited the proceedings of a multi-disciplinary conference in 1962 at which the main recommendation was to discard the term 'brain damage', pointing out that it was being misused to cover a heterogeneous collection of disorders with differing aetiologies and differing manifestations. Unfortunately, alternative terms, such as 'minimal cerebral dysfunctioning' (Paine 1968) and 'clumsy children' (Walton 1962) from medical workers, and 'hyperactive-distractible syndrome' (Cruickshank 1961) and 'psychoneurological' (Johnson and Myklebust 1967) from psychologists, are open to similar objections. No current writers seem able to avoid using the term 'brain damage'.

The failure to agree on terms implies a weakness in our understanding of the phenomena and the field remains full of challenge.

Unequivocal evidence of brain damage exists in cerebral palsied children. With an approximate prevalence rate of about 2·5 per thousand (Rutter, Tizard and Whitmore 1970), enough evidence has been accumulated since Little produced one of the first descriptions of cases in 1843, to arrive at a generally accepted definition: a disorder of motor functioning resulting from a permanent non-progressive defect or lesion of the immature brain. There are well-defined sub-types such as the athetoids, who show writhing movements that are due to extra-pyramidal damage, and the more common spastic whose stiff movements are linked with cortical and pyramidal damage. Furthermore, of greater interest to psychologists and educators is the fact that, in a large proportion of these children, the lesions affect learning and behaviour in ways that cannot be accounted for by simple motor difficulties and distorted experience, and are likely to be a direct extension of the effects of their brain damage.

Uncertainty arises once we leave such relatively well-defined groups, most of whom show hard neurological signs and in some cases histological and EEG evidence to support the diagnosis, and consider the groups that Strauss and workers with similar orientations, such as Cruickshank (1961) and Gallacher (1960), have studied. They have applied the concept of brain damage to children who show a certain symptomatology—but no clear aetiology. For the majority of children described in the literature as brain-damaged over the past decade or so, hard evidence about site and extent of brain lesions is rare: EEG studies are often inconclusive, for as Schulman (1965) points out, on certain criteria between 10 and 55 per cent of normal subjects show EEG abnormalities; *post mortem* studies are rare, and medical histories, usually concentrating on difficulties around birth, although suggestive, are rarely objective enough.

But the symptomatology, the learning and behavioural characteristics are of extraordinary interest to psychologists and educators. Although only tenuously linked with neurological data in our present state of knowledge, provided the learning and behaviour can be described systematically and meaningfully, and predictions made about future behaviour, under certain conditions, we are in a sphere where valuable psychological and educational contributions can be made.

Brain damage as a behavioural category

'. . . not a nice handicap. Such technical descriptions as catastrophic behaviour, perceptual impairments, perseveration, disinhibition, mimism, short attention span, exogenous behaviour, learning disabilities, Strauss' syndrome, neurological impairment and hyperactivity are translated by the outside world as spoilt, bratty, bad-mannered, ill-behaved, badly brought up, undisciplined, obnoxious, and by other children as queer'. This is how one parent quoted by Birch (1964) summarised the behaviour characteristics of the brain-damaged child. The five most frequently quoted characteristics listed by Clements (1966) in recent publications are: hyperactivity; perceptual motor impairment; emotional lability; poor co-ordination; and attention disorders. Most clinicians would agree with this ranking and many believe that the characteristics co-vary sufficiently to form a syndrome. A few sublime and several dubious studies have been made under these headings in the last decade and we can now briefly consider some of these, bearing in mind such questions as: what theories (if any) are directing the observations, what psychometric and other techniques are in use, what is known about the incidence of some of these disorders, their educational implications, and what therapeutic and educational measures might alter the behaviour?

1. *Hyperactivity*

Hyperactivity figures large in the literature on brain damage in children, partly because of its nuisance value, which is implied by descriptive terms such as 'restless, disruptive, disorganised, destructive'. Not only is there a strong element of 'social definition' here; there is also an overlap with the behaviour of some types of emotionally disturbed children and indeed the behaviour of many young normal children in certain situations (such as in the playground). Cruickshank (1961) followed Strauss' emphasis on the importance of hyperactivity as a prime neurological characteristic, and distinguished between *sensory hyperactivity* (which most people would term 'distractibility', and we will deal with this later) and *motor hyperactivity*. The criteria he used for determining the presence of hyperactivity are not satisfactorily explained. Simple rating scales are dangerous in this area, in that different observers may be singling out different aspects of a child's activity, in accordance with social definitions that have not been made explicit.

More objective measures of hyperactivity have produced some surprising results: Schulman (1965) has cast doubt on its very existence. Using an actometer, in the form of a modified self-winding watch strapped to the child's wrist and ankle, the total day activity levels of thirty-five boys of roughly ESN intelligence were recorded: no significant differences were found between those designated as brain-damaged and those who were not. Furthermore, the total day activity level did not correlate with the activity level recorded in more structured situations, such as in the classroom. There was a slight correlation between the presence of brain damage and structured activity levels, but in a negative direction, i.e. the more brain-damaged were less active. The authors are quick to point out some limitations in their study: for example, the selection procedures for entry to the particular residential school from which the sample was taken tended to exclude overactive and troublesome children, and since hyperactivity is to some extent situationally determined, there is clearly a need for many more measurements within different controlled settings.

The Hutts' (1963, 1964, 1970) work has been valuable in this respect. Starting with a bare experimental room, a child's movements are plotted on numbered squares on the floor space, and objective measurements of levels and directions of activities can be recorded, in response to various controlled conditions in the room, for example the presence of a box of bricks, the presence of a passive adult, an active adult, etc. The use of this technique in measuring a reduction in a child's hyperactivity following certain drug treatments has been demonstrated.

Repeated observation of clinicians and teachers that certain children are hyperactive has not yet been demonstrated objectively, using measures that are independent of social definitions and where environmental conditions are rigorously controlled. It may emerge that certain types of activity, and their relative 'aimlessness' in the eyes of the adult observers, are of greater significance than their frequency. Hyperactivity is of course related to the next behaviour characteristic that we will consider, namely disorders of attention.

2. *Attention disorders*

These are more subtle than hyperactivity. One can assume that very hyperactive children, such as certain youngsters who have had meningitis, and whose behaviour in many situations is highly acrobatic, are also showing attention disorders—since they are rarely sitting or standing still enough to focus their attention on any particular activity, and therefore fail to learn much about it. But one cannot assume this works the other way round. Attention disorders have been clinically observed in children who are not overtly hyperactive, including cerebral palsied children who are physically incapable of much motor activity, and this presents us with considerable problems of measurement. Cruickshank and his co-workers (1957, 1961, 1966, 1967) attached great importance to distractibility, considering it to be a major factor contributing to the perceptual difficulties of brain-damaged children: his techniques of measurement included various figure-background tests, such as marble boards and tachistoscope presentations of common objects against complicated backgrounds; in his very thorough 1957 study (revised 1965) of 325 cerebral palsied children, the latter showed much greater difficulties compared to the controls. This was interpreted largely as a function of distractibility, and the inability to refrain from responding to irrelevant stimuli was observed in auditory and tactile, as well as in visual tasks. Cruickshank followed Strauss in advocating radical educational measures, largely concerned with reducing distracti-bility—by providing relatively distraction-free classrooms. Ingenious suggestions concerning the development of work material, such as reading books in which the stimulus value of a word is heightened against a perfectly plain background, were also made (Cruickshank 1961).

The effectiveness of this type of educational regime has not yet been demonstrated (Cruickshank 1967) and it has not gained widespread support. Roy Brown's (1965, 1970) work challenges some of the basic assumptions. Using formboard errors as a measure of distractibility amongst twenty-eight severely subnormal children attending a junior training centre, scores on ten trials, within the setting of an ordinary noisy, highly decorated classroom, were compared to those obtained in a relatively bare, distraction-free experimental room. No differences emerged: indeed there were slight suggestions that performance declined (distractibility increased) in the so-called experimental room, and Brown attributed this to the familiarity and accompanying security of the ordinary classroom, compared to the experimental room, suggesting that 'distractions' are not distractions if one is used to them. However, Brown's work needs extending since the unfamiliarity of the experimental room would have decreased over a longer period of time. Furthermore his sample was assumed to be brain-damaged, by virtue of their low IQ, and although this is a reasonable assumption, most workers would restrict the concept to selective, and not generalised brain impairment. Brown's more fundamental challenge lies in his view that much of the distractibility noted in the subnormals may be due to poor environmental experiences, such as prolonged hospitalisation.

Schulman's (1965) study tends to dispute this line of reasoning; his tests of distractibility (e.g. card-sorting tasks, with and without external distractors in the form of a buzzer) were the only ones that correlated positively with careful ratings of brain damage amongst thirty ESN children. Incidentally the external distractors did not especially affect the scores, suggesting that the distractibility came from within. Abercrombie (1968) makes interesting clinical observations in this connection: noting the apparent hesitation and distress that some brain-damaged children show with certain tasks, such as copying a diamond, she hypothesised that attention impairments might be due to a failure in selective inhibition, e.g. that in attempting to copy a diamond, the feedback of information to the child included messages in different modalities (visual, somasthetic, etc.) and that these are competing messages amongst which the child cannot effectively select.

Future studies will need more careful controls over the types of children studied, the nature of the task given (whether simple or complex), the types of external distractors and the types of social and educational demands that are being made on the child—a reminder that attention, like hyperactivity, is in part a socially defined phenomenon, a response to adult demands to attend to certain 'figures' and ignore certain kinds of background.

3. *Motor incoordination*

Motor difficulties are obvious in most frank cases of brain damage, such as the cerebral palsied, and several workers (Walton 1962, Stott 1966) have suggested that mild, sub-clinical motor impairments may, by analogy, be indicative of brain damage on the one hand and the likelihood of educational failure on the other, and that such impairments may be common amongst the normal school populations. Standard neurological interviews have traditionally looked at motor performance, both gross motor movements (balance and symmetry, etc.) and fine specific motor movements (control of hand and facial muscles, etc.), using techniques of observation which, although adequate for detecting hard signs of neuropathology, are not usually fine enough to detect minimal motor disorders.

Efforts have therefore been made to develop finer standardised scales of motor proficiency and several versions of Oseretzky's original 1931 scale are now available (Sloan 1955, Stott 1966, Rutter *et al.* 1970). Reliability and validity studies are still under way. Whiting *et al.* (1969) for example found a low correlation between the Stott scale ratings and ordinary assessments, particularly among ten children attending a child guidance clinic who were rated as clumsy by teachers, parents and the psychologists: only four were detected on the Stott scale. In the Isle of Wight studies (Rutter, Graham and Yule 1970) a short 12-item version of Sloan's revision was developed: thorough reliability studies showed an 0·69 correlation between test and retest and there was an acceptable level of agreement with clinical assessments. Several suggestive group differences emerged: for instance, a fairly high percentage of the control group (160 randomly selected nine- and ten-year-olds) were rated as severely clumsy (5%) while among the children classified as retarded in reading this percentage increased to 12 per cent.

Another motor test, utilised by the same team, is of 'motor impersistence'—inability to sustain a voluntary act, such as closing eyes, protruding tongue, for a period of twenty seconds. Although our present knowledge of the underlying neurological basis of these tests and all their educational consequences is limited, these motor tests are promising tools.

Valuable work on many aspects of the development of motor skills in children is shown by Connolly (1968, 1970) at the Spastics Society's Motor Development Research Unit at Sheffield. This concerns work with normal as well as cerebral palsied children, and includes experimental intervention in such processes as the development of hand control. Operant conditioning techniques have been applied in attempts to alter certain motor functions, and the possibility of using augmented feedback from relatively unimpaired sensory channels has been raised. These applications of psychological principles to the treatment of motor disorders is much to be welcomed in a field where the results of conventional treatment such as physiotherapy and surgery are in most cases ambiguous (see Wolf 1969 for a review of the results of treatment amongst the cerebral palsied).

4. *Emotional lability*

There is a rough parallel between the motor hyperactivity, distractibility and motor incoordination that we have already described, and comparable

E

'erraticness' on the emotional side—children designated as brain-damaged are frequently described as over-excitable, inhibited, explosive, over-reactive, and minor changes of routine are alleged to provoke outbursts of rage or grief. Some evidence linking such characteristics with brain damage can be seen in adult and animal studies (Williams 1970), while with children such studies are complicated by difficulties of measurement and lack of normative data (normal children's emotional reactions are wide and varied). Schulman *et al.* (1965) attempted an objective study of emotional lability but used very limited measures, namely changes in children's performance in an operant conditioning situation, under conditions of stress (provided by a loud buzzer). No significant changes were found using these techniques. Rutter *et al.* (1970) suggested that there was an astonishingly high rate of behaviour disturbance amongst the ninety-nine brain-damaged children under study (mostly cerebral palsied and epileptic), over 34 per cent compared to $6\frac{1}{2}$ per cent in the general population, using teachers' and parents' questionnaires, and psychiatric interview data. No specific kinds of behaviour disturbance such as those we have described under the heading of emotional lability were noted, and the ratings of so-called 'psychiatric' disorder consisted of a multitude of motor, intellectual, emotional and social phenomena.

In a survey of literature about the emotional and social adjustment of physically handicapped children, Kellmer Pringle (1964) discusses the inadequacies of many studies, particularly those that rely too much on personality tests, largely of the paper and pencil type, designed for the non-handicapped. In an area as complex as emotional lability, far finer research tools will need to be developed.

Birch and his co-workers (1964) have provided some very important guiding concepts in pointing out that we never observe brain damage directly—we observe its functional consequences and these are a product of the whole gamut of the damaged child's relationships with his environment, including factors such as frequency of hospitalisation, delayed entry into school, family reactions, community attitudes and so on. Different parents react differently to children who, in theory, might have exactly the same lesions and initially show the same behaviour patterns, such as distractibility or emotional lability. In a fascinating longitudinal study of differences in the behaviour of very young babies, Thomas, Chess and Birch (1968) show the possibilities of rating levels of activity, rhythmiticity, adaptability, sensitivity, distractibility and general mood, resulting in rough classifications such as 'intensively reactive' or 'placid and easy' at the extremes. Given such behavioural characteristics, the question then arises: are the parents' reactions matched or mismatched in relation to these? In other words, their child-rearing patterns may either be harmonious or dissonant in respect of a particular child's 'early temperament'. The outcome, the later behavioural characteristics, is determined by this interaction, not solely by organic factors, and certainly not by environmental factors alone.

Little is known objectively about the child-rearing practices concerning handicapped children: Hewett (1970) presents some relatively objective studies on 180 families with cerebral palsied children, finding little evidence of psychiatric distress. Cashdan (1966) considers the question of whether the parents of handicapped children tend to understimulate their child, thus providing an additional handicap. Wall (1955) mentions the need of parents and teachers to adjust the demands carefully to the level of development of the particular child, and emphasises the importance of coming to grips with the psychological implications of handicap.

5. *Perceptual motor impairment*

Unevenness in intellectual functioning in various tests, such as the scattered uneven profile on standardised intelligence tests, has traditionally been highlighted in brain-damaged adults (Wechsler 1958), largely in cases that have shown normal abilities in certain directions, emphasising that the damage is selective in its effects on an otherwise normal or near-normal brain. A great deal of data is now available concerning children. The best commentaries are to be found in Abercrombie (1964a), Birch (1964), Nielsen (1966) and Francis-Williams (1970). These are largely centred on perceptual motor disorders (though some studies have included language disorders), an umbrella term referring to failures in the processes that normally mediate between perception on the one hand and the organisation of movements on the other. One of the commonest examples quoted in the literature is the failure to copy a diamond (see Abercrombie 1965 for an imaginative essay on this subject). The exact nature of the failures no doubt varies, presumably occurring anywhere in the link between sensory input, perception, central organising processes, executive planning, and motor movement, together with possible failures in handling the feedback of information that is necessary for the successful completion of any task and in intersensory integration processes (see Wedell 1968, 1973 for a very clear exposition of these processes).

Substantial work on frankly brain-damaged children (notably cerebral palsied, in which the incidence of perceptual motor difficulties is very high), has contributed greatly to our understanding of learning processes

in normal children, and bears on Piaget's (1956) emphasis on the importance of sensori-motor processes as a groundwork for the development of
later perceptual and higher conceptual skills. Wedell's (1960) very carefully devised studies of seventy-three cerebral palsied children and forty
controls showed the former to have far greater difficulties with tests
involving the matching of figures, copying patterns of bricks, assembling
cut-up figures. Low scores were recorded in 25 per cent of the cerebral
palsied children, compared to less than 3 per cent of the controls, on tests
that were designed in such a way as to exclude motor control as an
important variable. Children with different lesions responded differenti-
ally: bilateral and left-sided spastics scored lower than athetoids and right-
sided spastics and this association of perceptual difficulties with right
(non-dominant) hemisphere damage links up with traditional findings
of work with adults.

Abercrombie (1964b) confirmed the high incidence of visual perceptual and visual motor disorders among cerebral palsied children in an
extensive study of thirty-nine cases and eleven controls, using the wisc,
the Frostig Developmental Test of Visual Perception and various matching
tasks, visual and tactile, together with careful assessments of sensory and
motor handicaps. In this sample twenty-nine out of the thirty-nine children
showed specific perceptual or visual motor difficulties in one or more of
the tests, and this was not attributable to either motor handicap, or the
consequential limitations of experience, since children with equal degrees
of motor handicap and who were not brain-damaged did not show such
difficulties.

Birch's contributions (1964, 1965) have been outstanding: he has
demonstrated that although brain-damaged children made substantial
errors in copying block designs, they were able to select the correct design
from a multiple-choice situation, confirming that their difficulty was not
in perceptual matching but in the perceptual action system. Birch has
shown the importance of intersensory integration processes, and their
vulnerability to brain damage. In his study reported in 1964 it was shown
that cerebral palsied children could visually match certain geometric
shapes as efficiently as the control group. But when visual cues were
reduced, for example one of the geometrical blocks in a pair was screened,
and the subject had to use kinaesthetic information (tracking with a
stylus) to compare with the visually presented block, large errors were
recorded among the cerebral palsied children. Although the results are
tentative, the suggestions are of at least considerable delay in the development of intersensory integration, which could seriously limit the utilisation
of information, and lead to educational confusion. His work offers tenta-

tive but exciting explanations of the mechanism underlying perceptual motor skills; clearly no one mechanism can explain all such skills and he postulates several autonomous ones, including a recognition-discrimination system that develops early in life, and a perceptual motor system, more complex and more vulnerable to brain damage, that develops later.

A great deal has been learned from such studies of perceptual motor disorders in cerebral palsied children. Work with non-cerebral palsied children, although subject to the difficulties of diagnosis that we have already mentioned, is important in that it offers some explanation of learning difficulties that may be applicable to very large groups of children, including those attending normal schools.

In 1966 Brenner reported on the application of a large battery of visual motor tests (including parts of the Bender Gestalt, Goodenough Draw-a-Man, Benton), and rated nearly 7 per cent of 810 normal school children aged eight to nine as showing visual perceptual and visual motor difficulties. Bowley (1969), using a large battery of similar tests including the Frostig, reported an incidence of 1·5 per cent, designated as showing 'minimal cerebral dysfunctioning', out of a total sample that had been roughly screened of over 2,000 children. Cruickshank (1967) mentions incidence figures of between 1 and 7 per cent of the general population showing learning difficulties of a comparable kind.

Several workers have attempted to use Wechsler's verbal and performance IQ discrepancies to measure incidence rates and this has led to some exaggerated claims. For example, Clements and Peters (1962) asserted that a discrepancy of 10 to 15 points would indicate brain damage. According to Field's (1960) work on the Wechsler standardisation data, this degree of discrepancy would place about 25 per cent of the general population as showing signs of 'minimal cerebral dysfunctioning'. A useful discussion on the validity of verbal and performance discrepancies is contained in Rutter, Graham and Yule (1970), offering modest support to the view that large discrepancies show some association with brain disorder. 14 per cent of 84 children with definite neurological signs (mostly cerebral palsy and epileptic children) had differences in the region of 25 points, compared to $7\frac{1}{2}$ per cent of the control group. According to Field's studies, differences of 25 points would be expected in 10 per cent of the general population (5 per cent having higher verbal IQs, 5 per cent having higher performance IQs). However, many clinicians might wonder whether such children were completely without learning difficulties, of a kind that might have been revealed by closer study.

Several workers have stressed the importance of early detection in order to plan remedial work, but few have yet studied the field systematically. Francis-Williams (1970) presents a valuable study of forty-four cases who were noted to have shown 'minor neurological dysfunctioning' at birth, but who had no gross birth difficulties or major neurological signs of any kind at the neonatal stage. Over half this group turned out to be of normal intelligence and 60 per cent of these showed deviations on certain tests, largely based on Frances Graham's work (1962, 1963) on perceptual motor skills in young children, and Joan Reynell's (1969) language tests. Dinnage (1971) provides a useful review of work in this field.

Educational provision and techniques

Educational provision and techniques in the field of brain-injured children are largely centred on perceptual motor disorders, which are regarded as a prerequisite to the acquisition of basic educational skills. In the USA the growth of special educational facilities has been strong in the past decade, with an accompanying boom in research, literature, diagnostic and remedial material. An early example is that described by Strauss and Kephart's (1955) work at the Cove School for brain-injured children, Wisconsin; we have mentioned the educational work of Cruickshank (1961) with its emphasis on providing a distraction-free environment. Frostig (1964, 1968) followed up her diagnostic test of visual perceptual development with a remedial programme concerned with the training of any specific weakness denoted by the perceptual tests, such as in figure-ground confusion, perceptual constancy, etc. However, her work at the Centre for Educational Therapy, in Los Angeles, is also concerned with language difficulties; indeed, she places emphasis on stimulation in all developmental areas, based on comprehensive diagnosis. Evaluative studies on these remedial programmes have not yet produced very convincing results. Useful recent reviews by both Cruickshank and Frostig can be found in Loring (1968). Gallacher's (1960) model study on the tutoring of brain-injured children suggested that individual one-hour-per-day tutoring might be more effective than group work for such children and that although the educational gains recorded were small, the possibility of using peripatetic tutors within the ordinary school system was raised.

In this country no specific provision has been made, it being generally considered hitherto that brain-damaged children could, on the whole, be catered for within existing remedial groups and special schools. The work of Tansley (1967) with ESN school children is noteworthy, with his emphasis on Kephart's (1960) detailed methods of motor training as a basis for improving perceptual and conceptual activities. A few preliminary studies of Frostig's remedial methods have emerged, such as Tyson's (1963) on a small group of cerebral palsied children and Lansdown's (1970) and Horn's (1970) studies on small groups of non-cerebral palsied children who showed perceptual motor difficulties. On the whole such work has shown gains in terms of the Frostig perceptual quotients, but not in educational attainments. It is likely that more highly trained teachers might produce more favourable results.

Surveys of experimental educational work in this field are provided by Bortner (1968), Tyson (1970) and Francis-Williams (1970). More sophisticated techniques, including the use of operant conditioning and a whole variety of electronic aids, such as the Touch Tutor (Thompson and Johnson 1971) are showing promise, but on the whole most of the educational and therapeutic measures rely on 'informed faith' rather than hard-based evidence, and the need for intensive studies of the efficacy of various educational methods deserves considerable priority. These must be based on a much more thorough understanding of the precise nature of the specific learning disorders.

Is there a brain-damage behavioural syndrome?

Having briefly described recent evidence on the main behavioural characteristics commonly thought to be associated with brain damage in children, namely hyperactivity, attention disorders, motor incoordination, emotional lability and perceptual motor impairment, we are now in a position to consider whether they constitute a 'behavioural syndrome'. The short answer is No.

Clinicians regularly report individual cases in whom virtually all the above characteristics occur, suggesting a considerable co-variance between the characteristics. These claims have not yet been supported by actuarial studies. For example, Schulman's (1965) findings were negative. The co-variance between eight well-known indices of brain damage, including standard neurological examination, EEG, WISC verbal compared with performance, Bender Gestalt, Drawing a Person, and the objective studies of hyperactivity and distractibility that we have already mentioned, was trivial. Clinicians might point out that some of the techniques of measurement were too crude and that the samples of children were really not comparable to those they would describe as brain-damaged. For example, Schulman studied thirty-five ESN boys who did not appear to show specific learning difficulties. In Paine's (1968) study this objection was overcome: 83 children, mean age 8 years, mean IQ 96, referred from various reputable sources, with a strong suspicion of 'minimal cerebral dysfunctioning', were put through a large battery of investigations, including neurological examinations, full medical histories, EEGs, WISCs and behavioural ratings; no significant intercorrelations were observed.

So on present actuarial evidence we certainly cannot regard brain-damage behaviour as a single entity and are unlikely to be able to do so in the future. There is little doubt that the behaviour is multi-dimensional; a complex matrix, probably merging imperceptibly with normal children's behaviour at one end of the scale, and the behaviour of the frankly and seriously brain-damaged at the other. A valuable survey of recent literature, emphasising the need for proper screening methods to arrive at well-defined populations whose 'central processing dysfunctions' can then be systematically studied is to be found in Chalfant and Scheffelin (1970).

The next decade: coming to grips with specific learning disorders

The term 'brain damage' should be abandoned: it implies a knowledge of aetiology where none exists: it carries implications of irreversibility and whilst it has served an extremely useful purpose in focusing our efforts and attention to an intriguing area of study, there is the danger that it will lead to stereotyped thinking. Under a more realistic, albeit vague title such as 'specific learning disorders', we need to intensify our efforts to identify the main dimensions of the behaviour and learning disorders that we have so far described. Most researchers would agree that the development of finer techniques than those currently employed by psychologists and neurologists is imperative, both for more effective clinical work and for more rewarding actuarial studies. In the latter, for example, simple 'pass or fail' scoring is usually too insensitive to pick up subtle behaviour deviations. The task of developing more subtle behavioural measures is urgent, so that more meaningful measurements can be made, many of which are likely to fall into certain constellations, such as those that are linked with the concept of distractibility.

Meanwhile, psychologists confronted with what must surely be a considerable percentage of children whose learning difficulties cannot be satisfactorily explained by reference to concepts such as subnormality, emotional, cultural or sensory disorders, can glean a great deal from the existing body of work in spite of the gaps in our theories, in our techniques of measurement, and in our educational and therapeutic measures. Improvement in these over the next decade represents an enormous challenge to psychologists, of many specialities. For physiologically minded psychologists there is a rich field, concerned with mapping out the relation-ships between lesions and behaviour, in collaboration with neurologists. For those more singlemindedly behaviouristic and less in need of the security that others find in their efforts to reduce the behaviour to physio-logical concepts, there is a tremendous field of experimental possibilities, including treatment possibilities that may be able to show modifications in behaviour in spite of certain damaged neural pathways. For educational psychologists confronted with large numbers of children with ill-defined learning difficulties, the development of finer assessment techniques that are of use to teachers in planning remedial work, and of experiments in various educational techniques within special units and ordinary schools, offers fields that are bound to be rewarding. For all concerned there is material that throws light on our understanding of normal learning processes.

J. A. Leonard

8. Mobility training for children in British schools for the blind

Introduction

In this chapter I want to describe the changeover from a traditional to a more contemporary approach towards an important aspect of a blind child's life: the ease and safety with which he can move through the environment. Psychology has had nothing to do with the creation of the more contemporary approach and not too much directly with the change-over. But my colleagues and I were able to help in a number of ways and to observe the process. Because few of my readers will have a detailed knowledge of blindness or problems of mobility, I hope I will be forgiven for taking up some of my allotted space in setting the scene. The issue to be discussed is a highly specific one, affecting perhaps not more than a few hundred children. But it does not differ too much from a good many other situations where, before a new technique can be accepted, one has to look at the attitudes towards the old technique and help to modify these attitudes.

Apart from the blind children themselves, it is of course the handful of teachers for the blind who are concerned with the teaching of mobility, who are the people who matter in this story. Their problems and their efforts to arrive at solutions deserve to be known more widely.

Blind education

There are, in the United Kingdom, some 1,200 children whose vision is so poor that they require special methods of education. Almost without exception these children and young people are catered for in some thirty or forty residential schools which take them from the infant stage right through to the completion of secondary education. At the secondary level youngsters are streamed more or less as their sighted peers, the bulk of them going to something roughly comparable to secondary modern schools, and something like 10 per cent to grammar schools. Of the latter there is one for boys and one for girls. Those leaving school at sixteen can opt to take advantage of special further education facilities, of those taking A-levels an increasing number go on to universities. At present there are various schemes in this country to bring about at least a measure of integrated education of blind and sighted children. So far this still entails living in one of the schools for the blind away from home and spending the day at a sighted school.

Degrees of blindness

It is becoming fashionable to speak about visually handicapped children rather than blind children. This change in terminology may help to emphasise the range of residual vision to be found among these youngsters. At the very top end are those who are able to read newspaper headlines, watch television and so on without any optical aids, but who cannot read any ordinary size print or handwriting. At the other end there are those who have no perception of light at all. But, as Gray and Todd have shown most elegantly for an adult population, vision which is impaired as far as reading is concerned may be perfectly adequate for the purposes of getting about safely, i.e. for mobility (Gray and Todd 1968, p. 22). As a rule of thumb one may say that perhaps something like half the youngsters have impaired mobility relative to their sighted peers. Any form of mobility training provided in schools is therefore one of those subjects which does not have to be taught to all the pupils in a school.

Onset of blindness

The great majority of youngsters at schools for the blind will have been born with their handicap, or will have acquired it in infancy. The time of onset of blindness is crucial in a number of senses, though it must be noted straight away that it is not possible to say which particular time is crucial. One cannot say, for instance, that even the majority of children who become totally blind within the first year of their lives can be considered 'congenitally blind'. The distinguishing criterion has to be the extent to which a youngster does or does not make use of visual concepts and imagery, the extent to which he shares the broad language properties of the sighted, and so on. Those born totally without sight lack many of the experiences which are common ground to all the sighted. The most obvious example here is of course anything to do with colour, which appears to be a uniquely visual experience. On the other hand, those born blind may well have acquired more skill in making use of their remaining senses, in particular hearing, than those who become blind in later life. At the time of writing it is also almost certainly true to say that those born totally blind will have acquired quite a number of other useful skills for living which those blinded in later life may find it hard to acquire. Conversely, and of particular relevance to the present topic, there is a broad category of 'skills of living' such as dressing and eating habits, conduct in public places, and so on, which a good many of the congenitally blind need to be taught in more or less formal ways if they want to share these with the sighted.

For practical purposes, therefore, the bulk of the population at present in schools for the blind are likely to be without a number of the experiences commonly encountered by a sighted youngster, and a whole class of these experiences are highly relevant to the problems of mobility.

Additional handicap

Until fairly recently, the incidence of a handicap in addition to that of blindness was common among those born blind, but not universal. After all, there have always been several hundreds of blind children who could not attend ordinary schools for the blind. On the other hand, the bulk of those who were at schools had blindness as their sole and major handicap. It would appear that this pattern is changing fairly rapidly at present and that the future may confront us with a multiple handicap syndrome as the norm and the single handicap as an exception. This is true not only of this country but also of other parts of the world. There are naturally very far-reaching implications here for the future of mobility training in schools for the blind if we have to think primarily in terms of youngsters who as well as being blind are spastic, deaf or mentally retarded.

Mobility

By *mobility* one means the ability to move at will and safely through any environment, whether this be the familiar surroundings of one's home or the wholly unfamiliar environment of the centre of a town visited for the first time. To the extent that one cannot share this level or degree of mobility with the bulk of the intact population, one's mobility is impaired. Clearly, different disabilities do this to varying degrees and blindness as such is of course not the most immobilising disability. But to put the matter into perspective, consider a fully sighted person suddenly bereft of all his vision. To all intents and purposes he would become, if not wholly immobile, very, very severely impaired in his mobility. On the other hand we know of not a few congenitally totally blind people who in one way or another manage to come pretty close to sighted mobility and do so without sighted help. Thus while in the intact human being vision so dominates our lives that we are almost wholly dependent upon it for mobility, it is clear that many of the mobility problems can be solved in non-visual terms. By this time we do have a pretty good idea about the extent to which the adult blind population as a whole is impaired in their mobility (e.g. Gray and Todd 1968) and we also know a great deal about the extent to which we can at present counteract this impairment (Leonard 1968).

For purposes of discussion it is useful to consider the problems of blind mobility under three headings: the avoidance of obstacles, orientation or navigation, and something which one might refer to as *cognition*. By *obstacles* one means anything which is liable to harm the person: contact with a wall, a tree, other road-users, falling up or down a kerb, stumbling over a low railing or falling down a hole. By *orientation* one means the ability to orient oneself in space, both in terms of moment-to-moment orientation and in terms of being able to follow a given route from A to B without losing one's way. In referring to the cognitive aspects of mobility, one wants to stress the role of memory and concepts, and the importance of having some kind of scheme of the world in general and of the route one is on in particular.

To cope with the problems of mobility, blind people make use of their remaining senses, their memory, their cognitive abilities and a range of aids. They either teach themselves or they are taught. The aids now available are the well-known 'white stick' or short cane, the long cane, the guide dog and the sonic aid. The best, i.e. the most highly mobile, blind people one can observe making use of long cane or guide dog in particular, can move at will through most familiar and unfamiliar environments with a competence and degree of safety which comes close to the 'core of sighted mobility'. The bulk of the mobile blind population is restricted to more or less limited repertoires of familiar routes and will tend to move about with widely varying degrees of competence relative to that of sighted mobility. The main change brought about during the last five years or so in this country has been an increasing acceptance of methods of formal training and the existence of sighted instructors. At the time of writing, youngsters at school make use primarily of the short cane, but increasingly of the long cane. They are not able to have dogs until after they have left school and are at least sixteen years of age.

Finally there is the problem of motivation. This brings one right back to the most basic question: should one encourage blind youngsters to be mobile on their own, let alone teach them to be so? I do not want to take too much space over this issue here, because it takes me well outside my own direct area of work: my main concern has been to demonstrate the extent to which it is or is not possible for blind people to become independently mobile on the assumption that independent mobility is indeed 'a good thing'. But for both ethical and practical reasons one has to question and re-examine that assumption. Ethically because one is dealing with a human problem, practically because at the time of writing, and for some considerable time to come, the attainment and maintenance of independent mobility, while eminently feasible, requires effort and courage from the blind person and resources which need to be provided by society. Even at the highest level, the blind person walking about by himself carries out a difficult task in a 'dangerous environment'.

The alternatives to independent mobility are either mobility dependent on a sighted guide, or no mobility at all. We know that about a quarter of the adult blind population opt for mobility with a sighted guide (Gray and Todd 1968, p. 27). We also know from that same source a great deal about the limits set at present to independent mobility in terms of time spent walking about, and the small extent to which people are adding new routes to their repertoire. We also know that most blind people are aware of the fact that their blindness limits their mobility (*op. cit.* p. 45).

One simple answer to our question would therefore be that blind people want to be more mobile, and that if they do want it, society should do something about it. A moment's thought will show the difficulties of obtaining a clear-cut mandate on those grounds: I have no doubt that almost every blind person would want to be as mobile as the sighted if this could be achieved without any effort. But effort is required, and when this was expressed in terms of willingness to attend a mobility training course of between one and three months duration, only about a quarter of the adult population said they would be prepared to go (Gray and Todd 1968, p. 46). That is the picture with adults.

When we turn to children, we are of course beset by a double embroilment: we have in any case a custodial attitude towards the young, and much more so in the case of the disabled young. Here it is not merely custodial but also protective. It is therefore not merely a question of whether a youngster wants to be mobile but also of the extent to which he or she should be encouraged to be so.

The grounds for encouraging mobility in youngsters are those of physical health, of getting to know about the world they live in, and of the principle of independence. The first two can and have been coped with to varying degrees in the past by mobility in sheltered environments, e.g. the grounds or immediate neighbourhood of the schools concerned, and by relying on help from partially or wholly sighted friends. The real argument for encouraging mobility must therefore rest on the importance which one attaches to independent achievement, in particular, or independence in general. By now most of those involved in teaching the blind would appear to agree that independent mobility is a desirable aim, that quite apart from any of the specific functions which it may fulfil, there is at least as much to be said for encouraging independence as for accepting the extent to which one has to be dependent on others. One would dearly like to know much more about all this, and in particular about the extent to which blind youngsters are affected in the growth of their personality as a consequence of limits placed on their mobility.

Where all this becomes 'apparently obvious' is when one considers the limitations placed on the activities of blind youngsters, particularly when they are at home during the holidays. It is very difficult for them to make friends and even when they have attained quite reasonable levels of mobility at their schools, they are more likely than not to find their parents most reluctant to allow them to exercise it.

It will be seen that one is here in one variant of well-known vicious circles: until it can be shown that blind youngsters can be safely mobile there will be considerable reluctance to encourage them—but one can only demonstrate the possibility of safe mobility by encouraging it and indeed by teaching it.

A perspective

It would be quite wrong to create the impression that no thought had been given to the mobility problems of blind children in this country until the last four or five years. It would be equally wrong to claim that all schools are now doing their utmost to apply the most up-to-date knowledge to the solution of these problems. We are in fact witnessing a most fascinating period of reappraisal and reorientation which may well lead to mobility instruction in the widest sense becoming a standard feature of curricular activities in our schools for the blind. This may entail not merely problems of timetabling and syllabus but also of employing extra staff who have qualified in this subject matter. Since it is hardly possible to teach mobility effectively to more than one or two pupils at a time, the administrative problems alone are quite formidable. But far more formidable are the changes in attitudes and outlook which are required from all concerned— parents, teachers, pupils and administrators.

Many blind people, now adult, will have gone through schools in which little if any encouragement had been given to mobility. Where it was allowed at all, it consisted primarily of learning to walk along a small number of fixed routes; if possible without the aid of even a short white stick; mainly for those who were enterprising enough to allow themselves to be taught by more able, blind pupils; accepting as inevitable a fair number of more or less serious bumps on shins, noses and foreheads; trying to appear sighted as far as possible and with no common standard of attainment. It is worth noting that under this regime quite a lot of boys, and a much smaller number of girls, did acquire levels of independent mobility which greatly surprised audiences when I showed films of this in the early sixties. For most people any degree of success constituted an important personal achievement.

However, since the end of the Second World War, things have changed to a greater or lesser extent. In a number of schools, mobility programmes of one form or another were introduced if only as an extra-curricular activity. And during the last decade Myers at Condover Hall, Hewitt at Royal Normal, and Mrs Tooze at Sheffield gradually introduced a more and more systematic approach in their mobility programmes, to mention three outstanding examples. In one way or another, whether as formal teaching or, with younger children, as play activity, sensory training was introduced. Routes were no longer meaningless pedestrian exercises but were linked with some objective such as visiting a special shop or friends in the nearby town. But it was not until the last three years or so that the schools started thinking seriously, and as a body, about introducing mobility as a formal subject and part of the regular curricular activity of the school.

This was almost certainly mainly due to the introduction in the middle sixties of the long-cane/orientation technique for blinded adults from the United States. In essence it provides full body protection by a combination of cane-handling as well as hearing techniques, and equips the blind person with a wide range of systematised techniques for orientation purposes. A good and easily available account of this can be found in Thornton 1968. I want to deal with the attitudes on which this method is based rather than on the method itself since in the present context it is the former which strikes me as being more relevant, and since we are likely to see many variations and changes in the actual method.

The new approach—mobility as a formal subject

In the first place, then, one now thinks of mobility in terms of any other subject and seeks to teach principles as well as techniques for applying those principles. Thus, one is not merely concerned with teaching a person how to cross a particular street but how to cross any street, or at least a class of streets. One teaches not merely a certain number of landmarks but how to find and use landmarks in general.

Use of all remaining facilities

Second, one encourages the use of all remaining senses for the purposes of exploration of the environment. This refers not merely to hearing and smell but also to touch. In point of fact, for a totally blind person touch is the only modality through which he can learn to obtain a reasonable working knowledge of much of his environment—yet tactual exploration of their environment used to be actively discouraged in blind children because it made them obviously blind and different from sighted children.

The useful environment

Third, one thinks of the environment as friendly, providing helpful information, rather than as hostile and full of hurtful objects. Note that for instance the same lamp-post can be an obstacle or a landmark depending on how it is encountered and what use is made of it: indeed, even a painful encounter can lead to recognition of one's position—but one can learn to avoid the painfulness of the encounter by listening out for the echo from the post or by contacting it with one's cane rather than with one's forehead.

In this context the use of moving traffic constitutes a most fascinating example. To most blind people who have not been formally trained this source of noise is primarily a danger sign; if they rely mainly on their hearing for avoiding obstacles and keeping parallel with the walls (through a form of human echo-location) traffic noise is a very considerable nuisance. Typically at the sound of a heavy lorry, one can observe even quite a competent self-taught blind person either stop completely or at least move closer to the wall. Yet moving traffic can become one of the best of dynamic orientation cues to help one steer and maintain a straight course. It is quite difficult to learn, but a most satisfying experience when one has achieved it.

A common standard

Fourth, there is the matter of the standard at which one aims one's training. At first implicitly, and latterly quite explicitly, one thinks of the mobility achievements of the sighted as the ultimate aim. Like a good many other ultimate aims it may well be quite some time before a sizeable number of blind people reach that aim—but the existence of it is a constant spur towards seeking to improve the present levels of attainment in blind mobility.

Included in this aim is a most interesting distinction between ends and means. As mentioned several times before, there has always been some sort of an aim to be like the sighted: at the limit, if one stood still or sat on a chair one could not be distinguished from a sighted person, and, moving away from that limit, there was the ideal that one should seek to employ as far as possible the means available to the sighted. When one talks about aiming towards the standard of the sighted today one tends to think much more in terms of the ends which can be attained than the means which are employed. Indeed, I personally take the view that it is only by a full exploitation of non-visual means that it is at present possible to attain the desired ends, even if these means do make one somewhat conspicuous. (In point of fact, a good many blind people using modern methods are rather less obviously 'blind' than those who went before them.)

The sighted instructor

Finally then, there is the point that as far as contemporary mobility training is concerned, one thinks of sighted people doing the teaching rather than blind ones as in the past. There is a role for blind people in contemporary mobility training programmes, but one has come to realise that there are three functions of a mobility instructor which it is very hard for a blind person to fulfil in the first instance: the actual teaching of the subject matter, particularly as it relates to the motor skill of the cane-handling technique; the provision of immediate and adequate knowledge of results to the student; and the ability to ensure the complete safety of the student while he is under training and until he reaches the phase in which one has to allow him to be, as it were, at risk. All these points seem quite obvious, but taken together with the first four already made, they symbolise or signify the changeover from a sitting-by-Nelly approach of learning to that of formal training; from skilled craftsmen mysteriously handing on their knowledge to apprentices to the formalisation of that knowledge and its transmission. Hence there is a very considerable amount of initial opposition to the new ideas.

In the context of this chapter and of this volume, perhaps the most important point to draw attention to is the role of the sighted instructor in providing knowledge of results or, more technically, 'detailed augmented feedback' (Annett 1969, p. 27). If one realises the extent to which blindness reduces the information-gathering ability of the person one also realises the problem for the blind of obtaining adequate knowledge of results. It is clearly useful to know whether one has managed to avoid an obstacle by a narrow or a wide margin; whether one has managed to cross a street straight or by zig-zagging; whether one continues to hold one's cane in such a way that it provides adequate protection; and so on. Yet in mobility as well as in the more general sphere of education for the blind there seems to have been an incredible lack of appreciation of the role of the teacher as an 'augmented feedback' device: essential in the early stages of learning and to be faded out as soon as the student is able to create his own standards and can provide knowledge of results for himself.

The new attitudes summarised

Thus it will be seen that there are a number of deeply ingrained attitudes which have to be changed among pupils as well as among the teaching staff before the contemporary approach to mobility training can have a chance of success: mobility becomes a proper subject matter rather than an extra-curricular activity; there is the full exploitation of all remaining senses acting in combination rather than the use of one or the other modality in a rather restricted way; there is the attitude towards the environment being a friendly rather than an inherently hostile one; there is the acceptance of a common standard, with sighted achievement the ultimate aim, coupled with the interesting distinction between ways and means; and finally there is the role of the sighted, qualified instructor instead of the highly mobile, blind person acting as the medium of instruction. Anybody who has been involved in bringing about a major change will realise that the greatest difficulty here as elsewhere has been and still is bringing about these changes in attitude. Compared with that, the acquisition of the new methods is almost child's play.

The growth of acceptance

The groundwork for all this had been laid independently by a number of teachers, as already mentioned. I was able to help this along partly by the experimental work which I have carried out in various schools for the blind from 1962 onwards, and partly by organising conferences. The experimental work was primarily concerned with evaluating various mobility aids and training schemes and thus demonstrating the feasibility, as well as the cost, of having mobility training in the schools, and also with the use of simple tactual maps for blind pedestrians. The evaluations (the first carried out in 1962, the last in the summer of 1970) have laid the foundations for comparing various aids to mobility and for future work on matching these various aids with different classes of blind users. In the most recent, and still unpublished study, we were able to assess the effectiveness of a long-cane/orientation scheme in a residential school setting. There is little doubt that some variant of this form of training is suitable for quite a wide range of people, but by no means for all. There is also little doubt about the high levels of attainment which can be brought about with suitable youngsters in a matter of thirty to forty training hours, spread over six to eight weeks.

The first conference on Physical Education and Mobility was held at Nottingham in 1966 and, quite apart from anything else, was apparently the first time that those involved in mobility work in UK schools for the blind met as a group. The third was early in 1968, a meeting of heads of schools which in turn led to the setting up of a working party. This produced a publication, *Mobility Guidance*, a collection of papers by teachers, about half of them from this country, dealing with mobility problems for all age-groups from about six months to eighteen years. Through the generosity of the Viscount Nuffield Auxiliary Fund it was possible to supply each school with three copies by the end of 1968. Since then teachers have had several meetings of their own on the topic of mobility, a number of them have by now been trained to teach the new technique, and an ever increasing number of schools are improving their mobility schemes and bringing them up to date. But it may not be until after the report of the DES Committee of Enquiry into the Education of Visually Handicapped Children, chaired by Professor M. D. Vernon, that we will be able to see whether mobility will really have become a curricular subject in our schools for the blind.

The cognitive value of mobility training

In this last section I want to discuss the role of mobility instruction in helping blind youngsters to understand the world they live in, using this as a specific example of the value of such training.

It is perhaps not until one works with congenitally blind people that one appreciates how much of our everyday world we take for granted and how little of it has been directly accessible to blind youngsters in the past. During my first study in 1962, quite senior boys were astonished to discover the irregularity presented by modern shop-fronts: they had thought in terms of a straight building-line. It also transpired that quite a few of the boys we were then working with did not know a good half of their own school grounds. Later on, time and time again, we ran up against the absence of concepts such as 'pavement'. That pavements could come in all sorts, and that one could discover quite a lot about the various properties of pavements, such as their width, by systematic exploration (and that this after all was very useful information) was an unknown quantity. Not to mention, of course, the whole set of concepts which relate to conglomerations of buildings such as housing estates, and towns. There is a sense in which a street may have only one side for a congenitally blind person, namely the side he is walking on: to represent a street by two double lines on a map caused difficulties with some people. The role of landmarks might have been well understood in the case of specific routes, but how to be sure of finding them as a principle was not. That cars are more than that part of it through which one creeps to get on to a seat, and that one can find out quite a lot about cars by systematic tactual exploration, came as a surprise to many of our youngsters. That one could usefully think of immediate space as extending beyond one's fingertips, or much beyond it at any rate, was equally hard. That one could have a systematic pattern of a town, in non-visual terms by making use of points of the compass as a frame of reference, was again not something that was self-evident. Yet, by starting to make use of this universal frame of reference in one's home or school-room it is surprisingly easy to extend the pattern.

The mapwork in particular has opened up new dimensions of cognitive appraisal for blind youngsters. It was again not the case that nobody had used maps before but nobody had had the time or the opportunity to study why it was so hard for blind people to use them. Partly this was due to poor construction, partly due to lack of systematic mobility training and application of procedures. Yet we were able to show that, with a hand-held map, congenitally blind youngsters were not merely able to walk previously unknown routes but also solve detour problems (Leonard and Newman 1967). Whether one uses meaningful verbal descriptions or tactual maps, it is quite clear that congenitally blind youngsters can have spatial concepts far beyond those attributed to them by V. Senden (1960)— but in most cases one has to go to some trouble to teach them. By now, the kind of maps which we, together with a brilliant teacher at Worcester College for the Blind, Mr J. Pickles, helped to originate are used in a good many schools, and indeed by an increasing number of adults. They are simple and relatively cheap for volunteers at local levels to make (their production forms an ideal sixth-form project, incidentally) and they enable blind youngsters to have a new appreciation of space: by enabling them to experience the symbolism of a map representing an area they are already familiar with, it would appear to be much easier to appreciate the symbolism involved in other forms of maps—and probably much more generally to appreciate the nature of symbolic representation. Here again, it was of course not enough to produce maps which were intelligible or which could be perceived tactually. It was equally important to help create a method of teaching the use of maps by starting with maps of familiar areas and having exercises of increasing complexity in which youngsters plotted routes and walked them, or walked along routes with a map and told us what they expected to happen next along the route, or what they might expect when taking the next turning to the left, and so on. In the end we had groups of three boys dropped with a map in an entirely unfamiliar area having to establish their position and make their way towards the school.

Thus, particularly for the congenitally blind, there may well be benefits of mobility training beyond the immediately obvious ones of being able to go safely and competently from A to B. I suspect that at least those whose additional handicap is not a serious bar to mobility will be able to share with their sighted peers a much wider range of knowledge about the world they live in, and that this may well reduce some of the misunderstandings and frustrations encountered at present. To me person-ally the most satisfying aspect of all this is that the formal training of mobility opens up new worlds to a wide range of youngsters where before only the most able and determined walked.

Conclusion

There is quite a good chance that mobility may become a new subject matter to be incorporated formally in the syllabus structure of our schools for the blind. The evidence already available suggests that it is possible to attain quite high levels of independent mobility by the suitable application of already existing knowledge. Quite apart from the immediate practical advantages of this, the new departure is likely to have far-reaching consequences for the development of congenitally blind youngsters.

D. M. C. Dale

9. Advances in the education of hearing-handicapped children

Detection of handicap

In the United Kingdom and several other countries, screening tests of hearing are conducted routinely in public health clinics with all babies at the age of seven months (Ewing and Ewing 1958). A second national check is made using pure tone sweep-frequency audiometry at the age of five, six or seven years, and in some areas a third such screening is administered to all children on entering high school. In parts of Japan and in Formosa audiometric screening tests are administered to all school children every year.

The aim, of course, is not only to detect deafness as early as possible but also by further investigation to ascertain its aetiology and extent, so that appropriate treatment or therapy can be administered without delay.

For this reason, 'at risk' registers have been drawn up in a number of areas so that particular note can be taken of the hearing of the children born. Mothers who have been in contact with German measles (rubella) cases during the first three months of pregnancy, for example, are much more likely to bear children with defects. In 1964-65 such an epidemic in the United States resulted in an estimated 50,000 children being born with defects—50 per cent of whom had a hearing impairment (Doctor 1970). A vaccine to prevent maternal rubella has been developed and licensed and is being distributed. For some time yet, however, mothers in contact with German measles during the first tremester of pregnancy will be placed on 'at risk' registers. So too will children born to parents where there is a history of familial deafness. Anoxia at birth, prematurity, cerebral palsy and meningitis are all likely to cause nerve deafness and the hearing of such children should be very carefully checked as early as possible.

Administrative difficulties have occurred in most countries in keeping 'at risk' registers up to date, but they are still felt to be very worth persevering with by most health authorities. Difficulties too have been experienced in maintaining the interest of public health nurses in performing the screening tests of babies. Due to the rarity of nerve deafness in infants (approximately one child in 1,000) nurses become discouraged after performing a large number of tests without discovering any abnormalities in hearing and begin to feel the tests are not necessary except in the case of the 'at risk' children. The tests, however, are so quick to administer and the materials used so inexpensive (tissue paper, rattles, a spoon and cup, etc.) that from the publicity point of view alone, it is generally felt to justify the continuation of the practice.

In school-aged children the prevalence of deafness is very much greater. In city areas it is not uncommon to find that no less than one child in fifteen has a significant hearing loss in one or both ears. Over 95 per cent of this deafness is conductive in origin and usually responds readily to medical or surgical treatment. Although not as severe as most of the nerve deafnesses, it is none the less significant to the child at the time and has been found to cause emotional disturbance in children as a result of their not being able to understand what is being said and often not realising why this is so. Middle-ear deafnesses can often fluctuate by as much as 40 decibels within a few days and this, of course, adds to the child's confusion. Teachers in ordinary schools and educational psychologists should be more conscious of slight hearing losses in the children with whom they are working than is at present the case.

Audiology

Apart from the very useful work mentioned below, conducted in the field of evoked-response audiometry, it must be said that audiology, since the Second World War, has to a large extent been rather disappointing. The splendid Harvard researches of Hallowell Davis and colleagues (1946) showed that the ultimate limitation of the hearing aid as a prosthetic device was a physiological rather than a physical one. The main developments in the years that followed were largely in the miniaturisation of the hearing aid through the use of transistors.

Three developments in the fairly recent past, however, are noteworthy: the possibility of transposing high frequencies which are heard least well by most nerve-deafened patients to the lower frequencies which are usually heard best (Johannson 1966); the use of low frequency amplification (i.e. below 250 Hz) for profoundly deaf patients; and the use of battery-operated radio transmitter microphones which enable the children to hear without the distortion caused by noise and reverberation in conventional body-worn hearing aids and without the inconvenience to children and teacher of trailing wires and desk fixtures which are possessed by most group hearing aids. Hearing aids incorporating induction coils and used in conjunction with radio transmitters and close-talking microphones are felt to have distinct possibilities for the future.

The increasing use of *evoked-response audiometry* (ERA) in the assessment of hearing loss represents perhaps the most significant advance in audiology during the last twenty years (Beagley and Kellogg 1969; Davis and Onishi 1969; Rapin and Grazianih 1969). The attainment of a completely objective measure of hearing acuity for pure tones has now been brought a great deal closer, and many patients whom it has previously been impossible to test by conventional audiometry have responded to this newer test. Children with central disorders and those who are mentally deficient or so handicapped physically that they are unable to cooperate in normal testing, as well as malingerers, have all been found to test out using electro-encephalographic (EEG) techniques in conjunction with a computer.

Individual hearing aids are available free of charge through the National Health Services of the United Kingdom, Australia, New Zealand, Denmark and some other countries, to all children whose average hearing losses over the three speech frequencies is 35 db or greater—and whose loss is irreversible. In Denmark and a number of areas in the United Kingdom two hearing aids are fitted. The majority of UK and Australian children are fitted with the Medical Research Council (Medresco) body-worn hearing aid, and the deafest children receive commercial instruments which amplify the lower frequencies. In recent years a National Health Service ear-level hearing aid has been available to the less deaf children. (It is perhaps worth noting that the body-worn Medresco aid is retailed to overseas countries by the contractors to the British Department of Health for £6 or £7— i.e. US $15-$17 as distinct from $300-400 and even $500 charged for some similar commercial instruments.) The use of hearing aids on a full-time basis has resulted in a large number of spectacularly successful cases of children, usually with average hearing losses of less than 85 db, learning to speak fairly clearly in colloquial language and to understand oral speech very readily. For children with hearing losses in excess of 90 db, however, the effect of hearing aids, although eventually beneficial, is not so dramatic. Remarkable audiological results appear to be being achieved at the Peninsula Oral School in California using carefully fitted ear-level hearing aids which amplify low frequencies.

The Listening-Reading-Speaking method appears to the writer to be a significant contribution to the field of applied audiology not only for the partially hearing child but also for many of the severely and profoundly deaf children. The Ewings (1968) have described the method for assisting individual children 'to read, to hear, to comprehend and to say new words'. In an increasing number of schools and classes in ordinary schools for deaf and partially hearing children in the South of England, a similar, but not identical method has been found extremely useful in group situations. The method can be used in a variety of ways, but one way is as follows: The teacher writes on the blackboard a paragraph describing the activity, story, historical event etc. which he wants the children to consider. This is written in colloquial language—as though one was talking to normally hearing children. Most of the language is written at a level which the majority of the class will understand, but several words, phrases and concepts are included which the teacher knows are unfamiliar to the class.

Using a group hearing aid, an induction loop, or a radio transmitter hearing aid, and speaking close to the microphone, the teacher then reads through the passage aloud at a near-normal rate, pointing not only to each word, but also to each syllable. The children then repeat the passage phrase by phrase, after the teacher. The third step is a lengthy one, when the paragraph is worked through once more for meaning. At this stage, visual aids and apparatus are introduced when necessary to make meanings clear. Teachers deliberately delay such aids in order to encourage the children to work out meanings from the context as far as possible. Then extracts from the passage are read without the children watching and they are asked to identify these. It is surprising how, after practice, even some children with 100 db losses can do this. Finally the whole passage is read again and some questions might be given for homework or a copy of the text given to the children to take to their parents or houseparents.

The method as described by the Ewings can be used very effectively by parents and houseparents as well as teachers.

Regional audiology services

Throughout nearly all Western countries very wide variations exist in basic audiological procedures such as the fitting of hearing aids, the making of ear moulds, speech tests of hearing and pure tone testing. Even wider variations exist where the more sophisticated tests are administered. It is suggested that some form of audiological service might help to ensure that more patients receive the benefit of the most up-to-date knowledge available

Audiology services include the detection of deafness in the community; the assessment of its extent in each case; and the audiological procedures used to help minimise each individual's hearing handicap. It is suggested that large *audiology centres* in the main conurbation areas and smaller *audiology clinics* throughout the remainder of a country could provide the basis for an effective audiology service if planned regionally. Overall numbers required for the large regions and smaller clinic areas would, of course, vary considerably depending on the density of the population and the economic resources available.

A key figure in such a scheme—particularly in the smaller audiology clinics—is an educational psychologist with additional training in audiology. There is a precedent for this in a number of clinics in the United States and throughout the whole of the Australian Commonwealth Acoustics Laboratories. Authorities such as Hallowell Davis of Central Institute for the Deaf in St Louis, have recommended it strongly: 'Hearing, our main topic, is certainly a province of psychology. Communication may use physical tools and have social aspects, but it is basically a psychological process. Tests of hearing are also squarely the province of the psychologist. The reaction of the individual to deafness and the basic problems of self-adjustment of education, and vocational guidance are clearly psychological. At first glance, it may seem that psychology has been slighted and that only one chapter deals with a single and rather special aspect of psychology; on the contrary, the entire book is permeated with it. In fact, the psychological aspects of the various sections give our book its unity' (Silverman and Davis 1960).

The educational psychologist's earlier training (often in teaching, in child development and mental measurement) together with his experience of atypical children—especially those with language disorders—frequently make him exceptionally well fitted for further training in audiology for children. To ensure that the educational aspect is kept well to the fore, it is recommended that teachers of deaf children should see all pre-school children and all school-aged children whose hearing losses exceed 25 db in the better ear. Virtually every case has had a medical referral and invariably is seen by an otologist. The otologist discusses the case with the audiologist and teacher of the deaf and a report goes back to the general practitioner and/or the school medical officer, and other specialists are called in where this is felt to be necessary.

Content of language syllabuses

A survey of the language syllabuses used by 261 teachers in 46 schools and units for deaf and partially hearing children during 1968-69 in the South of England and Wales revealed broad patterns under which language topics were presented (Dale 1971).

4-7 year olds
1. Our homes and families
2. Our class and our school
3. Exploring our district
4. Story telling—frequently those about boys and girls or about animals

8-12 year olds
1. Current events
2. Our homes, school and district
3. Children and their families in other parts of the United Kingdom
4. Stories and studies of children and their families in other countries and in other times
(2 and 3 often involving visits or field-trips)

13-17 year olds
1. Current events—sometimes becoming the central theme around which the following other subjects turned
2. Local, national and world history and geography
3. Home management
4. Social living
5. Occupations—in some cases the syllabus became increasingly orientated to vocational guidance and placement and life after school days were over

Teaching methods

Language.   The Listening-Reading-Speaking method of language presentation has been described above. *Activity methods* have proved extremely effective in presenting language to deaf children. Essentially, they consist of placing a child in a stimulating milieu where he feels that communication is necessary, and then providing him with the appropriate language. For example, a doll which needs washing and an empty bath tub are given to the child. If he or she indicates to the teacher a gesture of a tap being turned on, the teacher quickly says 'Would you like some water? Where can we find some water? Let's go and get the water . . . etc.' As soon as the child begins to use language, teachers are encouraged to improve on the child's imperfect version as the lesson proceeds—e.g. if a child says 'Water?' the teacher would say 'Where is the water, please?' and ask the child to repeat this before continuing.

The running battle between advocates of oral and manual methods has been waged throughout the past 150 years and still appears to dominate the thinking of a large proportion of workers in this field—often, it must be said, to the exclusion of virtually all else. For most hearing-impaired children oral methods seem to be favoured. In recent years, however, it does seem that the argument has begun to centre more around what proportion of children should be taught orally and what proportion taught by combined oral and manual methods. Of the 174 people who presented evidence to the Department of Education and Science Committee to investigate 'The place, if any, of fingerspelling and signing in the education of deaf children' (DES 1968) not one suggested that purely oral methods were appropriate to all children. The percentage of children who are felt to fall into this category of needing some form of manual assistance, however, varies a great deal—some would say 40 to 60 per cent and others 5 to 10 per cent. More research is required in this area. In the United States during the last three years, a rapid development has occurred in the form of the *Total Approach*. Theoretically this involves using all methods to communicate with deaf children—oral, aural and manual. In practice it looks little different from the *simultaneous method* (Hardy 1971).

An interesting recent innovation in the field of methods of communication has been that of *Cued Speech* (Cornett 1970). Devised by Dr R. O. Cornett at Gallaudet College in Washington DC, it has as its first objective the early establishment and consistent use of natural language in which the information furnished by the lips is indispensable. Its second and third objectives are the use of clear speech and maximum capacity in speech reading. Cued speech is based on the following hypothesis: 'In Cued Speech eight configurations and four positions of one (either) hand are used to supplement the information available on the lips, in order to make each syllable look different from all the rest. Syllables which look alike on the lips always look different on the hand. Syllables which look alike on the hand always look different on the lips. No syllable can be read from the hand alone.'

Little research has been conducted into this use of Cued Speech. After observing its use by parents and teachers in the United States, Australia and England, it appears that Cued Speech is easy to learn but difficult to use as rapidly as is necessary when speaking at a near-normal rate. The writer feels, however, that every effort should be made to use it where difficulty is experienced in communicating orally and aurally, before one resorts to conventional manual methods involving finger spelling and signing.

Speech.   Teaching profoundly deaf children to speak intelligibly remains one of the biggest problems confronting teachers of such children today. A Department of Education Survey in 1964 of 264 children aged over fourteen years in schools for the deaf showed that only thirty-eight had reasonably adequate speech.

One of the factors which has kept research workers out of the field of speech therapy for deaf children has been the lack of accurate measuring devices.

A research just completed at London University Institute of Education entitled 'The Construction of a Test of the Intelligibility of the Speech of Deaf Children' (Spencer 1970) indicates that a valid, reliable and at the same time practical test has been produced which could prove to be of real value to teachers and research workers. The test is in two sections:

1.   A test of initial or final consonant articulation using 41 single-syllable words. These are tape-recorded and audited by normally hearing high school or teachers' college students using a multiple-choice technique.
2.   A test of rate of utterance where children say five groups of eight simple words in series.

The test has been designed for deaf and partially hearing children aged seven or above.

The significance of the construction of such a test is that answers should now be able to be sought to such questions as: 'Is individual speech teaching more effective than group speech work?' 'Are three individual speech sessions per day more effective than one a day, or one a week?'; 'Is emphasis on the teaching of correct articulation helpful or harmful to the overall intelligibility of speech?' At the present time, answers to these questions are largely dependent on the opinion of the teacher or parent. Such opinions are, of course, not nearly accurate enough to make weekly or even monthly assessments of progress.

It seems likely that various forms of electronic speech translators may well have much to contribute to intelligible speech production by both deaf children and deaf adults.

The education of hearing-impaired children in ordinary schools

The manner in which children with impaired hearing are integrated into ordinary schools varies very considerably depending on such factors as the hearing loss of the child, his intelligence, home background, personality, the size of the class in the ordinary school, the ability and aptitude of the teacher of the ordinary class and the amount of specialist service available to him. Over half the children in the United Kingdom who wear hearing aids are able to attend their local schools with occasional visits from teachers of deaf children or remedial teachers. Types of unit provision for the more severely handicapped children at the present time include the following, where the hearing-impaired children are:

1.   Attached to ordinary classes and withdrawn each day to a unit classroom to be helped by a teacher of deaf children;
2.   Attending a unit classroom for most of each day but being attached, usually in ones and twos, to ordinary classes for such subjects as physical education, art and craft, and in secondary schools, technical subjects;
3.   Attending a special class for approximately half of every day and the whole deaf group is attached to an ordinary class for the other half but accompanied almost all of the time by the teacher of deaf children. During these integration periods the two teachers work in the one room (Dale 1968).

With the build-up in the United Kingdom of the specialist visiting-teacher service from four to over 200 teachers during the past twelve years, and the consequent increase in guidance to parents of deaf children, and such varied methods of educating the children as those outlined above, it is to be expected that more and more children will be educated outside special schools.

Problems Encountered

It is clear, however, that not all integration schemes are successful. In the United States, for example, a report made in 1965 to the Secretary of Health, Education and Welfare by his Advisory Committee on the Education of the Deaf commented unfavourably on the integrated programmes, saying that the 'integration seemed more imaginary than real' and that although the children shared lunch halls and playing areas, there was next to no contact between the children—'There appeared to be a glass wall between the two groups.'

In an effort to obtain more friendships with normally hearing children near their homes, as well as improved academic attainments, the writer is currently experimenting with a form of individual integration for six children from a partially hearing unit in North London. These six children (mean H. loss 75 db) have now been enrolled in their own local primary schools. The following special provision has been made for them:

1.   A teacher of the deaf visits each child daily to assist with speech training and to supervise the programme generally.
2.   Three additional teachers have been appointed to work half of each day with two children.
3.   A language master, cine loop projector, tape-recorder, film strip and slide projector have been provided for each child.
4.   Parents are now able to receive up to two pages each day from the associate teachers, telling them of significant educational and social happenings at school.

After eleven weeks, the results are encouraging.

The effect of parental influence on linguistic attainment and social adjustment in deaf children

Throughout Professor Philip Vernon's book *Intelligence and Cultural Environment* (1969), concern has been expressed over the differences between peoples in their levels of technological advance, of education and civilisation or backwardness. Although no one will deny the importance of the geographical and economic handicaps of disease and malnutrition in the production of such differences, Vernon asserts than man to a great extent makes himself and fashions his own environment, and it is he who must be changed if he is to achieve a more prosperous and healthy existence: 'It is not only the poor circumstances of the parents but their backwardness and resistance to change which result in the underdevelopment of their children's capacities.' In the education of deaf children, although a large number of workers believe that home management has a similar influence, little objective data exist to confirm this. An investigation was therefore undertaken to ascertain the extent to which home management appeared to influence the linguistic attainment and social adjustment of a group of severely deaf children (Connor 1971).

The manner in which many of even the most able parents interviewed were missing opportunities to assist their children gave cause for very real concern, and must to a certain extent be responsible for the very low attainments achieved. Checking the performance of hearing aids daily has been shown to be essential for ensuring their satisfactory performance (Silverman and Davis 1960; Dale 1967). Yet twenty-two of the parents interviewed said that they did not ever check the child's hearing aid. The advantage of speaking close to the microphone of a hearing aid has been common knowledge to audiologists (and hearing-aid users) for the past twenty-five years yet parents in thirty-three of the sixty homes visited did not ever do this. Only eight said they did this daily. Daily diaries kept by the parents concerning the family's activities have been found to be an excellent aid to reading. Again only eight of the sixty homes were keeping such diaries. It is often recommended that a child should have books by his bedside and available at other times. Parents are encouraged to tell stories from the excellent books now available. Nineteen of the sixty children did not belong to a children's library, although these were accessible to them all. This negative list could be needlessly extended, but suffice it to say that teachers do have a responsibility to see that parents are better informed about their opportunities and responsibilities to assist their deaf children.

Higher education

With the disappointing results being achieved by most deaf children, it is not surprising that so few have succeeded in the field of higher education. In the United Kingdom it appears that fewer than ten ex-pupils of schools for the deaf or units in ordinary schools have obtained degrees. The United States have tackled the problem by establishing an institution— Gallandet College—which caters for over 1,000 deaf students. The standard of achievement, however, rates among the lowest of all such colleges in the country. Special teaching and interpreting facilities are offered at sixteen colleges of further education throughout the USA and in recent years four other institutions have provided advanced technical education. A National Technical Institute for the Deaf has been established within the Rochester Institute of Technology. Three hundred and fifty students are currently enrolled, and a final establishment of 750 students is envisaged.

In the United Kingdom, an interesting development since 1971 has been the enrolment of fifty hearing-impaired students at the newly established Open University. Reading materials are sent out, weekly tutorial classes are arranged and a one week summer school is offered. These residential periods, with interpreters, continuous typed television accompaniment of lectures and discussion periods, and hearing aids in-corporating induction loop systems, have proved most beneficial. By strengthening the tutorial work with an increase of individual tuition, this facility seems to represent exceptional opportunities for highly intelligent hearing-impaired scholars.

F

Sir Cyril Burt

10. The gifted child

The beginning of the scholarship system

'You, Citizens, are all brothers. But the God who created you has mingled gold in the composition of those who are born to be rulers, silver in those who will act as their executives, and in those whose task will be to manufacture goods or to cultivate the soil he has mixed brass or iron. Although most children resemble their parents, nevertheless occasionally a golden parent may beget a silver child, and a silver parent a child of gold, and indeed every kind may spring from any other. Therefore, the rulers have received this all-important charge from God, that first and foremost they scrutinise each child to see what metal has gone to his making, and then allocate or promote him accordingly; for the oracle has predicted that our state is doomed to disaster when its guardianship is handed over to men of baser metal.'* Here in picturesque outline was Plato's scheme for his brave new world. It is the first explicit mention of the need to select and educate those who are most highly gifted by nature to serve in the more responsible positions in the state.

The proposals thus advocated have been taken up and elaborated, with various modifications and minor criticisms, by a long list of philosophers from Aristotle down to Hegel and his British followers. Yet for a thousand years not the faintest attempt was made to put Plato's suggestions into actual practice. In the end it was the struggle for survival, not the exhortations of the philosopher, that led to the deliberate selection of the fittest to direct and administer the government of a European state. During

---

* *Republic*, **III**, 415 A–C. I have used 'executives' to translate the Greek word that is more usually rendered 'auxiliaries' and generally taken to signify 'soldiers'; it plainly had a far wider meaning. In discussing the differences in natural ability, which provide the basis for the hierarchical organisation of his ideal state, Plato recognises there may be 'certain admixtures', i.e. that nature produces gradations rather than clear-cut demarcations; but (as Adam remarks in his commentary) to make his new points plainer to the ordinary citizen Plato depicts the main distinctions as sharper than they really are.

the Dark Ages civilisation all but perished. At length Charlemagne, fresh from the defeat of his barbaric enemies and inspired by stories of 'The grandeur that was Rome', decided to institute a systematic search for men of high ability, who, unlike his fellow-warriors, could read and write, preferably in Latin, to assist him in organising a new and 'Holy' Roman Empire. At his invitation Alcuin of York came over to found and direct a 'palace school' at Aachen, and doubtless composed the famous rescript, *De litteris colendia*, requiring abbots and others in responsible positions to found schools and select scholars.

Unfortunately, when Charles the Great died, the palace school died with him. As Macaulay records, 'No sooner was he interred, than the imbecility of his descendants began to bring contempt on themselves and destruction on their subjects: nothing more was left to the abject heirs of an illustrious name—Charles the Bald, Charles the Fat, and Charles the Simple.' England, however, thanks to her insular position, was preserved from much of this constant disruption, and quickly settled down to a period of relative peace and stability under a single monarch. Almost at once an urgent demand arose for lawyers, justices, court bureaucrats, and clerks to assist in the elaborate administrative system set up by the Anglo-Norman kings. The need for talent created a search for talent. Reading and writing were still restricted almost exclusively to the Church—'the mother of all professions'. But, since the clergy themselves were celibate, they had constantly to be replenished; and, as their records amply show, were recruited from the abler sons in every social class.

Under the Plantagenets the monastic schools rapidly expanded. Early in the thirteenth century the new University of Oxford, with its unique college system, was already gaining a European reputation. Often the generous benefactors who founded a college also founded a school, and bequeathed funds to assist youths of proved ability who were unable to support themselves. Just after the death of Edward III, William of Wyke-ham, his former chancellor and himself of humble origin, endowed a 'New College' at Oxford 'for 100 clerks', and a 'grammar school' at Winchester for '70 pore and needy scholars proficient in the grammaticals'. This marks the beginning of the British scholarship system.

Towards the close of the Middle Ages merchants and others who gained their living by commerce greatly increased in number, and began to form a powerful middle class, midway between the nobles and the peasantry. The conduct of trade requires not only reading and writing but also arithmetic. New schools were accordingly set up in London and else-where, which produced a great and growing multitude of educated laymen. Under the Tudors and the Stuarts more than a hundred endowed grammar schools were established all over the country. Suitable scholars were generally selected by the 'governors'. Such schools and such scholars were urgently required by Elizabeth and her successors to provide and train what we should now call civil servants and municipal officials, many of whom were drawn from the newer middle classes. Moreover, during the Reformation, and again under the Commonwealth, there was a pressing need for intelligent 'secretaries' to defend the drastic changes that had been introduced both in religion and in government. My own school, Christ's Hospital, was founded in the heart of London by Edward VI at the instigation of Ridley. Year by year, as 'Founder's Day' came round, we young scholarship winners listened to the old Bidding Prayer: 'that there may never be wanting a succession of fit persons for the service of God in Church and State. I bid you pray for all schools, colleges, and universities of this land'.

The ideal of a classless society

'The Platonic ideal', it has been said, 'rests squarely on the supposition that men are created unequal.' In practice this time-honoured principle, tacitly assumed if not explicitly stated, often led to regrettable abuses. Greek civilisation itself had been based on slavery. Aristotle, we may remember, sought to justify it by maintaining that 'some men are slaves by nature and others born free'. The natural slave, he argued, is by bodily constitution fit only for physical and manual labour; the natural free man alone is 'fitted for the political life'. Still, even Aristotle himself would have been quick to criticise the injustices of the feudal system and the tyrannies of the autocratic Tudors.

Our two greatest Lord Chancellors, More and Bacon, have each attempted to follow Plato's example, and plan in imagination an ideal commonwealth. Of the two instructive fantasies, More's *Utopia*, written a few years after the accession of Henry VIII, is by common consent at once the most fascinating and the most influential. It professes to relate how More himself, while serving on one of Henry's embassies to Holland, encountered a kind of Portuguese Captain Gulliver. This 'ancient mariner', while sailing round the world with Vespucci, happened to land on an unknown island, in size very much like England; and his detailed description is to a large extent a witty and satirical comment on the state of the country at the beginning of the reign. Plato's ideal republic was based on class distinctions; More's is virtually a classless society. In contemporary England there was a king and nobles who ruled; there were knights with their retainers to fight; clerks to read, write, and study; ploughmen to till the ground. As in Plato's community, each man had one job, and one job only. But the citizen of Utopia combined and carried out nearly all these tasks for himself. There were indeed 'philarchs' elected as supervisors, one of whom was chosen to be 'prince'. Nevertheless, every self-sufficing citizen was expected to rule himself, to make his own tools, and to cultivate his own field or garden; his leisure hours were spent in study; and, though he detested warfare, he was at need a soldier; every child was educated, and educated alike.

More's Latin romance was the forerunner of many later attempts to describe a model society, from Bacon's *New Atlantia* and Campanella's *City of the Sun* to Morris's *New from Nowhere*, Wells's *Modern Utopia*, and McDougall's *Island of Eugenia*. John Dewey, a behaviourist, a pragmatist, and 'the most influential educationist the United States have produced', likewise advocated the 'abolition of all divisive class-distinctions'. Being itself an embryonic community, the school should, he argued, at once reflect, and embody, the principles needful for an ideal society and thus help to promote and foster 'social solidarity' (*Democracy and Education*, 1916). Quite recently two British investigators have started their enquiries with 'the hypothesis [and the manifest hope] that the abolition of selection and the reorganisation of education along comprehensive lines would help to establish a truly classless society';* and Mr Michael Duane puts the underlying assumption into explicit terms by declaring that 'all children are born equal in intellectual ability'. Manifestly unaware of the long and chequered history of the schemes they now revive, most of these modern enthusiasts completely ignore the many criticisms to which such schemes have been subjected.

The doctrine of innate mental equality, with its obvious corollary that all observable differences are results solely of environmental conditions, has had numerous champions in the past. It found its most vigorous and systematic exponent in C. A. Helvétius (*De l'esprit*, 1758; *De l'homme*, 1773). His conclusion was the oft-quoted maxim 'l'éducation peut tout', and his arguments exercised a powerful influence on the leaders of the 'utilitarian school' in this country—Bentham, the two Mills, Godwin, and their numerous disciples.

To designate 'an ideal community in which all are equal and all bear

* Julienne Forde, *Social Class and the Comprehensive School* (1969) and Frances Stevens, *The New Inheritors* (1970), especially chap. VIII 'Towards Equality'. So far, their results, as they frankly admit, have revealed no signs that the gathering together of children from all ranks of society and the whole range of mental ability tends to produce a greater mixing of social classes.

rule', the poet Southey suggested the name 'pantisocracy'. He and Coleridge planned to found a 'pantisocratic settlement' on the banks of the Susquehanna. Lack of funds prevented this chimerical scheme from being realised. However, in his later years the Poet Laureate related how, in his study at Keswick, he was visited one evening by a stranger, handsome and impressive, except for an ugly red scar around his neck. The visitor announced himself as the ghost of Sir Thomas More, and proceeded, in a series of *Colloquies on Society*, to expound how the humanitarian principles he had urged upon his royal master might be applied to correct the many ills from which England was now suffering under the heel of the Industrial Revolution. The envy, jealousy, and class conflicts that flourished in a social system that was still semi-feudal were to be forestalled by training each child to perform for himself 'all that was needed for the happy life'; and in the reveries of the Lake poets, as in that of 'Poor Susan', 'the happy life' was a life of rustic simplicity in rural England—'amid green pastures in the midst of the dale'.

Just before and just after the French Revolution various attempts were made to put the notion of a classless society into practice. In 1794 'Gracchus' Babeuf, 'the first to propose socialism as a practical policy', established a Société des Égaux in Paris, and advocated the elimination of all class differences with such obstinate insistence that he himself had ultimately to be eliminated. In America several egalitarian communities were founded by religious as well as by political enthusiasts. One of the most famous was a new village called Harmonie, built on an old camping ground of the Kickapoo Indians in Indiana by the companions of a German pietist named Rapp; and similar settlements were founded in the 1770s by a small group of British Shakers led by 'Mother Lee', a former Manchester factory-hand. Robert Owen, usually hailed as 'the father of British socialism', was a successful Manchester cotton spinner, who decided to set up a model firm (with Bentham as one of the partners) in the little town of New Lanark. With Helvétius and Godwin, he firmly believed that 'the characters of men are formed solely by circumstance', and could therefore be moulded by education, provided it began early enough (he was the first to open schools for infants). Finding himself hampered by the long-standing laws and customs that prevailed in Britain, he bought land from the failing Rappite community, and invited all who cherished the same ideas to join him in his 'new social programme'. It prospered so long as he was in charge; but three years after his return to England, it had to be wound up. Owen lost £40,000 by the venture. A little later Étienne Cabet, a Frenchman who declared himself 'tout épaté' by More's *Utopia*, started another 'Utopian colony' in Texas. But, like every attempt to set up a classless community, it collapsed almost as soon as it was left to run by itself.

These romantic speculations and abortive experiments did not escape the criticisms of contemporary philosophers and reformers. Of these the most vivid and outspoken was the historian of _The French Revolution_. In his various social and educational pronouncements Carlyle might well be described as a Plato with a strong dash of temper. The criticisms followed two main lines. First, as Adam Smith, another Scot, had already contended, an essential prerequisite of social progress and economic productivity is the division of labour. If each citizen of Utopia was to be jack-of-all-trades, each would assuredly be master of none. Nothing but inefficiency could result.

Secondly, Carlyle never tired of declaiming against 'the Helvetian doctrine of mental equality'—'any man equal to any other, Quashee Nigger to Socrates or Shakespeare'. 'The lower classes', he argued in _Shooting Niagara_, 'need both governors and guides. . . . Let the fittest to rule bear rule. . . . Let them found schools, not of the verbal or vocal sort, teaching the bare rudiments of reading aloud and writing on their slates'— 'the arts Babblative and Scribblative', as Southey had called them—but 'of a practical kind, so that each may learn and labour truly in that state of life unto which it shall please God to call him.' And then 'let the few wise take command of the innumerable foolish'. These injunctions were hammered home in the lectures on _Heroes and Hero-worship_, where Carlyle expounds his theory of 'the influence of great men on history', a theme taken up in one of William James's earliest papers (later reprinted in _The Will to Believe_, 1907).

The need for a scientific approach

All the foregoing theories and counter-theories, it will be noted, were defended almost exclusively on _a priori_ grounds. But the controversies they aroused have served admirably to clarify and pinpoint the basic issues. And these issues, as will now be evident, are essentially questions of fact. Are men born equal in character and capacity, or are some more highly endowed than their fellows? Do different occupations vary so widely in their difficulty and in the qualifications they demand that some can be performed efficiently only by those who are gifted by nature with the requisite aptitudes, or is it true, as Watson declared and some present-day educationists still argue, that, provided you start early enough, you can 'train any individual to follow any vocation you like to choose—doctor, lawyer, teacher, factory-hand or captain of industry, tinker, tailor, plough-man, or thief'? And how would those who, like Carlyle, uphold the doctrine of mental inequality discover and train those exceptional indivi-duals who are fitted to be 'the nation's leaders'? Finally, what evidence is there for the theory that the progress and prosperity of different countries is largely determined by the number of able men that each produces?

The first to attack these basic problems by scientific methods was Sir Francis Galton. The distinctive feature of scientific research, he maintained, was measurement. Accordingly, he set himself to devise means for measur-ing not only the various characteristics in which individuals appeared to differ but also the correlations of one characteristic with another. And in the earliest of his many publications in this field, *Hereditary Genius* (1869), he claims to be 'the first to treat the subject in a statistical manner, and so arrive at precise numerical results'.

He begins by accepting the traditional notion that mental activity has three main aspects—intellect, emotion, and will—and concludes from his biographical studies that 'those who may be accounted men of outstanding achievement' are characterised not merely by high intellectual ability but also by an intense emotional interest in whatever task they have taken in hand, and by a resolute will to work hard, intently, and persistently. The starting point, however, was to be an investigation into the first of these qualities, since intellectual capacity must necessarily set an upper limit to what each can achieve. His preliminary results clearly indicated, so he maintained, that the phrenologists and faculty psychologists had laid far too much stress on 'special aptitudes'—observation, inventiveness, language, and various scientific, artistic, and practical abilities; far more influential was 'a general capacity or factor entering into all we say, or think, or do'. And the differences in this all-important quality, so he tries to prove, are largely innate. Carlyle, whose writings had done much to direct Galton's attention to these problems, had expressed a similar view: 'I have no notion', he writes in *Heroes and Hero-Worship*, 'of a truly great man that could not be all sorts of men—Poet, Prophet, Priest, or King, or what you will'. And this somewhat novel hypothesis was later fully confirmed by various British factor analysts. For this 'innate, general, intellectual factor' Galton's usual name was 'general ability', though at times he adopted the single word *intelligence*—a term which Spencer had used in much the same sense, and which Binet subsequently popularised. It still seems necessary to repeat that Galton and his followers used 'intelligence' (in those days a word almost confined to scholars) simply as a convenient shorthand label to designate a hypothetical factor defined as above. The critics who imagined that 'intelligence' was an observable quality readily recognisable in everyday life, and that these early investigators set out to determine its nature, but failed to realise that it is 'largely the product of environmental agencies', are not demonstrating a new conclusion which Galton and his followers failed to appreciate but merely using Galton's term in a new and different sense. Galton himself repeatedly declared that all observable characteristics are always the joint effects of both nature and nurture.

Who are the gifted?

No one denies that certain forms of mental deficiency are inborn or that the most celebrated instances of genius—a Leonardo, a Shakespeare, or a Newton—owe their exceptional achievements to innate talent. Galton, however, went on to show that, between these two extremes, every grade and shade of innate variation may be discerned. Differences in mental capacity, like differences in bodily height, are a matter of degree; and, like differences in height, they are distributed roughly in accordance with the so-called 'normal curve of error'. Thus, so far as ability is concerned, the assumption of so many philosophic writers that mankind can be sub-divided into clear-cut classes, types, or races, differing sharply from one another in their level of intellect, is wholly mistaken. It follows that any definition of 'giftedness' will be entirely arbitrary. Different writers adopt different borderlines, often without specifically stating what precisely they have in mind.

In most of my own investigations I have used the term *gifted* to mean 'the brightest three per cent in the general population'. With a scale based on a conventional standard deviation of 15 points, the borderline would therefore be approximately 130 IQ. This proportion and this borderline were adopted because, when I first began my researches in the London schools, I found that they roughly described the kind of pupil who obtained 'a junior county scholarship' to what was then known as a 'secondary school', a 'grammar school' in current terminology. In recent years the proportion of pupils admitted to so-called 'grammar schools' has greatly increased, and varies widely from one area to another. Hence in many post-war enquiries a variety of borderlines are used: thus terms like 'bright', 'gifted', and their various synonyms may denote the top 5, 10, 20, or even 25 per cent of the school population. Many of those who criticise my findings are in fact talking about pupils of an entirely different category from those to whom my own conclusions relate.

The award of a scholarship or free place was originally decided by an annual examination in English and Arithmetic. Our psychological surveys revealed that this failed to discover many extremely bright children coming from illiterate and poverty-stricken homes. It was therefore resolved to make far more use of teachers' assessments, and to introduce a group test of intelligence which served to check and standardise the assessments of teachers from different types of school. Doubtful cases were re-examined by personal interview, and usually retested with individual tests.

The majority of these gifted children—over 58 per cent—came from the manual or 'working' class, particularly from the ranks of skilled labour, and only 41 per cent from the non-manual or 'middle' class. However, of the adult population, i.e. of the parents, only 15·3 per cent belonged to the middle class. Evidently the percentage, though not the absolute number of scholarship winners of middle-class origin was far greater than the percentage coming from the working class. Present-day writers constantly complain that 'a disproportionate number of the pupils in our grammar schools are selected from the middle classes', and denounce the disparity as 'a gross injustice to the lower classes'. It should, however, be recognised that scarcely any of the parents in the manual classes had sufficient ability to win a junior county scholarship. Hence, to the old-fashioned hereditarian of fifty years ago it came as a startling surprise to discover that so many of their offspring possessed such high IQs as were discovered by the tests. On the Mendelian theory of inheritance, however, this is just what we should expect. I may add that a recent survey of gifted children in New Zealand yields almost exactly the same proportions: 40 per cent of the pupils with 'high IQs' (over 125 points) were drawn from the non-manual classes.*

The after-careers of the gifted

All the gifted children discovered in our London surveys were followed up for the remainder of their school careers, and, so far as they could still be traced, during later life. It appeared that, by the age of thirty or a little later, nearly 80 per cent of the gifted boys from the manual classes were successfully pursuing what in our classification was rated as a 'middle-class' occupation. Of those who (so far as ability was concerned) had seemed fit to go to a university, less than half actually entered: since the last war the proportion has of course greatly increased. Nevertheless, as the after-histories obtained both in London and in Terman's research plainly prove,

* The detailed figures for the eight occupational classes into which the London population was divided are given in Table III of my paper on 'The Gifted Child' in the *Yearbook of Education* (1962); and Table IV sets out the New Zealand figures for comparison.

it was possible, even with the crude methods of those early years, to arrive at a reasonably satisfactory assessment of gifted children, and a reasonably successful prediction of what they were likely to achieve.

What then were the causes for the apparent failures? (1) Undoubtedly in many cases the initial assessments were at fault. Judged by the results of subsequent retests and by reports from the grammar schools to which scholarship winners had been allotted, at least 5 per cent of the candidates had been wrongly selected; and similarly, one may guess, at least another 5 per cent had been wrongly rejected. Nevertheless, most of these mistaken allocations were confined to cases near the borderline. Much of the inaccuracy could nowadays be avoided by improved methods of assessment, and especially by a greater reliance on the record cards, which every teacher should be trained to compile. But no scheme can be infallible. (2) A more serious and almost unavoidable set of causes arises from accident, disease, or prolonged ill-health. According to my own case-histories this accounts for nearly 15 per cent of the casualties. (3) A few, though not as many as are commonly supposed, result from unpredictable fluctuations in mental development, such as are frequently noticeable during adolescence. There are 'late bloomers' who mature slower than usual, and precocious youngsters who often drop behind. (4) Success in an academic career, particularly at the traditional type of grammar school, requires not only a high degree of general ability but also certain specific aptitudes, such as verbal facility and the capacity to deal with abstractions. Many of those whom a psychologist would pick out as highly gifted are weak in literary and academic work, but excel in practical and technical activities. The group tests of intelligence in common use fail to detect this type of child, and, when cast in the form of multiple-answer tests, favour those with an 'analytic' or assimilative type of mind, i.e. the intuitive, creative, and inventive individuals. This could readily be corrected by an appropriate marking of the English essays and an inclusion of more open-ended questions. (5) Academic success calls also for a particular type of temperament. Not every child of superior intelligence is prepared to spend long hours at sedentary tasks, poring over books, listening to lessons, and working out solutions to mathematical problems. Many bright youngsters, especially those from the manual classes, do not possess the requisite motivational drive—the ambition, the patient industry, the desire to do well at the task of the moment, which success both at school and in later life demands. (6) Finally, the child's home circumstances may impede or prejudice his progress. His parents and companions may set little store by intellectual or scholastic accomplishments; there may be no quiet room where he can do his homework; and in all probability he is secretly looking forward to the day when he can at last quit school, earn his own living, and enjoy his own independence.

The education of the gifted

In the ordinary classroom the curricula and the teaching methods are, as a rule, geared to the abilities and needs of the average pupil; and, in this country at any rate, there has been little or no investigation or discussion as to how they should be modified in order to realise to the full the potentialities of the more gifted individuals. The surest clues, I think, are to be found by considering what are the distinctive characteristics of gifted children as a group.

1.   To begin with, their IQs by definition are well above those of the majority of their classmates. Now an IQ measures rate of mental development. Hence, if the mean IQ of the gifted is 150, that at once suggests that their potential rate of educational progress is half as fast again as that of the average child. Ground which most children can only cover in three years, the gifted can master in two. It follows that the most obvious way of dealing with such children is by accelerated promotion. They will follow the same courses as the rest, but will be moved up to a higher class or form much sooner. In many schools this is still, as it was in my own school, the sole concession made to their superior capabilities.

2.   All cognitive capacities are correlated positively. Hence the gifted child is usually gifted all round. Compared with the average child, he is more alert, more thoughtful, more imaginative, sharper in the uptake, richer in his memories, and able to express himself more clearly and precisely. All these specific traits should therefore be exploited and exercised in the classroom. But, what is less frequently noted, such children are far more acute in perceiving relations. They are more systematic in organising their ideas and percepts into relational patterns, and so are quick to grasp meanings and implications. That is why the best tests of intelligence are tests of reasoning. Now reasoning is a teachable technique, though in the classroom little attempt is made to teach or train it. I would therefore urge that the instruction given to the gifted child should not only be more advanced in level, but also richer and more meaningful in content; and every effort should be made to instil a habit of critical and logical thinking.

3.   The gifted child has a far wider range of interests. At home he spends a greater proportion of his time in reading, often delving into cultural subjects that are never touched upon in the ordinary syllabus. His

hobbies are semi-scientific—building ingenious models with his Meccano, trying out chemical or electrical experiments, observing the stars, collecting fossils, or taking the kitchen clock to pieces. So far as possible, the school should cater for all these varied interests by providing suitable textbooks, encyclopaedias, and other books of reference, and a laboratory or work-shop with appropriate apparatus and materials. In the poorer districts both infant and primary schools should strive to supplement parental deficiencies by supplying what the home of a gifted child in the middle class would automatically include—toys, picture-books, and opportunities for hearing and acquiring good conversation.

4.   Gifted individuals differ far more widely among themselves, particularly as they grow older and their special abilities emerge and mature. Hence a lock-step type of promotion cannot do justice to their wide variety of talents. The pupils in each class should therefore be sub-divided into 'sets', and each child can be encouraged to work at his own chosen 'projects'. The timetable should be so arranged that for certain subjects, notably mathematics, literature, and languages, each can attend a class corresponding to his own capacities and attainments.

Briefly then it may be said that for the gifted the curricula, syllabuses, and teaching methods must not merely aim at a higher level; they must provide a deeper, broader, and more diversified type of education than is generally prescribed for the ordinary mass of pupils. The moderately gifted can, I believe, be satisfactorily accommodated in a comprehensive school, provided it is adequately staffed and equipped. This would have the advantage of correcting many of the faults of selection or streaming at the earlier ages by constant regrouping at a later stage. On the other hand, what I have called the highly gifted (as their own comments, letters, and autobiographies abundantly testify) can only develop to the full if trans-ferred to a school organised expressly to meet their very exceptional needs, such as one of our older public schools. No one can expect a compre-hensive school to provide, for the two or three cases it may happen to contain, all those scholarly facilities which youthful prodigies like William Hamilton, John Stuart Mill, or Francis Galton secured at home. The widespread assumption that, when bright, dull and average are brought together under one common roof, bright, dull and average will freely mix with each other, and so achieve a better mutual understanding, is not borne out in practice. As the recent studies by Miss Ford and Dr Stevens have shown, 'children of exceptional ability hardly ever form regular attachments to average or duller pupils of their own age; they choose each other as their friends'; and all too often the exceptionally bright youngster from a working-class family can find no friend at all. In our own survey of maladjusted children, Miss Howard and I found a disproportionate number of our cases among these 'able misfits'. In a school like Christ's Hospital, where bright youngsters come from every social stratum, class differences cease to matter. And in such schools the pupils learn far more from each other than they do from their masters. I have no space to touch on the specially gifted, those boys and girls who, often with no very high IQ, exhibit an outstanding talent for art, music, drama, or the dance. These plainly need transference at an early age to a school suitably equipped and staffed for the specialised training they require.

The contribution of the gifted

The after-careers of the more successful of our gifted group throw a newer light on an old and oft-debated issue—namely, the part played by gifted individuals in the life and progress of the nation. Galton ends his book on *Hereditary Genius* by reviewing the historical evidence and summarising its practical implications. He freely acknowledges the influence of environmental conditions—climate, geographical position, mineral resources, migration, conquest, and cultural diffusion; but these he regards as no more than accessory factors. What chiefly determines the rise and fall of nations, he believes, is the presence or absence of men of outstanding ability and character, ready to seize and exploit whatever opportunities the situation of the moment may afford. And his 'programme of practical eugenics' embraced not merely a scheme for 'breeding a large supply of individuals endowed with health, energy, and high intelligence' but also plans for discovering the 'highly gifted', providing them with a first-class education adapted to their needs, and directing each into an appropriate career.

His views were vigorously challenged by the environmentalists of those days—Grant Allen, Buckle, and Kidd; and William James answered by defending what he called 'the great-man theory of history'. McDougall took a more eclectic line. In his *Group Mind* he concludes that there are five principal factors which determine the rise both of great nations and of great civilisations: innate intellectual and innate temperamental qualities, intellectual culture and moral traditions, and social or political organisation. However, the arguments of all these writers are for the most part little more than speculative generalisation, based on *a priori* preconceptions, eked out and illustrated by a few spectacular 'facts from history'. There is no attempt at any rigorous scientific confirmation.

As a statistical psychologist it seemed to me that McDougall's list of 'factors' might well serve as a provisional hypothesis to be tested and verified by the method of factor analysis. This was a technique which had already been fruitfully employed for the causative study of differences between individuals; it was therefore an obvious step to extend it to a causative study of differences between nations. Accordingly, with the generous help of my colleagues at University College, particularly Mr Hugh Gaitskell (at that time Reader in Economics) and members of the departments of history, geography, and engineering, I endeavoured to collect a variety of data for a large sample of countries, which would indicate their cultural and economic status at two different dates (wealth, standard of living, industrial productivity, commerce, education, social mobility, and attainments in art, literature, science, engineering, and so forth). Estimates for progress and expansion in these various respects were then correlated and factorised in the usual way. To identify the chief factors that emerged we attempted a kind of case history for each country under much the same headings as had been devised for class studies of individual children.

All the intercorrelations proved to be positive. Evidently there was a 'general factor' operative. It accounted for just over 40 per cent of the total variance. This result appeared to offer a sufficient reply to those who had maintained that 'the social psychologist's search for a general explanation of the rise and decline of nations is as futile as the quest for the philosopher's stone'. A partial corroboration may be found in Bertrand Russell's 'attempt at a new social analysis'. 'The fundamental concept in social science', he contends, 'is Power, in the same sense in which Energy is the fundamental concept in physical science.' Like energy, power manifests itself in a variety of forms, but is itself a hypothetical 'general factor', entering into all these different manifestations. However, in his interpretation of the detailed evidence he appears to lay far too much emphasis on the motivational aspect. 'Those who desire power', he says, 'are the most likely to achieve it.' Yet, as a later chapter seems to concede, 'naked power' —a strong motivational drive unassociated with an equal intellectual competence—is more likely to ruin a country than to augment its progress (B. Russell, *Power*, 1938).

So far as our own evidence can be trusted, the dominating characteristics of those nations that had the highest factor-loadings for the 'general factor' would appear to be intellectual rather than moral or motivational. With each the most distinctive feature was the emergence of an unusually large number of able individuals during a single generation, and their acceptance by the community as leaders in their own particular spheres. Plausible as it is, James's 'great-man theory' is really an over-simplification. The successful nation must possess a large number of individuals endowed with moderate ability as well as the master-spirits of historic fame who are said to have swayed its destinies. There is a popular theory that this innate superiority is the unique speciality of some particular 'race'—the 'Whites', the 'Aryans', or the 'Nordics'. Whatever modicum of truth this notion may contain has, I am convinced, been grossly exaggerated in the past. What is far more important is the range of individual variation within the race or nation. This, it would seem, is largely the result of the blending of two or more racial stocks which differ somewhat in their innate qualities, but do not differ very widely.

When the effects of the general factor have been ruled out by partial correlation, a second factor is discernible. This is certainly motivational rather than intellectual, but acquired rather than innate. In some degree it corresponds to what McDougall has termed the 'group spirit'. I would prefer to describe it as a passion for efficiency in one's own field of work as distinct from the motive of self-interest, which seeks a maximum wage, power, or profit for a minimum expenditure of effort and care. It includes all the qualities that Max Weber summed up under the phrase 'Protestant-ische Ethik'; but it has been by no means confined to Protestant nations. It is an attitude due largely to tradition, instilled during early childhood by the family and the school, and later on by the whole social environment—friends, club, church, trade union, as well as by whatever types of propa-ganda are active at the time.

Our investigation was planned merely as a preliminary pilot study, and was unfortunately interrupted by the outbreak of the war. But the main conclusions derive a further confirmation from a recent research by McClelland (*The Achieving Society*, 1961). Choosing twenty-nine nations for which data were available, he assessed first actual achievement in terms of gain in electricity produced (measured in kilowatt-hours *per capita*), and then what he termed the 'need for achievement' by examining the content of the reading books used by the children at school. 'Need for achieve-ment' is defined as 'a motivational force controlled by reason'. It is, we gather, a traditional attitude handed on more particularly by the teachers in the schools, and adopted most readily by children of higher intelligence. Dr McClelland finds a positive correlation of 0·46 between the two assessments.

If the inferences I have here attempted to summarise can be accepted at their face value, then, I think, we may safely conclude that the activities and achievements of those who are pre-eminently gifted by nature are of paramount importance for the prosperity and progress, not of nations only but of all mankind. Yet giftedness by itself is not enough. Ideals and incentives are of almost equal moment; and the effective exercise of both is largely dependent on the way such children are selected, trained, and inspired by the teachers who have charge of them.

G. *Robb*

11. The education of gifted children

It is not the writer's intention to attempt an exhaustive description of the provision made for intellectually gifted children in each country. The basic reason for this is the lack of any universally agreed definition of giftedness in the intellectual or, indeed, in any other sense. The American literature uses the term *giftedness* to connote the top 20 per cent of the school population, as does the Scottish Education Department in *Primary Education in Scotland* (1965). In so far as the concern of this chapter will be with those youngsters who are as disadvantaged by that curriculum appropriate to the majority of their classmates as are the slowest learners, this connotation of giftedness seems much too blunt an instrument to be useful. It may well be considered that a reasonable provision is made for the majority of the top 20 per cent of the children in our schools and for this reason the term *giftedness* in the intellectual sense is used within what follows to refer to those children who: (1) on an individual test such as the Binet or the WISC, administered by a fully qualified educational psychologist, show an intellectual level associated with an IQ of 145 or more; and (2) demonstrate an unusually mature use of language relative to their age, or evidence of some other talent possessed to an unusual degree.

It used to be thought that if nature gave a child a first-class brain it also gave him a second-class body. The image of the short-sighted, puny, intellectual giant dies hard, but there is strong evidence to support the view that, in fact, the bright child is healthier, heavier, better looking, better at social relationships than children of lower general ability than he. This evidence derives mainly from the work of Lewis Terman and his colleagues, carried out over a period of twenty-five years from Stanford University, California. He studied in depth some 300 children of an original group of 1,000 whose IQs were found to be above 130 on the basis of individually administered intelligence tests. His team reported on this longitudinal survey at intervals of five years in a series published under the title 'Genetic Studies of Genius'.

In the latest book, *The Gifted Group at Mid-Life* (1959), Terman adduces quite properly the major findings reported in the previous four books. In addition to those qualities of being healthier, heavier and better looking, as quoted above, he states that the findings of the study are that as children the gifted group were much less frequently absent from school because they were popular with their contemporaries and a joy to teach. High school, college and university made few demands upon them that they could not meet without stress from their resources, and, in adult life, a significantly high proportion of this gifted group achieved membership of the American equivalent of the Royal Society, made original contributions to commerce, the arts, and the sciences; and on the whole they divorced less frequently.

This catalogue of advantages was found to be enjoyed by those youngsters whose IQs were between 130 and 170. One of Terman's colleagues, Leta S. Hollingworth noted, however, that in the group of those children whose IQs were found to be even higher than 170, there was a significantly high proportion of maladjusted children. 34 per cent of this 'stratospheric' group were rated by parents and teachers as being seriously maladjusted or almost completely withdrawn from social intercourse. A third to a quarter of them were only fair in their attainments in school.

W. D. Wall quotes Terman as saying about this group 'While the mental age at 6 might be 11, physical development would be accelerated by only 10 per cent and social development by only 20 to 30 per cent.' It should be stressed that this research occurred at a time when it was possible to achieve an IQ of more than 170 by reference to extrapolated norms of Form L and Form M of the Stanford-Binet. Currently, of course, one cannot attribute an IQ of more than 170 and remain psychometrically respectable. Clearly the number of children upon whom the test has been given at this level of ability is likely to be so small as to render reliance on IQ alone even more than normally fallible. Nor is it suggested that the Binet concerns itself with the whole range of intellectual abilities. Clearly it favours the verbally apt.

So it would seem that there were children of Terman's concern who were positively disadvantaged by their comparative intellectual excellence. For the causes of this apparent paradox I think we must concern ourselves with the relative development of the main component of the personality. The child in Hollingworth's (1942) stratospheric group might be described as below, as having an intellectual development which greatly exceeds the levels of development of the emotional and social aspects of the personality:

Physical _____

Intellectual

Emotional _____

Social   _____   Increment
                                  of
                                  disadvantage

I think it not unlikely that just as the hypothetical 'round' person is equally developed as far as the social, emotional and intellectual factors of his personality are concerned, so is it likely that if an individual, child or adult, is developed in any one of these factors disproportionately with respect to the other two, then he is very much at risk of becoming an unbalanced personality. For example, most of us can immediately call to mind professors or academics who may be national or international authorities in their field, but who react to real or suspected criticism within that field in a manner appropriate to an adolescent with a grievance. The peevish professor is not entirely a fiction. There are also academics who are both well informed and relatively emotionally mature, but who are ominously well suited by the cloistered life. These are often unable to form a warm relationship quickly with those they teach, are not good teachers, and find it difficult to get on well with other people. Such are to be seen typically propping up a corner and an empty glass at parties, and who escape as soon as politeness allows. Have they been adequately prepared for life?

The classroom context

If it is the case that a child consistently gets the hang of a lesson in ten minutes where it takes the other children a further ten minutes or even longer to do so, there is a considerable risk that he or she will be bored by school. It is almost certain that he will cease to regard it as an intellectually exciting or rewarding place. In the writer's experience, very often indeed do youngsters develop a syndrome which might be described as 'marital deafness'. When one's wife wishes to talk to one at a time when television or a newspaper have greater attractions, there is a certain survival value in being able to do one thing while apparently doing the other. Upon being challenged, 'you are not listening to a word I'm saying', one starts to replay the mental tape-recording one had better have been making. This resort may well serve to meet the needs of the gifted child, but he is especially at risk during the last year of the infant school and the first year of the junior school (ages seven to eight) because it is in these two years that the highest number of basic seminal facts and words are taught. If the gifted youngster is 'tuned out' at a time when some such word or fact is taught, it may very well present him with considerable difficulties in the future. This is because it is exactly those most basic of words or facts that are the most difficult to infer from context. Provided, though, the relationships between the particular gifted child and his contemporaries or teachers are good, no doubt he can ask for help and expect to get it. If, however, he has behaved in such a way as to alienate the tolerance or affection of his contemporaries, and possibly to threaten the security of his teacher, it may well be the case that he cannot ask for help, and may not get it if he does.

Of the many such children known to the writer, two main reactions to under-challenge have been noted. In those cases where the child concerned has been certain of the love of both parents, the worst that has happened is that he has become bored, listless and apathetic concerning school. It is distressingly frequently the case, however, that when an intellectually gifted child has reason to doubt the love of one or both parents, he has reacted to this threat to his *amour-propre* by throwing his intellectual weight about, being arrogantly, aggressively and consistently first with the right answer. Since nobody likes always being second, especially if one has been really trying, such children have soon become unpopular with their classmates, have often been found a threat or its rationalised euphemism, a 'smart alec', by the teacher concerned.

The writer remembers very vividly indeed the case of a boy referred by the teacher concerned because 'he doesn't want to do the work of the class except when it's nature study and then he wants to run the lesson'. This boy had a Binet IQ of 168, was bored to death with what was happening in the classroom, and used not infrequently to resolve this by going out into the forest which literally surrounded the school. He became, as a result of his wanderings, an authority on the fauna and flora of the forest. He could scarcely read. At a time when he had not been attending he had missed some basic words and had found it too stressful to ask for help. It has to be admitted that the teacher had not sought to resolve his learning difficulties with diligence.

Both the child's parents were divorced and had invited him to decide with which of them he would live after the divorce. Does it seem surprising that a youngster with these stresses imposed, sought self-reassurance by using the only tool available to him, his comparative intellectual superiority over his classmates. The writer persuaded the teacher to let the child teach the class from his store of knowledge in nature study and it was some of the best teaching the class had had for some time. We teachers too frequently fail to grasp the opportunities existent in the lodes of expertise possessed by certain of our children.

Certain educationists, persuaded of the fact that we are not meeting the academic needs of these children in the ordinary school, advocate the establishment of special schools or full-time classes in order to meet their needs. They argue by analogy that if it is appropriate to set up special schools for ESN children then it is no less so to establish special schools for intellectually gifted children. If such a school were set up it would probably be true to say that such children would leave it more intelligent, and almost certainly more informed, than they would leave any other school. If these two qualities are seen as advantages, then no other advantage or desirable result is evident to the writer. It seems a horrible piece of social engineering, approximating as it does to Aldous Huxley's 'Alpha Environment' by providing an optimal environment for an élite few. Sir Alec Clegg has, as usual, something very valuable to say in this context. 'To segregate a small minority of children according to the size of their brains, and educate them in isolation was an odd way of preparing them to work with all sorts of men. In the age of the atom bomb it is surely more, not less important, that men should learn to behave with humility and compassion towards other men and other races less fortunate than they' (NUT Conference, 1968).

It is, of course, the case that certain of the public schools do seem to provide a segregated education for an élite few. While one would be very surprised indeed if such schools set up to concentrate exclusively on the development of the intellectual prospects of the children for whom they have responsibility, it has happened that parental expectations, pressures and demands, have led to the children believing that, to their parents, academic achievement is all-important. This imbalance in the relative development of the intellectual, emotional and social aspects of the personality cannot but disadvantage the individual concerned. One cannot view with equanimity the not irrelevant statistic that the Oxbridge students' suicide rate is six times that of the other universities. The situation has not significantly changed from that which Hollingworth (1942) observed: that an unhealthy emphasis on intellectual development puts the individual child at risk of becoming maladjusted.

If, then, one accepts that whatever is to be done for these children must be done fundamentally within the normal school framework, there are two courses by which we can attempt to meet these children's special needs.

Acceleration

By acceleration is meant the placing of a child in a group of older children whose intellectual and academic needs are closer to his than are those of his contemporaries. This resort is not new in principle and has equally clear advantages and limitations for the intellectually gifted child.

For example, to place an intellectually gifted child of seven years in a group of ten-year-old children will not disadvantage him academically, but in other respects he would be likely to be unsuited by such placement. For example, he may well be able to think of a ten-year-old way up the tree, but his are still seven-year-old legs. The other children will have lived half as long again as he, and will thus have had more experience of disappointment, success, failure, frustration than he. Similarly, if one were to consider placing a bright ten-year-old in a group of thirteen-year-old children, again it seems likely that he would be able to keep up, but would be very much at risk of being made an involuntary isolate because the other children simply would not be likely to have the same interests in common. Further, given that the onset of puberty is known to occur between $10\frac{1}{2}$ and 18, it could be that some of those youngsters will have achieved puberty, with significant effects on the direction and strength of their interests. Therefore, acceleration, whilst having manifest advantages, has implicit limitations. It has been the practice in small rural schools within which teachers have responsibility for an age-range as compared to an age-group for the very bright young child to be taught as part of the older group. Further, it is common practice in those areas when secondary selection procedures still exist, for head teachers to be allowed to suggest that certain children be given the opportunity of taking the 11-plus one year early. In the writer's experience considerable advantage has resulted from placing intellectually gifted children (as operationally defined above) in a group of children who are two years older than they. Very exceptionally indeed has a chronological age-group of two years six months been contrived. A greater chronological distance than this does not seem desirable or even feasible.

Enrichment

Enrichment depends upon the fact that gifted children almost certainly require a much shorter time to grasp a lesson than do the majority of their contemporaries. If, for example, it is the case that a gifted child masters a lesson in fifteen minutes, when it takes the other children twenty to thirty minutes, it is open to the teacher to occupy his time better by one of two means: either by introducing, for that child's benefit only, subjects not offered to other children; or to arrange that the child concerned covers the same range of subjects as the other children but is allowed to progress more swiftly through them. In terms of difficulty, there is no reason why in a school offering junior sciences, some of the other sciences could not be taught, and, likewise, if, and it is an essential 'if', appropriate facilities, i.e. teachers, books and materials, are available in the school for teaching a language other than French, this might well be used to complement the normal curricular experiences offered to this child so as to reduce the number of occasions upon which he has to 'mince in time', to keep pace with the others. This has advantages but does, of course, increase the number of occasions upon which other children are likely to see this child as being singled out and it could well mean that they see him as something of a teacher's pet. In this event the odds are high that unless the teacher takes positive action, that child will become an involuntary isolate. Many children indeed of this intellectual calibre deliberately and consistently under-function in order to remain acceptable to their classmates.

When either of these two resorts are used there is the possibility of the other children beginning to see the gifted child concerned as receiving some kind of favoured treatment. The writer thinks it necessary the teacher makes it quite clear to the gifted child, and to all the others in the class, that he does not view the gifted child as in some way nicer or better, or more deserving of his attention than any other child. The point does need stressing that explicit action has to be taken here and great care must be taken by the teacher not to convey this impression unintentionally. The risk of doing this is real, large, and there is no mystery about its source. When a teacher attempts to inculcate a particular skill, and the child makes it clear that the teaching has been effective, the teacher has a justifiable reason for self-pride or, at least, pride in his professional competence. While this is both understandable and defensible, it would militate against the best interests of the individual child and the teacher's relationship with the group if the teacher did not take care to make it clear that the very bright child, because he is quicker and more accurate, does not have a special corner in his heart because of that alone. In a properly run classroom, children are made to compete only with themselves and the wise teacher finds something in each child to praise. It needs, therefore, considerable professional skill not to allow one's justifiable pleasure in professional competence to prejudice the acceptability of the individual gifted child to the group.

The more one considers the means by which the needs of intellectually gifted children can be met, the more it becomes apparent that one is describing the same facilities and, indeed, to some extent, the same techniques by which one can meet the needs of ESN children or, indeed, others of different handicaps. Perhaps in this context 'special' education is a misnomer, since it seems to connote those qualities that distinguish good education from that which is not concerned with the individual needs of particular children. The writer would like to offer the following two statements as bases for determining greater relevance in the opportunities given children in school. They do not relate exclusively to any level of ability.

1.   Education is what you retain when you have forgotten all that you have learned.
2.   The mark of an educated person is not so much what one knows at any one time as how well one can find out.

Those teachers who find the second statement in particular something with which they agree, should find in it a firm directive to take a constructive but hard look at the present content of the curricula we offer our children. Does it not seem more important to give children the skill to find out than to continue to teach them a selection of those subjects currently offered them in school, the more so since this range may change as a function of the staff available in that school? There are a large number of schools in this country who see it as one of their major responsibilities to prepare children for university or other forms of higher education. I have not yet visited one which explicitly taught the skills of reference, and surely one has only to point out the advantages to university students of having skills of reference for the desirability of this being given to them in school to be placed beyond doubt.

There is a need for some research to find out which components of those skills possessed by the successfully educated adult can be taught to children of different ages, and by what means.

There are a few teachers who would wish to give their children this skill but who may not be certain how to go about it, and it would certainly be optimistic to believe that to issue texts on 'Psychology of Study', or even to teach from this, would meet the needs of the situation. But there is a means of self-help here. If an individual school or any discussion group of teachers wished to make a start in this respect they have only to form a series of pairs. Each member of the group would then be required to find out about some subject on which he is quite uninformed at the beginning of the project. A suitable undertaking would be that each member of the group would contract to make himself sufficiently informed on the topic concerned, which might be Persian poetry, Chinese pottery or some similarly sufficiently esoteric subject, as to be able to give a lecture or write an essay on it in a month's time. His colleague would note the steps taken in order to inform himself, i.e. libraries visited, the experts consulted, the reference books used, the visits paid. The roles would, of course, then be reversed so that both members of each pair evolve a statement of the methods used in order to become informed about the topic concerned. By collation at the end of the agreed period of each of the modes of tackling the problem, certain common features will become evident. Clearly this will normally include basic competence in our skills of reference such as the use of the *Oxford Dictionary*, the *Encyclopaedia Britannica*, the Librarian in Charge, local experts, and a convenient museum or art gallery. Why not then teach the common components of this group skill of reference to children? This has manifest advantages, in the first instance for intellectually gifted children but also for all children. It is the writer's belief that if, say, a junior school could borrow a set of encyclopaedias for three weeks only, that the greatest return from this restricted period of access would come if sufficient practice were given in the use of the index as to make the children's fluency of reference become equivalent to that of the teacher. To teach the fluent use of a dictionary or an adult-level reference book or encyclopaedia is to have made the optimum use of the reference sources concerned. Even if the school thereafter had to return the encyclopaedias, other sets exist, and provided the children know how to make the best use of them wherever they are, a very great deal of the teacher's pedagogic responsibilities will have been met.

As a profession, teachers tend to be chronically cellular. Perhaps this is due to the fear of being seen to boast, but very rarely indeed has the writer heard teachers spontaneously swopping tips and discussing techniques. If it were possible to share out equally the total expertise contained in any group of teachers, each member would be considerably enriched. Therefore in a situation where a teacher believes that he or she is not at present fully meeting the intellectual and academic needs of any intellectually gifted child, some better use of total current resources seems indicated. One means of doing this would be for the class teacher to record at a staff meeting all the subjects which her colleagues had read at college or university. This done, a further itemising of resources should take place. This should comprise those facts and pieces of expertise known or possessed by the teachers concerned as a result of the development of their enthusiasms and hobbies. Some will know about Hi-Fi, others about the brewing of beer, still others about national modes of embroidery, and some may know about butterflies, fishing or photography. The total reservoir of expertise thus made available to the class teacher should be borne in mind when she chooses a project to be the individual responsibility of the gifted child, in the pursuit of which he should be encouraged to go out of school with tape-recorder and, on some occasions, a camera, on information-seeking and recording expeditions.

While it is common practice for schools to bring in the fireman or policeman, there seems to be an unjustifiable limitation in the range of such visitors to the school. Why not use any articulate enthusiast? A rural school headmistress once confided to the writer that one of the best lessons she had ever heard was given by a man who was not well educated at all, but who had developed a remarkable capacity for predicting local weather changes and, on another occasion, that she was astonished at the level of questioning put to an aeronautical engineer whom she invited to talk to her group of nine-year-old children about why aeroplanes stayed up, why the sky was blue, and so on. I think it very likely to be true that we are un-adventurous in the extent to which we seek to involve in our schools those people who are important components of the society for which we are preparing our children. Unless the personality of the individual gifted child thus involved with projects strongly contra-indicates it, the likeli-hood is that it would be of considerable advantage, not only to the gifted child but to his classmates, to have him teach from the store of knowledge he will thus accumulate.

It may indeed be a useful way of introducing other children to this mode of enquiry if, on subsequent projects, the gifted child is made the coordinator of a small group of children, say, four, one of whom should be of considerably lower ability than the other children. In this way, provided the teacher ensures that the same careful, explicit teaching in the skills of finding-out is given to all members of the group and, ultimately, to all her class, significant profit for all the children in the class can result from the teacher's initial concern with the gifted child.

The writer can recall a palaeontology club being run in a junior school. The president and vice-president were intellectually gifted children and, on the day of the writer's visit, the other child concerned was one dull by any standards. The other two children were not patronising him. They took care to ensure that he knew what they wanted him to do and this ESN boy's self-respect gained enormously from being genuinely involved with these relatively esoteric activities. Perhaps there is a lesson here. May it not be the case that some of us, moved to compassion by the academic difficulties manifestly encountered by some children, thereafter perhaps on occasions fail to demand enough of them academically or intellectually? Do we not also prejudice the range of opportunities we thus offer them?

The size of the problem

Cyril Burt in the *British Journal of Statistical Psychology* in November 1963 questioned the view that intelligence was normally distributed and adduced evidence to suggest that there were more children at the extreme ends of the scales than statistics would lead us to expect. He was kind enough to quote some work of the writer's in Lincoln City that suggested there may be many more children at the top end of the scale than would be consistent with normal distribution. Since then, experience in many schools and authorities throughout England and Wales leads the writer to the view that at least 2 per cent of the children in school are as consistently disadvantaged by that curriculum appropriate to the majority of their contemporaries as are those children comprising the bottom 2 per cent of the scale of ability. And it may be as much as 5 per cent. (The proportion of children in ESN schools in England and Wales is almost exactly 2 per cent.) The truth is that we see only the tip of the iceberg here. The work of Rosenthal and Jacobsen (1970) has shown us just how determining teacher expectations can be, as have those results of enquiry into streaming: 'Expect C stream performance and that's what you'll get.' In schools where it is necessary for some of the most intelligent of our children to deliberately under-achieve in order to remain acceptable to their contemporaries, is it surprising that the real level of their capacities is not always realised by the teacher?

Current activities

In July 1968, the DES published in their 'Reports on Education' a pamphlet concerning the education of gifted children. This statement makes it clear that the DES sees the problems experienced and posed by the gifted child as a respectable matter for concern. While not viewing as desirable the segregated education of intellectually gifted children, the DES sees special schools for the musically gifted child as the only economic way to provide that intensity of tutor-child contact required for the best development of the young pianist, cellist or ballet-dancer. Hence the Yehudi Menuhin and the Royal Ballet Schools.

The National Association for Gifted Children

The National Association for Gifted Children (NAGC) was formed as a result of a national conference at Attringham Park, Shrewsbury, in

November 1964. It is essentially a group of parents and teachers who cooperate in looking after the interests of intellectually gifted children. In almost all cases they concern themselves with the problems experienced by these children. They have organised a series of conferences throughout England and at local level cooperate with certain of the larger interested authorities by providing opportunities for the youngsters concerned at weekends, which are complementary to those experiences offered to them during their normal school week. Although not a few head teachers have expressed hostility towards some, but not all, of their children being given these extra opportunities, this hostility has now to a large extent disappeared. Partly this was due to those organising the NAGC activities making available to the schools concerned the contacts with computer firms, factories, museums, which in the first instance were available exclusively to this Association. This is yet another example of how specific concern for an individual problem can rebound to the advantage of all children.

N AG C

Schools Council

The Schools Council formed a working party to concern itself with the gifted child in the primary school. This, while under the chairmanship of the author, has still to report and, therefore, at this time the findings are confidential. It is, however, possible to say that the members of the working party felt extremely fortunate in being able to call upon the services of Dr Eric Ogilvie, then on the staff of Weymouth College of Education and now the Principal of Northampton College of Education. Dr Ogilvie wrote to all local authorities in England and visited all those who responded, these visits involving the setting up of teachers discussion groups and requiring him to carry out a most extensive and arduous programme throughout some eighteen months, at the end of which he presented the working party with a lengthy, cogent and helpful report embodying a description of the local authorities' practice and provision for gifted children. Dr Ogilvie's report suggested certain courses of action to the Schools Council and these recommendations, if approved, will be given practical expression in the light of specific advice being made available to teachers in primary schools who are aware of the problem and who see it as a responsible matter for concern and seek to provide more appropriate and not better things for the gifted child.

Two local authorities in particular, Essex and West Sussex, have pioneered in this field. In north-east Essex four groups of children, deemed by head teachers and psychologists to be intellectually gifted, are brought together in groups of six or seven, two afternoons a week in their last four school terms. They meet at a geographically convenient secondary school, chosen because of the library facilities immediately made available. The teachers concerned have not pursued any formal course of training explicitly directed at the education of intellectually gifted children (there is no such course in existence at this time). They have been given the brief to explore as many ways as are open to them how to teach these children the skills of reference. Given that the mark of the educated person is not how much they know at any one time but how well they can find out, it seems by far the most profitable use of such opportunities to give these youngsters the skills of finding out. In West Sussex a limited experiment with similar intentions is also under way. In neither authority has this work been going long enough for it to be possible to form any judgments about its value.

Brentwood College of Education

The work which is being carried on at Brentwood College of Education with gifted children has been reported on in detail in the book *The Gifted Child and the Brentwood Experiment* edited by Dr Bridges. It seems a pity that no articulated programme has been devised or offered to the children such that inference can be made of the appropriateness of some of the activities offered to those children in the ordinary school. Despite this there can be no doubt that two very important results of this work are apparent:

1.   The children themselves are described by their teachers as becoming more tolerant and helpful than they were prior to having these opportunities offered them;

2.   The children report that they experience great relief from being able to have each other's company on this weekly basis.

Many of them have told the author that they did not wish to come to Brentwood more than once a week and they did not wish in any sense to leave their own classmates, but quite consistently they say 'what a relief it is to find that one is not always first with the right answer', 'It is great not to have to be careful about putting your hand up first', or 'to find that you get the answer wrong sometimes'. For what it is worth, Moreno-type enquiries confirm the spontaneously offered comments of the head teachers, that whereas at the beginning of the experiment none of the children were very popular, at the end of the year none of them remained involuntary isolates and most of them tended very frequently indeed to be chosen by the other children as companions.

Statement of aims

There can be no doubt that at the present time any teacher seeking to offer intellectually gifted children something different from that which is appropriate to the majority of their contemporaries will be accused of attempting to contrive a favouring treatment for an élite few. The refutation of this piece of polemic lies in the 1944 Education Act, which requires all of us to provide that education which is suited to the age, ability and aptitude of the individual pupil. What the author seeks is not 'better' things for gifted children but more appropriate things. There can be no doubt that were we to divert some 1 per cent of our total educational budget towards a more appropriate treatment of such children, the return and the benefit to society would be enormous. This argument of expediency may commend itself to politicians—I do not suggest it is one which would commend itself to those professionals concerned with education. We should do the right thing by these children as a simple matter of conscience and not because it will be of great advantage to us as a society. If we fail to recognise their special needs then we are conniving at the continuation of a system where some of our youngsters are denied the possibility of realising some of their potentialities. If we do seek to meet their needs in an appropriate way then we may with justification hope for the evolution of a society characterised by an aristocracy of achievement arising out of a democracy of opportunity.

12. Advances in training educational psychologists

The background

In February 1913 the editor of *Child Study* wrote a paragraph welcoming the London County Council's appointment of Mr Cyril Burt as School Psychologist. This appointment has been widely regarded as the birth of the profession of educational psychology in this country. Indeed, as Keir (1953) records, Thorndike described this step as 'the first appointment of an official child psychologist in any civilised country'.

It is axiomatic that the early stages in the growth of training arrangements in any profession must be initiated and fostered by those who can have had no similar training themselves. Thus the pioneers in the training of educational psychologists in this country were mainly educational psychologists whose preparation for the training role rested upon the experience which they had had themselves as educational psychologists working in the field. It is therefore interesting and quite characteristic to find that the first training arrangement instituted in England and Wales began in 1923 when Cyril Burt was closely involved in the organisation of a postgraduate course in educational psychology at the old London Day Training College (Burt 1969). It is not only interesting but also highly prophetic to see that this course extended over two academic years and led to a Masters qualification.

In 1918, courses which led to the Bachelor of Education degree as a postgraduate qualification in Education and Psychology had been established in Scotland. The B.Ed. qualification has prepared students for a wide range of careers (Nisbet 1962), including that of educational psychologist.

In 1929 the Child Guidance Training Centre was established in London with assistance from the Commonwealth Fund of America. This was the first centre in this country which attempted to provide inter-disciplinary training for the members of the three-man child guidance team: the psychiatric social worker, the psychiatrist and the educational psychologist. It is probably fair to comment that at that time the Child Guidance Training Centre emphasised different aspects of the work of the educational psychologist from those emphasised by the earlier trainings which have so far been noted. In essence the Child Guidance Training Centre stressed the *team* approach to child guidance work, laying emphasis on the psychiatric approach to unravelling children's problems. Another training course with a clinical emphasis was established at the Tavistock Clinic, where educational and clinical psychologists were trained alongside each other.

Another stage in the development of training for educational psychologists in this country came at University College, London, where in the 1930s the University of London approved the establishment of a one-year course leading to a postgraduate diploma in educational psychology. This training course was novel in that it was a university-based course which required entrants to the course to be psychology graduates. So by 1939 there were already a variety of different approaches to training educational psychologists in England and Scotland.

The events of the war, particularly the effects of evacuation of children, war-service on the part of the fathers and war-work by mothers, all leading to disruption of family life, brought the problems of children's behaviour to the fore as never previously. The legislation which followed the 1944 Education Act recognised these and other problems by laying down categories of the maladjusted and the educationally subnormal. The need for local education authorities to identify (or ascertain) maladjusted and slow-learning children was one of the main reasons, though not the only one, for sharpening the country's awareness of the need to recruit more educational psychologists for work in child guidance clinics and in what were becoming known as school psychological services.

In 1948 Schonell and Wall began training educational psychologists at Birmingham. Like the Scottish trainings, this was based on an education department of a university, but unlike the Scottish trainings it required candidates to be both Honours graduates in psychology and to be trained teachers with several years of teaching experience before admission to the course. It was the first of the English courses to be accepted by the Department of Education and Science as a course to which experienced teachers could be seconded on full salary, an important step in the development of training courses since this represented a means whereby students could enter educational psychology and feel financially secure during the period of professional training.

In 1951 Dr Wall took up his appointment with UNESCO. He was followed in his post at Birmingham by Dr Mia Kellmer Pringle. For

G

several years thereafter no fresh courses were started, although the Leicester LEA instituted an interesting experiment in in-service training. The annual output of educational psychologists in England and Wales between 1949 and 1959 varied between ten and seventeen persons (Department of Educational and Science 1968, Table 5C1). The need to expand these numbers was of course referred to in several publications, notably the Underwood Report (Ministry of Education 1955).

The Underwood Report represented a milestone in the development of training in educational psychology. Ostensibly the report dealt with services which the country needed for maladjusted children, but in fact it also produced a blue-print for the development of child guidance services. It called for the expansion of training in educational psychology, recommending a target of one educational psychologist per forty-five thousand school children to be reached within ten years of publication of the report, i.e. by 1965.

This overall target had in fact been passed before 1965. But it had soon become apparent that the need for educational psychologists had been growing very much faster than the Underwood Report had been able to foresee. Even with an additional one-year course for psychology graduates with teaching experience started at the University of Manchester in 1961, demand greatly exceeded supply.

Recent new developments

In 1963, two new courses were started at the Education Department of the University College of Swansea and represented the first training arrangements based in Wales. The first of the two courses was a conventional one-year training course, whereas the second, an integrated course of four years' duration, represented an attempt to do two things. The first objective of the integrated course was to ensure that a good psychology graduate could enter a training course for educational psychology directly on completion of his graduation, knowing that he had a direct route to professional qualification in his chosen career. This removes some of the uncertainty about the future which faces a psychology graduate who enters teaching with a view to later qualification as an educational psychologist. The second objective of the integrated course was to bring together the components of postgraduate training in education, teaching experience and the year's professional training. In this way the different parts of the training programme can be deployed so that the best use can be made of them in the preparation of future educational psychologists.

In 1966 the Department of Psychology of the University of Nottingham launched a new course for training educational psychologists. This represented a new development in that for the first time Masters degrees in psychology were awarded to students who successfully completed the course. The course was, again, a one-year course and it was not until 1968 that a two-year postgraduate course leading to a Masters degree in educational psychology was instituted by the University of Sussex. The title of this qualification is interesting in that it represents a specific recognition of the subject of educational psychology as an academic discipline in its own right. The length of the course, a two-year postgraduate period for psychology graduates with teaching experience, is also an interesting acknowledgment of the need to incorporate more material in the professional training of educational psychologists.

In 1969 the B.Ed. training in Northern Ireland which had hitherto been similar to the Scottish pattern was augmented by a qualification on the line of the Nottingham Masters degree though with some variations. So by 1970 the conventional pattern of a one-year training course for experienced teachers with a psychology degree had already been broken by a number of different establishments in a variety of ways. If we survey the new developments and examine the curricula of the different training courses then we can summarise the directions in which new developments are occurring as follows.

First, there is a move to lengthen the professional component of the educational psychologist's training. This is obvious, notably at the University of Sussex with its two-year postgraduate course, and is a reflection of the educational psychologist's need to be aware of the much greater volume of research work which has occurred in the discipline in recent years. Secondly, the higher levels of performance achieved at the end of his training are increasingly being recognised by the award of a higher degree. In 1970, at least three universities, Belfast, Nottingham and Sussex, were awarding Masters degrees on the completion of an educational psychologist's professional training course. (In Scotland the B.Ed. qualification has been replaced by the M.Ed.) Thirdly, there is probably a greater emphasis on the research aspect of the educational psychologist's work than has hitherto been the case. The Birmingham course's requirement that students complete a dissertation as part of the course, as well as carrying the normal full load of clinical experience and lectures, has been adopted by other courses. Fourthly, there is an increasing tendency to shorten, if not eliminate, the teaching experience components of the educational psychologist's preparation. Whereas fifteen years ago some training courses were demanding a minimum of five years' experience as a teacher before taking students for their professional training, this minimum has now dropped in most cases to three years' teaching experience. An alternative is the two years' teaching experience and a course leading to the certificate of education, which the Association of Education Psychologists normally accepts as part of its requirements for membership. Fifthly, there is an increasing awareness of the value for some educational psychologists of integrating their postgraduate study and experience.

These new developments were being initiated during the 1960s, a period of considerable strain on the profession of educational psychology. The great demand for educational psychologists in other branches of the education service, such as colleges of education, universities and the inspectorate meant that in the middle 1960s the numbers of educational psychologists employed by LEAS actually dropped, in spite of the growth of the training courses (Department of Education and Science 1968, Table 5.3). This position was one of the factors which led the Department of Education and Science to establish a working party to examine among other issues the training of educational psychologists. The report of this working party, the Summerfield Report (Department of Education and Science 1968) focused attention on new ways in which training might develop in the future. A selection of these issues will now be discussed.

The future

Duration of training.   Conventionally, training for educational psychology has been a divided process. The intending educational psychologist, having completed his degree, has often been required first to obtain a qualification for teaching, then to proceed to teach for a period of two or three years, and then to take up a one year's course of professional training in educational psychology. Thus he is usually expected to take a training which occupies at least four years after graduation. The Summerfield report suggests that 'postgraduate training for educational psychology can be shorter, more concentrated, more directed and no less effective' (p. 90).

The proposal which Summerfield advocated for shortening the postgraduate training of educational psychologists was in essence a condensation of the four-year period to two years by omitting the minimum two years of full-time teaching employment, which had previously been the middle part of the postgraduate training sandwich. At the same time

Summerfield argued that the two years which would then be available should be restructured so as to make the experiences obtained therein more effective and more directly concerned with the educational psychologist's future employment.

This proposal for shortening the duration of training, although only one of three proposed routes to training educational psychologists, has probably been the recommendation which has aroused most reaction. The Summerfield report regarded teaching experience as important but not essential. The arguments for and against the experience of the teaching situation for educational psychologists were discussed at length in the report. These arguments have in their turn been criticised by Curr (1969), who argues for child guidance and teaching to be seen as one profession. Similarly Currie (1969) presents the case for recognising that 'teachers consult us as *educational* psychologists and that the educational aspect of the designation is as essential as the psychological aspect'. She argues that teachers turn more readily and confidently to people who have additional expertise within their own field than they do to members of a different profession. On the same theme Moore (1969) contends that the educational psychologists in the long run should be more concerned with teachers than with children and advocates linking the normal career in educational psychology with teacher training and recruiting educational psychologists from teachers rather than from psychologists. Not all professional reaction to this point has followed these lines and for a selection of viewpoints the Spring 1969 issue of the *Journal of the Association of Educational Psychologists* should be consulted, alongside the arguments analysed in the Summerfield Report itself.

Differentiation within the profession.   One aspect of the omission of the teaching component remains to be considered. The resulting two-years' postgraduate training which the report advocates seems to be an inevitable consequence of increasing knowledge, which has already been recognised by some training courses in this country. If two-year postgraduate training courses without teaching experience are introduced, will this development lead to a brand of educational psychologist who by virtue of different experiences and different behaviours will be different from other brands of educational psychologists already in existence? Shall we see more special-isation in the types of educational psychologists that trainings produce?

Burt (1969) has already argued for three different types of what he calls 'school' psychologists, along the lines of the American nomenclature. He argues first for a child psychologist whose principal task is to make intensive studies of children suffering from various disabilities. This person is not unlike the 'clinical child psychologist' of North America and is similar to the child psychologist whom Morris (1969) sees emerging in Scotland. Then he argues for what he calls a 'remedial psychologist' whose work will be most closely involved in the effective treatment of intellectual and emotional disabilities. Thirdly he argues for an educational psychologist whose concerns are more those of administration, organisation and research advice. In fact Burt, to some extent, solves the problem of increased knowledge by arguing for specialisation and concentration within the field of educational psychology itself.

In order adequately to decide whether specialisation of this sort would be useful or not it is important to obtain a fairly clear idea of the range of tasks which educational psychologists are expected to do and the extent to which they feel that they need more skills to do justice to the problems confronting them. It is fairly easy to examine the duties of British educational psychologists in 1965, as reported in the Summerfield survey. But what we need to have for training is a glimpse of the future. We train today for activities some years hence. What will be the activities which society will demand of its educational psychologists some years from now?

Pretraining.   Another issue is the increased attention which is likely to be paid to pretraining, within the contexts of conventional training arrangements. There are different ways in which pretraining can be carried out. For example, it is possible to visualise a situation in which earlier specialisation within the psychology degree is developed. Murrell (1969) has argued for pretraining of this sort in relation to occupational psychology, and the analogy can be applied to educational psychology. This approach has its dangers. If carried to extremes one reaches a situation in which the university degree course becomes frankly a professional training rather than a broad experience in a particular discipline. However, it would enable psychology graduates who wish to specialise in educational psychology to have some of the required ideas, skills and approaches already acquired by the time they complete their first degree. The B.Ed. course in some colleges of education may be of some relevance here, although Murrell's comments are made in the context of the psychology degree. Admittedly this will force the student into an early occupational choice but as Murrell himself points out there is no hard evidence that an eighteen-year-old is less likely to make a good occupational choice than, shall we say, a twenty-one or twenty-four-year-old.

Another way in which earlier specialisation within the conventional training might take place occurs at the point at which an educational psychologist takes his postgraduate certificate in education. At the moment there are few certificates in education which cater specifically for psychology graduates wishing to specialise as educational psychologists. It is possible that the time available during this year and the experiences which this year can provide for the students concerned could be used to better advantage than has been the case hitherto. The increased number of psychology graduates wishing to enter the teaching profession has not as yet been met with a realisation by the education service that persons with qualifications in this particular discipline might need training which is radically different from that which has been obtained hitherto. At a time when the whole pattern of teacher education in this country is under review, ways in which people with special skills need special types of training should be considered. This is a change which the current developments in teacher training may well include.

A third point at which pretraining of educational psychologists can be tackled occurs, of course, within the teaching process. Here it is possible that in the future we shall see much greater attention paid to the knowledge which intending educational psychologists gain while they are acquiring their experience of the teaching process than has been the case previously. The dangers of casting intending educational psychologists upon the sometimes stormy waters of the teaching experience may result in a product which is not ideally suited to the needs of the profession of educational psychology. Bad experiences can produce bad educational psychologists. The opportunity to use the period of teaching in such a way that the teaching experience itself is adequately structured should not be missed. At the same time there is little doubt that local authority school psychological services could well play a much greater part in the practical experiences gained by the intending educational psychologists during this period of two or three years' teaching. This could, admittedly, turn the experience into one not so much of teaching as of education. These experiences could involve the educational psychologists in some of the work of other educational services, e.g. the youth employment service, or possibly services based in other departments.

The educational psychologist as psychologist.   Another point which needs consideration is the advocacy of greater unity in the future training of educational and clinical psychologists. Tizard (1970) has argued this point: 'Traditionally, in this country, there has been a distinction (in training and in function) between the clinical psychologist who works in hospital clinics and the educational psychologists who work in local education authority child guidance clinics. It is evident from the overlap between disorders that this distinction is a false one. If child psychologists are to be maximally effective they must have both clinical and educational skills and they must be able to function equally well in the hospital as in the school. The (artificial) division between local authority clinics and hospital clinics has retarded the development of child psychiatry. The hospital psychologist who has no experience of schools is operating with his right hand tied behind his back, because many of the children he sees will have educational difficulties. Similarly, the psychological assessment of children referred to psychiatric clinics by schools often requires skills which up to now have been the prerogative of the clinical psychologists. Some means must be found of providing a clinical *and* educational training for all psychologists who will work with children.'

This is a commendable attitude, but if the proposals are accepted there is a danger that some problems are solved at the expense of creating others. If clinical psychologists and educational psychologists are each to be trained in the other's skills, this would increase the training period required. We do need some psychologists who combine some of the skills of educational and clinical psychologists and these could be the child psychologists who have been mentioned by Burt (1969) and Morris (1970). But if *all* psychologists working with children were to be trained to acquire all the skills of clinical and educational psychologists the length of training would increase.

Post-experience training.   So far we have considered ways in which current training arrangements are likely to be modified. Another point refers to a different aspect of training, that is, post-experience training. One of the problems of our current society is the way in which individuals need retraining in their professional skills at an ever increasing rate. A Californian study indicates that the half-life of the curriculum used in the initial university education of an engineer is now five years and reducing. This obsolescence of professional competency means that, increasingly, much more attention will be paid to post-experience training in educational psychology as in other professions. In what ways will this professional post-experience training take place?

There are clear signs that the current four- or five-day refresher courses which have been provided in the past by the British Psychological Society are no longer adequate. Some of the specialist psychologists, particularly those working with certain groups of handicapped children, have already started to provide courses for educational psychologists wishing to acquire specialised skills in work with spastic children or children with hearing loss, for example. But what is wanted is something much more radical than this. There are many educational psychologists working in the field whose learning experience since their initial twelve-months' training perhaps twenty or twenty-five years ago has been no more than attendance at a few three- or four-day refresher courses.

The tradition of the sabbatical year has been an important part of university education and has been a valuable and necessary weapon in the prevention of the hardening of obsolete ideas in university teachers. For a long time there have been arrangements for teachers to be seconded for full-time courses of advanced training, but educational psychologists have not as yet had the opportunities to return to refresh their skills in an intensive and lengthy post-experience situation. This type of development is needed. What is less certain is how this sort of training should be provided. There will be considerable advantage in one or more of the current training centres developing into an institution where post-experience courses for serving educational psychologists are available. Advantages would accrue to the initial training of new entrants to the profession, who would be in close contact with experienced and mature educational psychologists at the very formative time of their own entry to the profession.

The range of needs which can be specified is now enormous. If we restrict ourselves to a brief examination of techniques alone, then we note the development of new assessment methods, screening procedures for early identification of handicap, application of electronic devices in group testing, use of computers for processing survey data, as a few examples of activities in which educational psychologists should be competent for their work to assimilate modern ideas. Within the next few years we certainly should see the establishment of post-experience courses much longer, much more intensive and much more thorough than any hitherto.

The voice of the profession.   Another way in which training is likely to develop is by the profession's greater control of standards of entry and qualification. At the moment training is mainly vested in the hands of the universities, and the acquisition of the university diploma or degree gives the educational psychologist the qualification which fits him for a professional post. In other countries, however, a system of certification is also required. In the United States, for example, the number of states requiring certification arrangements for school psychologists has been steadily increasing and as far back as 1964, thirty-seven of the states had already established certification arrangements (Traxler 1967). Under this system a certification board is established which vets qualifications of different sorts, e.g. foreign qualifications, as well as qualifications from newly instituted training programmes, in order to see that the background and experience of a school psychologist are enough to enable that state to award the school psychologist its licence to practise. There have been advocates of a similar system for certification, allied to the keeping of a national register, to be instituted here. There are also dangers in implementing this type of arrangement and Frost (1969) has pointed out some of these. However, the pressures for registration and certification will probably increase and in the future the profession itself may take a greater part in its own government through the twin organisations of the British Psychological Society and the Association of Educational Psychologists.

Conclusions

There is little doubt that the present structure of training arrangements is very much of an *ad hoc* pattern. It was for this reason that the Summerfield Report argued strongly for the introduction of purpose-designed training centres for educational psychology. It is difficult to see how this request can, in the long run, fail to be met. The financing of training centres for educational psychologists must be centrally supported so that these centres have the opportunity to develop their particular skills and activities to their best advantage. At a time when no training centre in England and Wales has a budget which remotely approaches that of a single college of education for teachers, the imbalance in the training arrangements of educational psychologists becomes blindingly clear. Nothing will develop the training arrangements for the whole profession as much as the establishment in the 1970s of one purpose-designed, adequately financed demonstration training centre, in which could be combined arrangements for initial training, post-experience training and adequate supervision for pretraining of students intending later to enter the profession. This is the most vital of the Summerfield recommendations and this is the one development which the training of educational psychologists needs above all others. The profession could then recruit members whose services to the community can be as effective as modern educational psychology makes possible.

Acknowledgments   The author is grateful to Dr Mia Kellmer Pringle for help in answering some queries. He is also grateful to Mrs Debbie Welfare for typing the manuscript.

Part Three

Adolescence

P. A. Osterrieth*

13. The draw-a-man test (Machover) at adolescence

Introduction

Can an analysis of drawings made by young people between the ages of eleven and seventeen add to our understanding of the psychological development of the adolescent? We should like to put forward a few tentative, and as yet incomplete, observations by way of an answer to this question.

The answer to our question has always tended to be a negative one because it has long been taken for granted that drawing evolved little after the age of twelve. In a previous article (Osterrieth and Cambier 1963) we have shown that we are unable to accept this view, which is the result of using essentially cumulative methods of analysis and assessment and which is based on the somewhat naïve assumption—relatively valid for the years of early childhood—that, as a child grows older, his drawings necessarily become 'better' and present a more objective view of the real world. No purpose is served by repeating all the arguments here, particularly as the analysis of work produced individually by adolescents and even adults has proved so worthwhile that drawing has already been widely included, for several decades past, in batteries of clinical tests. But is it not possible that these drawings which play such a large part in individual clinical examinations can reveal something of the general psychological state of adolescents at particular ages? Could it not also be concluded that a knowledge of the distribution of certain characteristics across successive age-groups would enable us to arrive at more confident interpretations when individual cases are being studied?

For some years the Centre for Genetic Psychology at the Free University of Brussels has been working on a genetic analysis of results obtained when directives inspired by K. Machover (1949) were given:

* This chapter was prepared in collaboration with Ch. Haesaerts and A. Querton (Centre for Genetic Psychology, Free University of Brussels) and translated by Mr and Mrs A. W. Hornsey.

'Draw a human being', then 'Now draw a human being of the opposite sex'. These instructions—slightly modified for subjects under twelve years old—were given under standardised conditions to a wide range of children in nursery, primary and secondary schools. The work of 1,363 children— that is to say 2,726 drawings—was then used as the sample to be studied. The selection was made so as to produce a completely 'normal' cross- section (without any sensori-motor, intellectual or scholastic bias) and so as to eliminate possible influences of school, class and teacher.

In analysing these drawings we have used an original 'breakdown- system' which has been established empirically and with reference to the relevant literature. The system (which we hope to publish shortly) has proved valid, either used as a whole or in part, in numerous pieces of research; it has helped to demonstrate how the most varied behavioural and situational characteristics can be reflected in drawings. In addition to the usual filing categories, the system analyses drawings under sixty-eight headings covering the whole range of variants in the depiction of the human figure, and each of them can appear under many different aspects. Thus, within the confines of our work, every figure-drawing can be defined in terms of a maximum of sixty-eight pieces of information relating to the figure as a whole or to particular details. Since it lends itself to computer analysis, the profile produced enables us to study changes in the drawing of both male and female figures in relation to the age and sex of the person that produced them, as well as identifying any more or less stable patterns of variables which might occur; it also makes possible a comparison of different samples (Osterrieth and Cambier 1969). From the point of view of genetic analysis, it has been shown that some variables are not linked to age, while the frequency of others rises or falls in a regular pattern. Still others have proved particularly characteristic of certain age- groups, attaining for a limited period frequencies markedly higher than at any other stage of development. We shall quote some examples from this last group which seem significant in an assessment of how far the drawing of adolescents is influenced by the psycho-sexual aspects of their develop- ment (in the widest sense) or which at least raise certain problems relative to this period of development.

The following data are based only on those drawings from the vast sample in which the sex of the figure was clearly indicated. Subjects, aged between 11:0 and 17:11, each drew a female and a male figure; the age-groups (11:0 to 11:11, 12:0 to 12:11, etc.) are each made up of on average 44 boys and 39 girls. For the sake of simplicity, but at the risk of over-simplicity, we shall only attempt to outline in this study the ages at which the different variables reach their highest frequency. (From this point, we shall refer to subjects in the age-range 12:0 to 12:11 as 'twelve-year-old subjects' or the 'twelve-year-old age-group' and those in the range 15:0 to 15:11 as 'fifteen-year-old subjects' or the 'fifteen-year-old age-group'.)

Drawing and psycho-sexual development

It is already established that sexual differentiation in the drawing of the human figure appears very early, in the choice of dress, hair style or accessories. These methods of differentiation occur in childhood and do not concern us here. Nor will we discuss the complex problem of differentiation through facial features.

But one would expect that the most obvious of the physical changes that occur during puberty would be reflected in the drawing of the human figure and would correspond to the objective or subjective changes in the adolescent's perception of his own body or to the changes in his awareness of the physical appearance of others. An excellent example is *the depiction of the breasts in female figures* since this is one of the most differentiating features appearing at adolescence. Our 'breakdown system' takes into account three different ways in which the breasts may be drawn: by discreet adjustment to the outlines of the figure; by accentuation of detail or size; by caricature or gross exaggeration; to which can be added specific indications through the medium of dress.

If one considers all these possibilities in the drawings of the female form drawn by *girls* (figure 1), while the breasts are absent from the pictures produced by seven-year-olds and occur only sparsely up to the age of ten (10%), the frequency of occurrence rises to a peak at thirteen (56%), falls off to sixteen (20%) and starts to rise again at seventeen (40%). Thus the frequency curve shows a definite high-point between eleven and fifteen; it could be concluded that this is the age at which the adolescent girl is most likely to emphasise the breast in her drawings; we feel also that it corresponds closely with the period during which the girl is actually experiencing a marked and significant change in this part of her body and one which is particularly symbolic of femininity. It is not surprising that she is concerned with these changes and that this concern is reflected in her drawing. But what is surprising is that, at the age when the frequency reaches its peak, it still only applies to the work of 56 per cent of the girls.

We doubt very much whether this figure is an accurate reflection of the real position; more probably it opens the way to possibilities of interpretations of a more or less projective nature. It is certainly not without significance that a girl's drawings fail to reflect changes occurring to her own body; nor is it any less significant that a girl should indicate features which she still does not possess physically but which she envies or fears. Without involving ourselves in such interpretations at this stage, it is at least possible to state that the fact that the breasts start to be represented

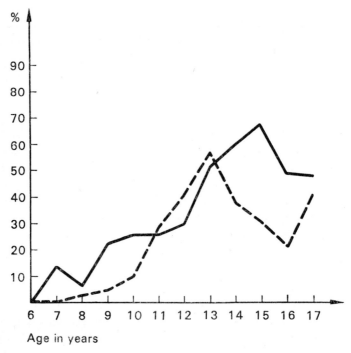

FIGURE I   *Depiction of the breasts.*

—————————   *Female figures drawn by boys*
– – – – – – –   *Female figures drawn by girls*

shows the girl's concern for her development and that this concern is characteristic of puberty. This concern is still more explicit, and may have positive or negative implications, in those cases where subjects use accentuation or exaggeration in their drawings. Taking these cases on their own, the frequency curve shows a definite upward-turn between twelve and fifteen, with its peak again at thirteen (38%) (figure 2).

How do the *boys* cope with the drawing of this essentially female feature? Taking together all the different ways of depicting the breasts, the frequency curve starts at zero at age six, rises gradually between seven and twelve (30%) and reaches a high level between thirteen and seventeen years, with a peak at fifteen (67%) (figure 1). If only the modalities considered under 'accentuation' or 'exaggeration' are taken into account, it is found that their frequency rises steeply at fourteen and fifteen, with a distinct peak at fifteen (45%) (figure 2).

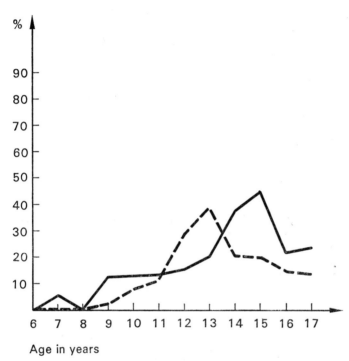

FIGURE 2   *Accentuation of breasts.*

━━━━━━━━   *Female figures drawn by boys*
▬ ▬ ▬ ▬ ▬ ▬   *Female figures drawn by girls*

Thus the frequency of the representation of the breasts in figures drawn by adolescents reaches high levels at:

11 to 15 for girls, with a peak at 13;

13 to 17 for boys, with a peak at 15.

The frequency of the 'accentuated' and 'exaggerated' variants furnishes proof, if such were needed, of the sensitivity of boys and girls to this secondary sex characteristic, whatever the particular shade of this sensitivity may be. It is surely not by chance that the frequency reaches its peak two years earlier for girls than for boys. This may indicate that what happens to the individual himself and seems important to him shows up earlier in his drawings than that which is only observed in others, however interesting it may be. It is perhaps also another example of the time-lag so often encountered in certain aspects of pubertal development between girls and boys. It is probably also not accidental that from age seven onwards, with the exception of the period from eleven to thirteen, there is always more evidence of preoccupation with the breasts in the drawings of the boys than those of the girls. Particularly at adolescence, boys seem more interested in this female characteristic than the girls are themselves and this interest is confirmed by the greater frequency of accentuated, exaggerated or caricatural representations among the boys.

We have discussed elsewhere (Osterrieth 1968) the category 'apparent age of the figure' and the difficulties of making an objective assessment under this heading. It is necessary to return to his point here in order to examine to what extent the frequency of 'depiction of the breasts' is related to the number of female adolescent and adult figures (as opposed to children) whose apparent age is compatible with this characteristic. Since, in fact, depiction of the breasts was used on occasion to determine the age of the figure, it is not surprising that the number of adolescent and adult females drawn by the girls in the thirteen-year-old age-group is higher than by the boys in the same group (82% and 71% respectively) and that the reverse was the case in the fifteen-year-old age-group (50% and 86%). But even so, even at the ages where depicting of the breasts is most frequent, its incidence is still 20-25 per cent below the total of adolescent and adult female figures actually drawn. Thus the factor 'age' is not inextricably linked with 'depiction of the breasts', a fact of some importance for any psychological interpretations. What is more, this discrepancy is slightly more marked in the case of the girls, confirming that they are less alert than the boys to this characteristic female feature.

One final point must be made in this connection: the female figures drawn by the girls more often take the form of a girl or a young woman than those drawn by the boys (61% and 20% at age thirteen); they are views of themselves as they are at present or soon will be. The female figures drawn by the boys, however, tend much more to suggest a mature woman (55% and 15% at age fifteen) and seem to be a mother figure or a future wife. Thus we can conclude that the concern with this feminine characteristic varies considerably with the sex of the drawer concerned, and this is a useful reminder of the dangers inherent in interpreting parts of a drawing without regard to the whole context.

'Depiction of the chest' falls under the same heading as 'depiction of the breasts', but it is obvious that considerations of the drawings of the *male figure* do not carry the same significance as those of the female figure. But one item has produced a surprising result: it concerns the inclusion of one or two breast pockets in the drawings. This did not occur frequently in our sample, not rising above 15 per cent for the boys' drawings except in the case of the thirteen-year-olds (28%) and not above 10 per cent for the girls' drawings except in the case of the eleven-year-olds (16%). It is strange nevertheless that we should find ourselves confronted once again with this two-year age-gap between the girls' peak and the boys'.

After the significant results shown by this first variable, we set out to find amongst the other headings of our system those which would present a similar evolution during adolescence and which could reveal the same sensitivity and complacence to physical appearance with the same undeniable libidinal undertones.

A heading 'depiction of the legs' was thought to meet both these requirements. One item listed under this heading, called '*shaped legs*, characterises those drawings in which the legs of the figure, whether clothed or not, are given a curved outline at the thigh, the calf or the ankle. This is a less marked feature than the first one discussed so it is even more revealing when it is indicated.

This item is almost totally absent from the drawings of children up to age nine. Beyond this age, in the female figures drawn by the *girls* (figure 3), its frequency rises abruptly at eleven and reaches its peak at fourteen (58%); it then falls to sixteen (27%) and starts to rise again at seventeen (50%). In the male figures drawn by the girls, the rise in frequency is much less abrupt and never reaches 20 per cent; the peak is at age seventeen (18%). In the female figures drawn by the *boys*, the rise in frequency is more gradual and comes later than for the girls; the peak is at age sixteen (54%). As with the girls, the male figures drawn by the boys are accentuated in this respect to a lesser extent; the peak is at age fifteen (24%).

It was to be expected that conventions of dress would lead subjects to give shape to the legs of female figures more often than to the male figures and the difference between the peaks is rather less pronounced than it was for 'depiction of the breasts'. In the case of the female figures we find yet again that the girls are two years ahead of the boys, though the peaks occur a year later than for 'depiction of the breasts'. The same two-year gap, again occurring a year later, but this time with the boys ahead of the girls, appears for the male figures. Although the subjects of both sexes together give their female figures shaped legs more often than their male figures, although each sex makes the legs in the figure of his own sex more shapely than those of the opposite sex; it is perhaps significant that boys and girls in the twelve to fourteen age-groups are about equal in their use of curves to depict the legs of their male figures and that sixteen-year-old boys draw curves to a much greater extent than sixteen-year-old girls.

There is another heading in our breakdown system which satisfies both our requirements with regard to pubertal development and inter- pretative value: it is *accentuation of the genital region.* Our breakdown

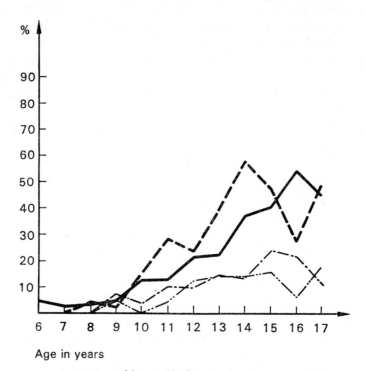

FIGURE 3   *Depiction of legs with shape.*

Female figures drawn by boys
Female figures drawn by girls
Male figures drawn by boys
Male figures drawn by girls

system allows for this accentuation to take the form of either contoured hips or thighs or emphasis on the pubic region by means of clothing or anatomical details. In the age-groups that concern us, the former type of accentuation appears particularly in the male figures drawn by the girls and the female figures drawn by the boys; the second method of accentua- tion occurs most frequently in the male figures drawn by the boys; accentuation of the genital region in female figures drawn by the girls is very rare. This distribution is of course partly affected by conventions of dress and is too uncertain at the different ages to be more than just an indication. Depiction of the actual genital organs is quite exceptional.

On the whole 'accentuation of the genital region' very rarely occurs earlier than the age of eleven; it does, however, become more frequent from twelve or thirteen onwards and this shows that it properly belongs to adolescence, although its frequency never reaches 30 per cent in our sample. It occurs more often in the boys' drawings than in the girls' and is somewhat more frequent in the male figures than in the female (respectively 28% and 27% for the boys and 26% and 7% for the girls). It is still worth noting that, whatever the sex of the figure drawn, the peaks come at fourteen years for the girls and fifteen for the boys. Once again we find the girls ahead of the boys in the depiction of a feature with undeniable sexual implications. Even admitting that the age-gap in this case is one year instead of two, it is nevertheless significant that it is still apparent even in a category where the incidence in the drawings of their own sex submitted by the girls is very low.

The features which we have discussed so far all have one thing in common. The curve of the breast, leg or thigh implies a curvilinear rather than a rectilinear outline. In fact our system provides a heading under which it can be indicated whether a drawing is predominantly curvilinear or rectilinear and there is of course a variant denoting a mixture of the two types which has a very high frequency. How does the variant *predominantly curvilinear* compare with the features discussed previously and which may have contributed to the drawing's being classed as curvilinear?

The growth of the frequencies of the factor 'predominantly curvilinear' show that this is another feature peculiar to adolescence (figure 4). From the age of nine, its frequency rises steadily; after twelve, the increase is very pronounced. Generally curves are used by the girls somewhat more than by the boys, but both sexes make more use of them when drawing a figure of their own sex.

The frequency curves can be listed in declining order:

1. Girls' female figure: sharp increase after age 10 (35%); peak at 14 (84%), then decrease;
2. Boys' male figure: sharp increase at age 12 (58%); peak at 15 (68%);
3. Girls' male figure: increase at age 12 (27%); peak at 16 (63%);
4. Boys' female figure: big fluctuations, plateau from 14 to 16 years; peak at 16 (46%).

The maximum frequency therefore reaches a higher level and occurs earlier when the adolescent is drawing a figure of his own sex (figure 5) and this applies even more to the girls than to the boys. For the female figures the girls are two years ahead of the boys once again, whereas, for the male figures, the boys lead the girls by one year.

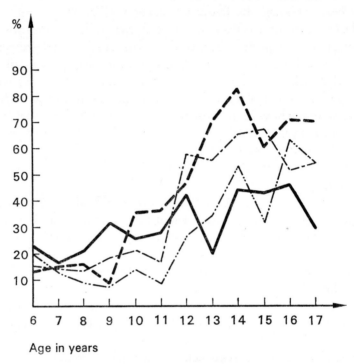

Age in years

FIGURE 4   *Indication of curvilinear predominance.*

━━━━━━━	*Female figures drawn by boys*
━ ━ ━ ━	*Female figures drawn by girls*
—·—·—·—	*Male figures drawn by boys*
—··—··—··	*Male figures drawn by girls*

Let us assume that all the properties noted under the headings discussed so far can be attributed entirely to a 'curvilinear factor', which increases with age and applies especially when drawing figures of one's own sex but which affects girls slightly more than boys. On the basis of this assumption, one would expect that curves in the body outline would occur more often and earlier in female figures drawn by the girls than in those drawn by the boys and that the same would be true of male figures drawn by the boys compared with those drawn by the girls. If we take ages and maximum frequencies alone into account, our observations confirm this hypothesis to some extent:

Heading	Confirmation (+) or Invalidation (−)	
	Maximum Age	Maximum Frequency
Depiction of breasts	+	−
Accentuation of breasts	+	−
Female leg curved	+	+
Male leg curved	+	+
Accentuation of genital region, female figure	+	−
Accentuation of genital region, male figure	−	+

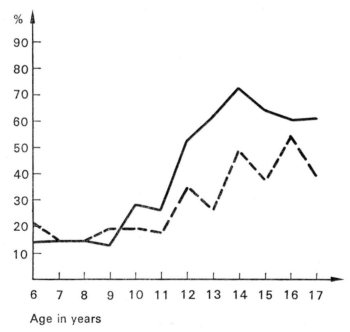

FIGURE 5   *Indication of curvilinear predominance.*

─────────────   *Figure of the same sex as the drawer*

─ ─ ─ ─ ─ ─   *Figure of different sex from the drawer*

But they only confirm the hypothesis partially and the discrepancy would be even greater if we were to consider all ages and not just the ages of highest frequency. The curvilinear factor alone, then, can no more account for all the phenomena observed than can a would-be 'degree of objectivity' factor. The difference between the frequency of the 'predominantly curvilinear' category and the frequencies of other categories, which are mostly much lower, indicates that other factors, related to the psychological significance of each physical feature, are involved. As to the interpretation which should be placed on the appearance of this curvilinear factor, which is typical of adolescence, we feel that it may perhaps be regarded as an expression of the adolescent's increasing integration of the body-image, of his more intimate experience and awareness of his own body, of a certain listlessness, of his receptivity to sensuality and of his more acute and delicate sensitivity, and all these facets of the adolescent's nature also affect his reaction to the opposite sex, though somewhat later.

Some writers have taken the view that the waist is a sort of frontier zone between the upper and lower parts of the individual and may be regarded as symbolic of his attempt to control his sexual urges. Machover (1949) in particular has put forward some interesting arguments in support of this view. We thought it appropriate therefore to analyse the drawings of our adolescent subjects to see if there was any relationship between the treatment of the waist and the phenomena discussed above.

In our sample, 'indication of a waist', whatever form it may take, is already frequent at age six and appears in 70 per cent of the drawings produced by both boys and girls at age seven; its frequency tends to decline at adolescence, following a peak at age eleven for both the male and female figures drawn by girls and at eleven and thirteen respectively for the male and female figures of the boys. 'Indication of a waist' is clearly not a typically adolescent feature, but it is worth noting that there is again the two-year gap between the boys and the girls in their drawings of the female figure. On the whole, a waist is indicated more in the female figures than in the male figures.

But if, on the other hand, we single out those drawings in which the waist is specially accentuated, we get frequency curves very similar to those for the other categories already analysed, showing a marked increase and peak during adolescence. This *accentuation of the waist* may take the form of a double horizontal line (as compared to the single one which is the usual indication), a jagged line, a more or less elaborated belt, bold lines on either side of the body or a combination of several of these features.

'Accentuation of the waist' is unusual in young children but shows a marked rise in frequency after age eleven (figure 6). For the female figures, the girls show a sharp increase at age twelve (this age being the peak with 64%) and this is maintained until fourteen; for the boys' drawings, the increase comes at thirteen and the peak is reached at fourteen (71%). For the male figures, the girls' drawings produce a period of higher frequency between ages twelve and thirteen, with a peak at sixteen (70%), while in the boys' the higher frequency comes at age twelve with a peak at thirteen

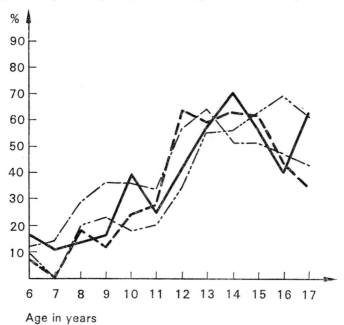

Age in years

FIGURE 6   *Proportion of accentuated depictions of the waist among drawings in which any waist is depicted at all.*

▬▬▬	*Female figures drawn by the boys*
— — —	*Female figures drawn by the girls*
—·—·—·—	*Male figures drawn by the boys*
—··—··—··—	*Male figures drawn by the girls*

(65%). For this category, like most of the others, the maximum frequency comes earlier and more suddenly in the cases where adolescents are drawing figures of their own sex but, for figures of the opposite sex, the frequency actually reaches a slightly higher level.

At present, we have not enough evidence to support the theory that an accentuated waist represents a barrier or indicates tension connected with sexuality. All we can say is that this feature seems to belong to the same group as the others we have considered as revealing the drawers' awareness of, and sensitivity to, the changes that are taking place in their own body and sexuality shown in others. We can however stress the point that, within the limits set by the categories we have analysed here. 'accentuation of the waist' is the feature (in terms of genetic development) which reaches its maximum frequency earliest in the male figures drawn by the boys and the female figures drawn by both the boys and the girls. In these three instances, it precedes by one or two years the time of the maximum frequencies for the other categories we have discussed.

Conclusions

We thought it would be interesting to analyse, in connection with a study of adolescence, some variables in the drawing of the human figure which conceivably are in relation to objective physical changes occurring at puberty and also to the adolescent's attitude towards his own body and others'. Clearly these variables cannot be considered in isolation, but must be put in connection with one another and with many others that we have not included here. Also, since we have mentioned only maximum frequencies, we have not been able to show the very revealing fluctuations and inversed relations that appear at other ages.

We have compiled the following table as a summary of the categories we have considered, combining the age at which they reach their maximum frequency and the frequency attained:

A. *Drawing of the female figure*

Category	Age of maximum frequency	Percentage
Girls		
1. Accentuation of waist	12-14	64
2. Depiction of breasts	13	56
3. Accentuation of breasts	13	38
4. Curvilinear factor	14	83
5. Shaped legs	14	57
6. Indication of genital region	14	7
Boys		
1. Accentuation of waist	14	71
2. Depiction of breasts	15	67
3. Accentuation of breasts	15	45
4. Indication of genital region	15	27
5. Shaped legs	16	54
6. Curvilinear factor	16	46

B. *Drawings of the male figure*

Boys

1.	Accentuation of waist	13	65
2.	Curvilinear factor	15	68
3.	Indication of genital region	15	29
4.	Shaped legs	15	24

Girls

1.	Indication of genital region	14	26
2.	Accentuation of waist	16	70
3.	Curvilinear factor	16	63
4.	Shaped legs	17	18

If one considers the ages, the maximum frequency for each of the categories discussed always occurs one to three years earlier for the figures of the same sex as the drawer than for the figures of the opposite sex (except for the indication of the genital region in the male figure). This maximum always comes one year earlier for girls than for boys. If however one looks at the actual percentages, they are generally slightly higher for the boys' drawings than for the girls'. This applies to three categories out of four for the male figures (exception: accentuation of waist) and to four categories out of six for the female figures (exceptions: shaped legs and, particularly, the curvilinear factor).

We present these few observations in the belief that the phenomena discussed here might perhaps confirm, complete or modify the present state of our knowledge of the psycho-sexual development of adolescents.

K. Lovell

14. Intellectual aspects of adolescence

Introduction

The Latin verb *adolescere*, meaning 'to grow' or 'to grow to maturity', has given us our word adolescence. This involves not only physical and intellectual maturity but at least a move towards emotional and social maturity as well. The affective and social impulses of adolescence have often been described and it is certainly not the present writer's place to discuss these matters. What is not well recognised, however, is that the changes in the general ways of knowing in adolescence have a bearing on these impulses. The onset of new intellectual structures allow the adolescent to handle hypotheses, and to reason with respect to propositions removed from perceptible or imageable data. It is the changes in the nature of the general ways of knowing, or in the growth of intelligence, which determine the changes in manner in which data over a wide area of experience are understood, and problems viewed and solved.

In *Advances in Educational Psychology* Volume 1 the writer has outlined the main changes in the nature of thinking, which take place in the pre-adolescent and adolescent years. The individual then reaches what Inhelder and Piaget (1958) call the stage of formal operational thought, the essence of which is the ability to invert reality and possibility. Instead of imagining what the world would be like if there was some simple extension of the actual in the direction of the possible, the adolescent can imagine what the actual world would be like if some hypothetical conditions were fulfilled. Thus when he is faced with a problem he can produce more complex expectations than he could as a child, he can elaborate a set of hypotheses and deduce the consequences, and after some kind of either outer or inner experimentation, select those hypotheses which are consonant with the evidence as being likely to be the correct ones. Moreover, since such thought no longer requires intuitable data but can deal with verbal elements, propositional logic is imposed on a logic of classes and relations; while formal operational thought may also be characterised as second-degree operations, for the individual can now structure relations between relations.

This new stage in the development of the intellectual structures should be regarded as a potential stage of growth. As indicated in the chapter in Volume 1, not all individuals attain it. Others will reach it in limited areas of their experience, especially when they are knowledgeable in respect of the content, and when credibility and logical necessity go together. An adolescent, or adult, may well reach mature ways of thinking in one area and show incomplete development in others, so that formal and egocentric modes of thought may exist side by side in the same individual. Again, no one lives at the level of formal operational thought throughout the waking hours. Even in the case of very able adolescents there is reversion to concrete operational or even pre-operational thought in certain situations, or in certain emotional states. There are, therefore, considerable inter-individual and intra-individual differences in respect of mature ways of thinking about situations. Further, it will be realised that many everyday problems simply do not call for formal operational thought for their solution.

At this point it is worth recalling the influences which appear to be at work in aiding the development of the general ways of knowing. These are:

1. Biological factors. The maturation of the central nervous system seems responsible for the unfolding, in fixed sequence, of the stages in intellectual growth. This fixed sequence has been found in all cultures studied to date.

2. The socialisation process. In all societies, there arises to a greater or lesser extent, agreements, discussions, exchanges, and oppositions in social intercourse. This factor is linked with 4 below, for now the general coordination of actions concern the inter-individual as well as the intra-individual.

3. Education and culture generally, particularly the type of concepts used and discussed in the system and the opportunities within it to consider possibilities. Obviously the influences just outlined differ markedly from society to society.

4. Self- or auto-regulation. The reflection of the individual on his own coordinating activities in 2 and 3 above, made possible by 1, seem to be very important for intellectual growth.

The third influence, as already stated, varies greatly across cultures, and between subcultural groups in some instances. It is the one which appears to play a greater role in the emergence of formal operational thought than it did in respect of the emergence of concrete operational thought. Such limited evidence as we have suggests that in areas where there is a lack of schooling and an underdeveloped milieu, the onset of the ability to elaborate a combinatorial system, and the notions of probability and chance are delayed (Peluffo 1967; Kimball 1968). Indeed, a most important problem for research is to identify further these features in the culture pattern, schooling, and child-rearing practices, and those value judgments and belief systems which tend to promote or hold back the growth of formal thought.

Having introduced the topic we now consider the implications in some general and specific areas of adolescents' life.

Temporal perspectives and temporal operations

A brief discussion of temporal perspectives and temporal operations will make clearer that the elaboration of formal operational thought both helps the adolescent to focus on ideas which are non-present and future, and helps us to understand his increased mastery of certain ideas in, say, history, or in mathematics, as in the instance of velocity or rate of change.

A pre-school child, at the pre-operational stage of thought, can recall the past in the form of, say, a story, and he can organise his actions in ways which are representative of the future. Since he can represent the past and future to himself he can be said to have a temporal perspective without having the ability to handle temporal operations. Thus when we represent to ourselves the past, present or future, we do not necessarily hold some abstract scheme of time, but rather we merely have in mind a number of events that can be put into some rough sequence. There is some suggestion, although no precise knowledge exists, that the growth of temporal perspective is affected by personality structure; for example, emotional stability and the extent to which the individual is dominated by the present. However, we can say with greater certainty that, because of differences in upbringing, there are likely to be differences both between, and within, groups of people in respect of the extent of their temporal perspective. Adolescents whose forefathers have lived in the same village for generations are likely to have different temporal perspectives from those who are recent immigrants. In the case of the latter, the memories of their childhood cannot be linked directly with the new background without reasoning being invoked. With the advent of logical thought, however, and hence of temporal operations, a person who is a member of many groups can pass from one perspective to another by reasoning about all the events he can recall, and by placing them in an abstract time. But this does necessitate the growth of logical thinking.

With the coming of temporal operations around eight to nine years of age (Piaget 1946; Lovell and Slater 1960) the child begins to be capable of putting events into a sequence according to the order of their succession; of marking off intervals of time between ordered points on a time scale and of placing smaller ones within larger ones; and of choosing a time interval as a unit and using it as a unit for measuring some other time interval. Early in the junior school the past is not clearly differentiated into various historical periods and the latter tend to be lumped in confusion. It is around ten to eleven years of age before 75 per cent of pupils understand the implications of historical dates well enough to link those simple dates with historical characters, although they may quote dates in history much earlier. Even so, pupils in the junior school and in the early years of the secondary school ascribe concrete properties to time; clocks and calendars give them a model of a steady and continuous state of change.

It is not until fourteen to fifteen years of age that 50 per cent of pupils correctly answer the following question, giving sound reasons: 'When you move the hands of the clock forward one hour in spring-time do you suddenly become one hour older?' It is the onset of formal operational thought that allows time on the clock to be regarded as a convention which has no effect on the changes it measures. Time is now looked upon in an abstract sense, independent of events. It will likewise be fourteen to fifteen years of age before children of average ability can consider together, say, the Renaissance, the Reformation and the sixteenth-century explorers.

So with the onset of formal operational thought the adolescent can pass from the concrete homogeneity of clock or calendar time to the abstract homogeneity of a duration which is a thread linking events without being dependent on them. He can now look upon ideas from the past through the present and into the future in a way not possible before. This helps to liberate the adolescent from the concrete in favour of interests and ideas that are orientated to the non-present and future, and helps him to look at any topic, social, political, or others, with greater continuity and perspective.

Social and political concepts and adult–adolescent communication

The advance in the general ways of knowing also enables the adolescent to consider differing social and political points of view, these manipulations being carried out without the necessity of committing himself to any particular one. Moreover, he can advance hypotheses and build theories, some simple, some complex, some very middle-of-the-road and some extreme, to explain the origins, and outcomes, of the issues in question. Indeed, the changes in the child's conception of politics with the onset of adolescence has been indicated by Connell (1971). Inhelder and Piaget (1958, p. 340) neatly state the position, ' Most of them have political and social theories and want to reform the world: they have their own ways of explaining all the present-day turmoil in collective life.' Thus just as the individual can elaborate hypotheses in respect of physical situations, so too he can in the case of social and political ideas and in the case of, say, ethical and religious concepts (cf. Goldman 1964) with the onset of formal operational thought. But it must be remembered that only few adolescents can do this with equal facility across diverse content-areas and there is likely to be considerable intra-personal variability. Even in late adolescence and adulthood, this intra-personal variability remains. Moreover, in the case of less able adolescents, instead of elaborating theories themselves, they subscribe to ideas passed on by peers, or picked up from books or via the mass media. But the tendency to break out of the present and from the immediate surroundings is there; they want to join in the ideas, ideologies and ideals of a larger group

If parents and children, teachers and pupils, adolescent and adolescent can operate at the level of formal operational thought—at least in some areas of experience—the range of ideas that can be communicated increases enormously. In discussion they will try to relate different variables, realise a multiplicity of possible links in an issue, try out ideas in systematic fashion, and go beyond the given data using hypothetico-deductive thought. Such communication will, of course, be carried out with greater ease in some circumstances than in others because personal experience varies, and personal feelings will enter into some issues more than into others. However, generally speaking, the discussion need no longer be in terms of the facts—the concrete evidence—but can go beyond these to hypotheses underpinning these facts. Moreover an entirely new range of conceptualisations can be considered, or old ones looked at in new depth and perspective. Entirely new topics—personal, political, social or scientific —may be discussed, or old topics argued in a new light. For example, whereas an average ten-year-old understands, say, 'king' as a person who rules his people, it is not until adolescence that the essential attribute of kingship is realised as that of a relationship with other persons.

The changes just discussed may also bedevil family communication in adolescence, or indeed any form of adult-adolescent or adolescent-adolescent dialogue. If for one reason or another an adolescent is able to operate at the level of formal thought but the parent or adult is not, there can be difficulties in communication and resulting conflict. Second—and this is rarely acknowledged when the alleged troublesomeness of teenagers is discussed—the adolescent can, for the first time, see the way in which adults run the world or do some specific thing, as one of a number of possible ways. When he or she tries to communicate this to parent, teacher or other adult, the latter persons may not, for one reason or another, consider the options. Third, the adolescent in forming theories about the ways in which the world should be run and often having his affective life thereby influenced, may join a group or organisation so that he can foster his new-found aims and motives—sometimes to the detriment of adult-adolescent dialogue. In making these three points it is in no way intended to imply that adolescents are always right and adults wrong. Adolescents can see possibilities not previously available to them and we should help them to do so, but they obviously do not have the experience to judge the value of the theories they elaborate. It is, however, imperative to bear these points in mind for they can render adult-adolescent dialogue more difficult at times than it need be.

Once again it is seen that it is the development of the general ways of knowing which greatly enriches the possibilities of adult-adolescent and adolescent-adolescent dialogue. In adolescence the issue of, say, peace, war or social life can be considered at a more complex level. Obviously, less able adolescents will be at a disadvantage, and communication may break down or be seriously impaired with them unless this is borne in mind. The content of the communication must be encoded appropriately for them, and the issue discussed in concrete rather than in formal terms.

Mathematical and scientific ideas

So far we have discussed the effects of the changes in the nature of the intellectual structures as they relate to very general but vital issues in the life of the adolescent. We must also bear in mind, however, that it is the development of the general ways of knowing which determines the ways in which certain new or particular knowledge—such as pupils often learn in school—is assimilated. Recent studies have thrown much light on the nature of the difficulties pupils have in understanding school subject-matter and nowhere is this more clearly seen than in the fields of mathematics and science, although it must be stressed that this is just as true in history, geography, literature and so forth. In Volume I the writer indicated the difficulties which pupils have in handling metric proportion

H

and probability before the onset of formal operational thought. In this paper we look very briefly at the growth of the concept of a function and at two other important mathematical issues, together with a passing glimpse at some concepts used in science.

Piaget *et al.* (1968) describe the growth of understanding the quantification of a function using the term in a narrower sense than is currently used in mathematics. They consider a function as the relationship between the magnitude of two qualities, the variation in one bringing about a variation in the other in the same proportion. Altogether 353 pupils were studied in five experiments, the ages of the former varying from six to fourteen years although the number of pupils taking any one experiment varied from 41 to 116. The upshot was that a function, as defined, is only slowly and laboriously grasped. In the case of young children the notion of a function is characterised by the putting into correspondence of two values; for example, the larger the wheel the greater the distance travelled each time it turns; or it appears in the form of some causal dependency—the weight of a piece of iron depends on its size. But with the elaboration of formal thought the pupil can tackle the ratios between successive pairs of ordered values of a variable.

More recently Thomas (1969) in the USA, and one of the writer's students (Orton 1970), have investigated the growth of some aspects of the growth of a function using the term as it is currently held in mathematics. Thus the function $y = f(x)$, defined on X as domain and with a subset of Y as range, gives a mapping of the set X *into* the set Y such that for each $x \in X$ there is a unique image $f(x) \in Y$. Functions involving proportionality are thus to be regarded as only a subset of functions in general. The data obtained from these two studies show striking similarities in respect of pupil difficulties. It seems that some aspects of the idea of a mathematical function can be grasped by pupils with flexible concrete operational thought. But it also appears that the early stages of formal operational thought are necessary before the pupil appreciates relations presented in all the major representations, by diagram, by graph, by ordered pairs, by table and by equation. Moreover, more advanced and flexible formal operational thought—Piaget's stage IIIb—is necessary before the composition of functions and the f-notation can be successfully tackled.

Another mathematical idea of great importance is that of limit. As long ago as 1948, Piaget, Inhelder and Szeminska produced evidence that children pass through a number of stages in their understanding of 'point'. Indeed it is not until the onset of formal operational thought that point comes to be regarded as without shape or surface area. But more recently Taback (1969) showed among verbally sophisticated American children who came from cultured homes, that few pupils below the age of twelve years, with a likely mental age of at least fourteen years, could conceptualise an infinite process and so arrive at a mature concept of a limit.

The study by Reynolds (1967) is also of importance for it involved pupils' understanding of mathematical proof. Such understanding will, of course, be vital regardless of the nature of the mathematics curriculum. Studying able British pupils of secondary school age in respect of their grasp of assumptions, generalisations, and proof by converse, deduction and *reductio ad absurdum*, he was able to show that the move from concrete to formal operational thought accounts for a great deal of the change in pupils' understanding of proof. His work also shows that when a problem is well structured and the assumptions and universes of discourse easily identified, with the pupil having to introduce no assumptions or hypotheses from outside the problem, the solutions offered by pupils more readily fit into the Piagetian cognitive-developmental model.

To conclude this chapter we will look at a few conceptualisations used in science, for they provide good examples of the changes in understanding that come about with the onset of formal operational thought.

Consider the concepts *force* and *pressure*. Ten-year-olds can be helped to acquire an intuitive understanding of force in terms of small bodies accelerating faster than larger bodies when the same steady push or pull is applied. And pressure can be thought of as push per square of area. It is, of course, the teacher's task to help pupils acquire these intuitive notions as they prefigure, so to speak, formal understanding, although while understanding remains at an intuitive level it will be restricted to a concrete context. With the advent of formal thinking, however, force can be considered in terms of the product of mass and acceleration, and pressure in terms of force per unit area. Turning to the concept of *gravity* we may note that the junior school pupil well understands from everyday experience that the earth pulls bodies to it. And, incidentally, it should be realised that with the coming of space travel the distinction between mass and weight is made much easier—at least intuitively. Thus children in the junior school and in the lower classes of a secondary school can understand intuitively, say, the term 'gravitational' as used in compound words where 'downhill movement of' under the pull of the earth is involved, e.g. gravitational flow of a glacier or other material. But not until the coming of formal operational thought can the pupil consider gravity in a formal sense, that is, as an intellectual construction indicating the magnitude of a force given by $\dfrac{km_1m_2}{d^2}$ (a frequently used notation).

Finally we may note that a whole new range of classifications becomes available in adolescence. The ten-year-old can classify, say, iron, wood and wool as primary products—although he may not use these actual words—for they are intuitive data. But not before the onset of formal operational thought, and some study of physics, will the pupil classify the subsidence and adiabatic heating of a high-altitude air mass, also rapid heat loss due to radiation at ground level on a clear night, as cases of temperature inversion.

It must be stressed, however, that we need to know far more about the thinking strategies which emerge in adolescence and which are termed 'formal operational' by Piaget .More information is needed about the characteristics of such strategies; the features in the environment that encourage their development; the conditions under which the individual can use, say, propositional logic, the proportionality scheme or certain motions of probability; the effect of content or the nature of the materials, or the situation involved in the task presented; and the effect of motivation Recent studies have suggested that formal operational thought may be less general than Piaget supposed and may be more specific to a wide variety of tasks in which a casual and logical analysis coincide.

James Hemming

15. Emotional and moral aspects of adolescence

The purpose of this chapter is to overview some of the factors influencing emotional and moral development in adolescence which have come to the fore during recent years. Emotional and moral aspects are considered together, because they are integrated in the perceptions, attitudes and behaviour of adolescents. The emotional and moral react on one another: the individual adolescent's feelings about himself and others affect his moral outlook; conversely, failure to arrive at a coherent system of personal values during the years of adolescence leads to emotional uncertainty and vulnerability to situational stress. Social relationships are also considered in their relevance to emotional and moral development. Indeed, 'emotional', 'moral' and 'social' may be described as entry words to fields of discourse that together describe a single area of interaction and development.

The total field is immense because physical development, hormonal influences, cognitive maturity, intelligence and perception are also closely involved in emotional and moral growth. But a limit must be drawn somewhere. This chapter will concern itself with setting the scene of contemporary adolescence, in contrast with the past, looking at some central concepts useful in describing adolescent development, and considering the special role of the school and the curriculum in the new situation. Moral development will receive particular attention in line with the increased interest in this field of late years.

The expanded milieu

The adolescent stage of growth was formerly conceived as a comparatively simple affair. The stability and security of childhood were regarded as rather suddenly shattered by the onset of puberty and the ensuing upsurge of development. This extension of capacity—physical, intellectual, emotional, social—was seen as projecting the individual into a period of *Sturm und Drang* during which the mature identity was painfully discovered, in preparation for the roles of adulthood: social, heterosexual, parental, occupational and civic. At the end of the period, the young person was expected to be safely back in the mainstream of life, ready to set the cycle going once more for the coming generation.

This description of adolescence remains valid so far as it goes but it has to be modified and extended to meet the new conditions now surrounding adolescents. The earlier description included a more or less intense revolt against the adult world, followed by a return to that world upon the attainment of adulthood. The adult world was conceived of as a neat pattern of social norms and personal and institutional authority in which the adolescents were a rather restless element whom time would bring back to conformity. For their part, the adolescents had the established social order as a well-defined frame of reference for their own struggles, challenges and explorations.

All this has changed. The uncertainties of adolescence, including the uncertainties of identity and status, now exist in a climate of general social uncertainty. Absolute authority has lost credibility, as much for adults as for adolescents. Furthermore, modern mass communications and rapid transport have established a global feedback system which ensures that every society in the network will change rapidly during an individual's years of adolescence so that the world surrounding a child at puberty is no longer there when he returns from his adolescent explorations to take up the responsibilities of adult life.

Nor is society—the constantly experienced setting of adolescent life—only beset by pressures of change; it is also challenged at its roots. Confidence in the status quo is weakening because formerly trusted authorities and hierarchies seem impotent to act constructively in the new situation, of which building international and multi-racial cooperation, population control, and the conservation of the human habitat on a planetary scale are only three of many issues with which 'the system' seems unable to cope.

All this influences adolescents profoundly. They are seeking a way of life and set of values in which they can feel confidence and with which they can identify themselves in their struggle towards self-actualisation. If they cannot find what they need they will seek to forge an 'alternative' system of values, or respond to the confusion they sense around them by nihilism and, possibly, iconoclastic destructiveness—both on the increase round the world.

This is a quite new situation, which calls for re-evaluation of the concepts which, in the past, provided us with a fairly clear pattern for understanding the adolescent phase. Now that adults, including the authority figures of society, are themselves in a perpetual condition of *Sturm und Drang* as they grope through present uncertainties towards an unknown future, adolescents, as never before, are thrown upon their own resources to make sense of their own lives. In the new context, emotional and moral growth becomes a personal achievement and not 'just' a matter of learning, imitating, identifying and maturing. At an increasingly early age, the adolescent is faced with selection between alternatives. The background to growth for our adolescents today is not *a* society or *a* culture, tidily stratified into upper, middle and lower classes, but a complicated congeries of subcultures, often in conflict with one another, with which the modern adolescent has somehow to interact to achieve personal integration and identity.

The interaction system and the self-concept

The classical way of regarding the adolescent was as an individual actualising his potentialities through a process of biological and psycho-social development. This still stands, but the modern approach goes beyond this to put more stress on interaction. The individual adolescent is, willy-nilly, drawn into a self-social interaction system such as has been described by Parsons and Bales (1956), Argyle (1969) and others. The influence of this interaction is especially formative for an adolescent because 'The self of the teenager particularly has the elements of an open-ended system.' (Otto, H. A. and S. T. 1969). The concept of growth taking place within a field of intense interaction is central to the contemporary outlook on adolescence.

In its turn, this view brings out the importance of the self-concept in the dynamics of growth, so that the former concentration on developmental factors has now to be supplemented by a proper awareness of how the self is perceived *by the individual concerned*. At one pole of the interaction system is the objective self of the adolescent—the individual observed in his environmental context. But, behind this behaving self, is the subjective self—the perception of self. This determines the quality and extent of interaction with the external world and modifies personal development as a whole, including emotional and moral aspects. Thus, an adolescent who perceives himself as inadequate, whether or not he is, in fact, inadequate, is liable either to withdraw from actual experience into fantasy or to project a false, compensatory image. In either case, the potentially formative interaction between individual and environment is diminished.

Hence, the nature of the self-concept has a powerful influence upon emotional and moral—as, indeed, upon all—development. An individual too much lacking in self-respect and self-confidence is likely to retreat from those very encounters upon which his continuing development depends. Or he may embark upon compensatory behaviour that reinforces the original inferiority.

We cannot here go into the processes by which the self-concept is originally formed. By adolescence it is well established, although modifiable. Suffice it to say that any unselected group of adolescents is likely to show the whole range, from unrealistic, depressed self-rejection to an objective self-acceptance and self-confidence. The ensuing interaction patterns are manifold and complicated. Gold and Douvan (1969) sum up the position: 'The level of an individual's self-esteem depends most heavily upon the evaluation he makes of the central components of himself and their integration. His own evaluation, in turn, depends mainly upon the evaluation reflected to him by the people who matter to him, by the standards of his reference groups and by the effectiveness of his self in helping him reach his goals. The continuing influence of adolescents' parents is evident here again. If an adolescent perceives that his parents are concerned for him, then his evaluation of himself is likely to be higher.'

The characteristics of any self-social interaction system are, it should be noted, likely to be self-perpetuating. Adolescents with assured self-confidence tend to be constantly reinforced in their strong position (Rosenberg 1965) while those who feel failures are likely to live up to their own expectations. The feeling tone of the experiencer tends to produce a feedback which confirms the feeling.

The problem is how to modify interaction systems that obstruct development towards maturity. Of some help here is the view that the attainment of mental health depends upon the fulfilment of a postulated 'true self' through the formative interaction between an understood, accepted, and trusted, self and the whole milieu of what is not the self (Rogers 1961; Maslow 1962, etc.). Since mental health is a concept that combines concepts of emotional, social and moral maturity, we have an indication here of how emotional and moral immaturity may be remedied by helping the adolescent to live *through* himself rather than in terms of the expectations of others. This is in line with modern educational principles generally. It is also, interestingly enough, in accord with the widespread feeling among adolescents that it is important to have the courage to 'do your own thing'. Kelly's personal construct theories (1955) are pertinent to this. Construct analysis seeks to find out the values an individual attaches to himself and others. If we can help him to a reasonable objectivity on both counts, we establish good conditions for continuing personal growth within the context of social life. Working at Tenterden Manor, George Lyward has arrived at similar conclusions in the treatment of high-grade maladjusted boys. From these various sources, and others, new insights on the emotional and moral development of adolescents are gradually emerging. We do not, any longer, expect to achieve formative results by concentrating on the dynamics of the individual in isolation but by helping the individual attain an objective self-confidence within the relationships of a formative social milieu. The person is both participant and product within a self-social system. 'The adolescent period', writes Ausubel (1966), 'is everywhere an interval of extensive and distinctive personality reorganisation.' The attainment of the valid self when both inner and outer worlds are in a state of flux is not an easy task for the adolescent. The full complexities of this situation require continuing study. We can here touch on only a few aspects.

Identity

A concept which has been much to the fore of late years in adolescent psychology, and now calls for re-examination, is *identity*. This concept overlaps to some extent with the self-concept, but is not synonymous with it. The sense of identity may be defined as an assured conviction about oneself within the social context (Carstairs 1963). It is a name for the awareness which brings the self-concept into relationship. Erikson (1950, 1968) has described adolescence in the modern world as particularly beset by a crisis of identity, which can lead to a confusion of values. Hence, a valid sense of identity forms part of the basis for moral and emotional maturity.

A difficulty arises because the objects for personal and social identification, through which a sense of identity is to be achieved, are today bewilderingly numerous, within the immediate social spectrum, and are often inconsistent with one another (Wall 1948). In earlier times, potential identifications were limited and conventionalised; today they are unlimited and open. Argyle (1967) writes: 'During adolescence, and during student life, there is still no need to decide on a particular identity, and young people are allowed to experiment with and play at various identities, before they finally commit themselves.'

The mass media and pop culture offer a wide range of identification figures, many of whom represent values and ways of life, including ways of feeling, quite different from those of the subculture in which personal life is set. This kaleidoscopic abundance of potential roles and identities, fed from both real and fantasy life, can be challenging and invigorating for the stronger personalities; for the weaker it may be overwhelming. Many young people feel, to quote one of them at a television interview, 'just lost'.

Another factor which makes the attainment of identity more difficult in the modern world is the sense of isolation, insignificance and alienation of the individual within the increasingly depersonalised financial-technical-political complex that society has become. Durkheim long ago saw this situation as imminent, and it is now acutely with us. Alienation is not total, or only rarely so, because individuals build their own groupings as some security over against the technological juggernaut which they are forced to serve, but do not understand. Alienation *vis-à-vis* the forces and bureaucracies governing the greater society is, however, quite disturbing and disruptive enough to upset security of identity.

As a difficult element in the emotional and moral development of adolescence, the identity crisis is likely to stay with us. We should perhaps accept this and add 'overcoming uncertainty about identity' to the list of developmental tasks that have come to be recognised as characteristic of the adolescent phase (Havighurst 1953, etc.). One point we need to notice is the increasing complexity of the task of attaining identity, which suggests the need for more educational help to young people to clarify their identity within the various groups in which they play a part. We should also notice that here, as in many other aspects of adolescent life, the very same problems that strengthen the robust may prove too much for the frail.

Conformity–nonconformity

The adolescent's choice of identifications has acquired an extra dimension from the range of conformity–nonconformity within society. It is an aspect of the milieu of modern youth which is receiving close study. All that can be attempted here is a general outline of a complex and changing situation which adds both vigour and risk to the moral and emotional development of adolescents.

A degree of nonconformity has always been recognised as an aspect of the challenge the adolescent throws out to constraining authority. What is remarkable about the present is the extent of the conformity–non-conformity continuum, and the range of behaviour that is tolerated by society for the adolescent and, indeed, for others.

This permissive situation is the logical correlate of the open, pluralist society which has emerged during the past few decades. Once concepts of absolute authority had lost their hold, and personal fulfilment became a recognised social value, then the exploratory extension of personal freedom of choice and behaviour—which is what is happening in the 'permissive society'—was inevitable. It was also inevitable that young people should explore the possibilities to a greater extent than adults.

Hence, the need to make a bid for independence by rebellion—long identified as a characteristic of adolescence—is now served by an unprecedented wealth of outlets. The individual may follow the tracks of comparative conformity, limiting his revolt to small-scale conflicts with immediate authority; or he may drop right out of society, for good, or for a time. In between lie a whole range of possibilities, including getting a haversack and a bedroll and thumbing and working your way around the world. An interesting variation is the insider drop-out, who does his A-levels or a job with steady application while demonstrating his nonconformity through clothes, hairstyle, sexual behaviour, drugs, or the general way he spends his leisure.

There have, of course, always been drop-outs, but formerly, their ranks were mostly made up of the failures and incompetents. The big difference today is that some of the most able and intelligent young people are also dropping out—adolescent challenge merges with, and matures into, social responsibility and social protest.

Describing conformity and nonconformity in terms of overt social behaviour is of course unsound because nonconforming subcultures—nonconforming behaviour generally—always attract conformist personalities who solve their ambivalent needs for revolt and conformity by identifying intensively with a rebellious group. Indeed, many way-out groups, like the Hells Angels, *demand* conformity (Thompson 1967), as distinct from the looser groups of nonconformists, among whom 'doing your own thing' is a declared value. Nor does nonconformity necessarily imply a leftist ideology. The skinheads, for example, were racialist, and reactionary about the role of women. The revolt of youth has its own variety and offers a range of attitudes and groups (Mays 1965).

When we consider together the urge of youth to rebel—to escape, to be adventurous—and the current openings for unconventional life-styles, what is remarkable is how strong the pull towards conformity remains. The picture of youth as in total revolt is a quite false presentation. For every out-and-out rebel, whether of the blatantly destructive or of the intelligently critical kind, there are many others in the same age-range and situation who accept without question the expectations of those in authority. At the height of any campus revolt the majority of students press on with their ordinary lives. It is only when those in authority behave with extreme violence or insensitivity that more than the activist minority recognise the struggle going on as something in which they have a part. The real position is that there is in modern society a climate of revolt, but also a great deal of conformity.

The number of conformist adolescents puts in question the popular assumption of an exceptional 'generation gap' today. That such a gap exists between some young people and some adults is obvious. Communication may break down completely. But in other families the communication and cooperation are of a frankness and friendliness which seem to be far in advance of the norms of 1910, or even 1930, when, for the most part, no communication between the generations on personal matters was expected, and the role accorded to young people was not to discuss but to obey.

The actual position is that the whole of society is in a turmoil of readjustment, during what might be called this post-autocracy era, and all people are taking up positions on the conformity–nonconformity continuum, with a majority of all age-groups seeking security in the storm by clinging to one pattern of conformity or another. This brings the avant garde youth, who are pressing on along the permissive axis—involvement, participation, shared decision-making, cooperative action, etc.—into sharp conflict with the solid mass of conformist adults who want to retain traditional authority systems, and are increasingly insecure because the authenticity of these systems is becoming less convincing all the time. This struggle for the future is confused by the existence of a minority of extremists who are not prepared to try to think their way through the complexities of the present and seek to smash and shout their way through instead. Their influence is amplified by the exaggerated attention paid to their activities by the mass media (Halloran, Elliott and Murdock 1970).

The situation is as one would expect on the basis of interactionist theory—the range of conformity–nonconformity existing among the young also exists among their elders. Sexual behaviour is an instance of this. The young are not as casual as some suppose (Schofield 1965; Corry 1967), nor are adults as conformist as some like to assume (Kinsey *et al.* 1948, 1953). The position is that prudery and socio-religious taboos have lost their domination of the human sexual impulse which is now regarded, by a proportion of all age-groups, as something of value in human relationships and experience rather than as a naughty indulgence (Heron 1963; Greet 1966).

It may well be true that young people are conducting their lives more frankly than adults in terms of these changes of attitude; it is not true that young people invented the changes. Young people are, as Margaret Mead has pointed out, nearer the future than their elders (Mead 1970) and some of them understand what is going on better than their parents, who may become rather resentful and vocal in consequence. But the actual situation is mis-described as Youth *v.* Adult. We are, rather, caught up in changes which some of all ages accept and seek to understand but which others of all ages seek to reject.

The spread of conformity–nonconformity through society brings us to the crux of the matter in the consideration of emotional and moral development among adolescents today. Their problem is to achieve emotional maturity and moral clarity within a society whose dominant characteristics are instability, variety and moral confusion. For the well-founded, secure personalities there is a wealth of experience available, combined with an incentive to think, which nourishes their robustness; for the frail and insecure the task of coming to terms with it all may well be beyond their powers, unless extra help is forthcoming to see them through.

We also have to consider how all that is going on is perceived by children—both directly and through the mass media—as they move into and through the adolescent stage. It is a curious world that the young adolescent looks out at and measures himself against. How is he to attain equanimity within it? How is he, to use the adolescents' own language, to 'get himself together'?

A new look at socialisation

The process that has been depended upon in the past to help young people achieve a viable set of values within society has been called 'socialisation'. Sandström (1961) writes: 'The general term "socialisation" is used to describe the process by which a young person adopts forms of behaviour that are in accordance with the norms and values of the adult environment. The concept is closely connected with the intricate problems of bringing up children to become good citizens of the community to which they belong.' Elkin (1960) more briefly states: 'We may define socialisation as the process by which someone learns the ways of a given society or social group so that he can function within it.'

Such quotations show that, even so recently as a decade ago, socialisation was commonly regarded as education for conformity; social maturity was equated with a good adaptation to the status quo. It is now clear that conformity alone is not enough. Social maturity—which brings in the concept of social responsibility—goes beyond acceptance and calls for the intelligent reassessment of social norms to meet new situations, and for a critical examination of the goals of society, and the roles of individuals within society. The concept of participation, for example, viewed as the appropriate relationship between individual and community within a democratic society, implies a constant renovation of aims, and modification of action, brought about by the confident application of every individual's thinking to the resolution of difficulties, and the improvement of social functioning. This sort of interaction—which is valued and spreading in our kind of society—is only one example of the active quality of social adjustment which is replacing passive acceptance as the desired social norm.

In these circumstances, the expectation that socialisation in terms of the *necessary* values of a democratic society will happen of itself is likely to be disappointed. An individual moving from childhood into adolescence is not subject to a single socialisation process but to a battery of processes in competition for his allegiance. The processes by which young people learn about the values in the community draw them into some kind of relationship with society but do not necessarily socialise them. The sub-cultural values that they absorb may be the antithesis of the values which the society as a whole depends on for its continuance; or they may so conflict with the individual's felt needs that they are discounted.

In a simple, static society, the value system in terms of which the child is socialised forms an integrated self-consistent structure of ideas, symbols and derived values. Children growing up in our society receive no such bonus for personal security but have to scramble for what they can find with which to structure their personal lives. If the result is sometimes rather rickety we can hardly be surprised. We can, in fact, no longer rely on a compact structure of social influences to socialise our young people. We have, rather, to train them to deal with a weakly structured system and help them to attain a well-structured individuality by autonomous selection from what is available. Society is not a steady current but a number of cross-currents. To go with the current takes an individual nowhere. Today everybody has to learn to swim. This calls for a new approach to the process of socialisation—and, therefore, to education.

How are we to find outlets for the energies of young people, who are bigger, stronger and fitter than ever before, in such a way as to develop and socialise them within the context of a fragmented but dynamic society? We may, perhaps, learn some of the answers from research recently conducted by Professor Philip Mayer and his wife among the Red Xhosa of the Transkei (1970). In this community, the thirteen to twenty age-group forms a youth culture in which, within a context of mutual responsibility, the young people socialise one another. The aggression and status-seeking of the young males are canalised and controlled through participation in organised cudgel-fighting. Sex-life is controlled by principles of behaviour upheld by the young people themselves, which ensure against premature pregnancies—the permitted sex-play excludes penetration—*and against the rejection of less-favoured individuals.*

Throughout, the socialising influence is mutual consideration and concern, which permits a ready outlet for adolescent needs while securing limits on behaviour that protect the individual. A cudgel-fight among juniors is stopped by seniors before a contestant gets hurt, or a fighter may shout 'Enough!' at any time without loss of face. Sexual relations are managed with a delicacy that acknowledges that an individual's feelings should always be considered.

Some interesting points of contrast and comparison with our own culture arise from this study. We have, in the past, attempted to socialise the sexual impulse among adolescents, and the physical aggression of young males, by suppression or sublimation, whereas, in Xhosa society, these impulses are used as the *means* to socialisation. Again, we have tended to assume that socialisation could take place only in supervised situations.

The points where the Mayers' study has new insights to offer are exactly those where socialisation is failing in our society—in the control of sex and violence and in the 'management' of our young people. Adolescent sex-life is in the throes of a kind of emergent uncertainty; the under-used vigour and status-hunger of young males is breaking out in all kinds of inconvenient ways, and the young are making ever-wider claims to self-government. This quandary points towards the need for a new approach to the socialisation of our young people—socialisation through the use of personal powers in place of socialisation by conditioning and denial; socialisation through the comradeship, interaction and responsibility of participant action, in place of socialisation through external pressure.

The problem of how to organise socialisation within our changing society would seem then to have three aspects. We have to find ways of using the powers of adolescents in the service of their own development; we have to provide community experience for young people in which the abiding values of our society are manifest in the way of life offered, and we have to develop personal moral insight to a point when valid decisions may be made in the circumstances of moral conflict or unexpected situations. All these are educational issues. Even though much of adolescent experience is gained outside the school, it is at school that the essential values of our society may be differentiated from the general confusion, that personal confidence may be developed, and moral insight fostered, through a common—though not standardised—community life. The last two sections of this chapter will, accordingly, touch on some of the specifically educational aspects of moral and emotional development.

Developmental morality

Since Piaget (1932) sought to show that moral awareness develops in stages, as the cognitive powers of the child expand, there has been a gradual acceptance of the idea that moral development is of the same order as other development: it is the outcome of a process of learning, maturation and interaction. We start with the dependent, egocentric baby; we hope to finish with the independent, morally mature adult. While the idea of developmental morality has been gaining ground, the concept of external moral authority as the basis for moral growth has, inevitably, been losing its credibility. The developmental aim has ceased to be obedience to external rules. In its place we have the concept of moral autonomy—the discovery and internalisation of values and principles that carry conviction because they have been confirmed by personal experience.

The work of Gesell and his associates (1946, 1956) and Bull (1969) gives support for sequential stages of moral development, with moral autonomy as the highest attainment. Kohlberg (1968) has postulated six stages, at any one of which an individual or a culture may become fixated: 'In some cultures people eventually pass through all the initial stages and reach stage six, the highest level, while in other cultures the highest level achieved may be stage two or three. The order of the stages is always the same because it follows an inner cognitive logic in the individual's comprehension of society.'

Such work implies that moral capacity is educable, and that it may be stunted when ideas and experiences necessary for its fruition are absent. How far an individual's moral development may be limited by inherited insufficiencies is not known and need not concern us here. The essentials with which we have to deal are that moral autonomy is the appropriate moral development for an open, changing society, and that our educational aim should be to maximise the opportunities for such development. This especially applies to the adolescent phase, because moral maturity is not attainable before the cognitive capacities appropriate to it have been acquired; and because, lacking appropriate moral education during adolescence, the individual is vulnerable to fixation at a premature stage of development.

One may summarise the outcomes of the various streams of enquiry in terms of three broad stages of moral development—the dependent, egocentric stage of responding to pressure; the socialised stage of imitating and conforming; and the independent stage of judging and innovating within a context of responsible social awareness. Moral maturity depends on a satisfactory transition from the egocentric to the social-conformist stage and from the social-conformist stage to the stage of moral autonomy.

The important transition from conformity to autonomy can hardly be attained without both individual effort *and* educational support. The process is one of dynamic interaction. Kay (1968) writes: 'Individuals must grow from the stage of social morality to that of personal morality. *Yet they must live in a social context while doing so.*' (my italics). But how is order to come from confusion? As we have seen, the 'social context' does not today offer a single voice of social conformity but a cacophony of discordant ideas.

Before seeking an answer to that question we have another conundrum to face. If moral autonomy is regarded as the desirable norm, how are we to prevent the moral order of society splitting into a host of individual moralities? This problem is not as difficult as it at first appears. Firth (1951), Kluckhohn (1951), Ginsberg (1956) and others have pointed out that there are certain values governing behaviour that underlie all human societies— they form a kind of deep structure of moral necessity without which productive human association is impossible. In addition, there are the values inherent in any particular social system, as, for instance, regard for the individual in a democracy. There are, further, situational values that are the correlates of purpose. Mountain climbing, for example, requires, by the very nature of the activity, courage, cooperation and willingness to make sacrifices for the common good. Thus, people of well-developed moral insight, living in the same kind of society, and facing similar situations of personal and social life, are unlikely to disagree about fundamental moral principles, however difficult it may be to apply these principles in new and unexpected situations.

The nub of the matter is the education of moral capacity. Wilson and his associates at the Farmington Trust have been studying what skills are necessary as a precondition to moral maturity (1967). The 'moral components' identified are the ability to identify with others (PHIL); insight into one's own and others' feelings (EMP); the mastery of relevant knowledge (GIG); the ability to formulate rules and principles to guide behaviour involving others (DIK); the ability to formulate rules and principles for the guidance of personal life (PHRON); and the ability to live up to the rules and principles formulated (KRAT). Wilson and his associates regard this list as, at present, tentative, but the actual components to be included in the list are not so educationally significant as the idea that moral development can be studied in terms of component skills, and that these skills are educable. Techniques for awakening moral awareness are the basis of the Schools Council's Moral Education Curriculum project.

We must here digress for a moment to consider the present status of moral education through religious belief, which was dominant until very recently. When religious beliefs carried almost universal conviction, the implied close tie between religious belief and morality had some social force. But such a tie becomes a hindrance rather than a help to the moral education of the community *as a whole* once religious absolutes become subjects of controversy, and once religious beliefs—as distinct from interest in religion—lose their grip upon the human intellect. Bull writes: 'The traditional binding of morality to religion has a fatal defect—that religious decline must lead to moral rejection.' In a recent ITA survey of Britain and Northern Ireland, those of the sample who were certain of the existence of God, and those who expressed uncertainty, divided almost exactly 50:50. Religious conviction tended to decline among younger subjects, with 64 per cent of the sixteen to twenty-four age-group categorising themselves as 'Not very religious' or 'Not at all religious'. Other studies, for example Eppel and Eppel (1966) and *Enquiry* (Schools Council 1969), also indicate a secularisation of moral outlook. Allowing for the fact that those with religious convictions feel morally strengthened by these convictions, it is nevertheless unrealistic to regard religious teaching as the main incentive to moral behaviour at a time when the authority of specific religious belief is influential among only a minority of the community.

Combining the insights of psychology, sociology and anthropology, the task of helping adolescents to attain moral maturity in a changing, confused society may be simplified to four conditions for facilitating moral development:

1.   Help with gaining self-respect and identity so that the individual may be brought into a courageous, participant relationship with others.
2.   Education in those skills upon which the attainment of moral maturity depends.
3.   Experience of living in a community where the values of a humane, responsible, democratic community govern relationships and daily life.
4.   The development of understanding and concern about the wider community—social involvement.

The only way of assuring that these conditions are met for all adolescents is to make our secondary schools into places where the fulfilling of these conditions is given a high priority, if not the highest priority. Miller (1967) has stated that schools 'now have to provide the social environment in which young people may find a way of life'. This view has gradually been gaining ground over against the more limited aims of the past. In responding to it, the schools may perhaps help to solve, through a single reorientation, a host of problems that are now being dealt with piecemeal.

Reality in the secondary school

Musgrove (1964) has described secondary and higher education as a conspiracy to stop young people growing up. If this does less than justice to many schools and institutions of higher education, at least it draws attention to a state of affairs about which young people are themselves complaining with mounting irritation. Evan Hadingham, the sixth-former who edited *Youth Now* (1970), a well-produced resumé of the current youth scene, echoes a number of sixth-form manifestoes when he writes: 'Education is not simply a matter of passing exams and reaching university, but of playing a responsible, active part in social and political life.' There is a feeling among non-academic adolescents also that schooling is not sufficiently about life.

This hunger for a closer contact with 'reality' is an important motivation in the attainment of moral and emotional maturity. Young people participate in a number of interaction systems—family, peer groups, school, society. The school, at the secondary stage, should be playing a major role in helping young people to interpret themselves in relation to these groups and these groups in relation to themselves. To grow mature personally, young people need a valid perception of themselves, others, society, the wider environment, and the nature of the human struggle in which they are participating. Hence, education should not be something experienced over against the world but should be an initiation into life, through which perceptions and concepts are extended and clarified.

An analogy may be drawn with what has happened to sex education. Although adolescents are sexually mature, sex was, until, say, a quarter of a century ago, excluded from the curriculum. There was no teaching about sex, no discussion of sexual relationships, and only 'safe' texts were set for English Literature examinations. This precluded the development of values in this area from school influence. Nowadays, sexual information, the discussion of values in sexual relationships, and texts with a frankly sexual content are included in most secondary schools. Many young people complain that sex education has not yet gone far enough, but at least this important interest of adolescents is accorded a place in education.

Today the bowdlerisation takes another form—lack of frankness and relevance in teaching about the kind of society in which we are living. To close this gap, the curriculum has to be integrated and extended in such a way as to provide a valid perspective on life past, a clear understanding of life present, and a sense of responsibility for the future. Such a curriculum can give the individual adolescent a sense of significance and participation as a person within a process of change and emergence. Without a valid perspective, personal life in a confused society easily loses contact with adequately rich interactions and may become meaningless. Apathy and cynicism are devoid of potential for personal development.

The slowness of secondary education in general to respond to the contemporary adolescents' contemporary needs has produced two consequences around the world, both of which are closely involved with moral and emotional development. One is a crisis of motivation, a weariness with the academic grind, an evaluation of school as 'alright'— but no more. The other is an upsurge of energy and experiment in an effort to give secondary education a closer relevance to the modern world, *including a closer moral relevance*. In 1960, Bruner wrote: 'A curriculum ought to be built around the great issues, principles and values that a society deems worthy of the continual concern of its members.' In the decade since, there has been struggling but definite advance in experiments towards this end, including the New Social Studies being worked out in New Zealand, the Curriculum Laboratory at Goldsmiths College, and the Humanities Project of the Schools Council.

Bruner and associates (1965) have recently been working on a curriculum which both transmits 'an organised body of knowledge and skill to a new generation' and also seeks to achieve five goals:

1.   To give our pupils respect for and confidence in the powers of their own minds.

2.   To give them respect, moreover, for the powers of thought concerning the human condition, man's plight, and his social life.

3.   To provide them with a set of workable models that make it simpler to analyse the nature of the social world in which they live and the condition in which man finds himself.

4.   To impart a sense of respect for the capacities and plight of man as a species, for his origins, for his potential, for his humanity.

5.   To leave the student with a sense of the unfinished business of man's evolution.

Such a curriculum synthesises cognitive, emotional and moral aspects. Its appropriate setting is a school community in which the same principles of relationship and responsibility obtain as those included in the curriculum. To combine an appropriate curriculum with an appropriate school community opens up for the adolescent a rich developmental experience with which he can identify because he recognises what it offers as the means to his personal fulfilment. As Wall (1968) has stated: 'We should remind ourselves that many of the most important educational aims are only indirectly a curriculum matter, and that many strictly curricular aims are only likely to be achieved if the framework and climate of the educational institution is perceived by adolescents to meet their needs as well as to embody and exemplify the ends the actual subject-matter proposes as "good".'

The pigeonholing of human potential into subjects, skills, and other categories is important in itself as a means of clarifying what we have to do, and what we are doing, to help adolescents grow up. But it is on the quality of the synthesis—the total experience—that our hopes for promoting moral and emotional maturity must rest. Well-integrated personalities are an unlikely outcome of fragmented curricula.

J. B. Mays

16. Social aspects of adolescence

Until comparatively recent times most discussion and research into adolescence has been undertaken either from a physiological or psychological standpoint or from a combination of both. The reasons for this are obvious enough and need not concern us here. It is only in the past few years, perhaps more precisely in the last quarter of a century, that a specifically sociological account of the nature of adolescence in contemporary industrial society has been forthcoming. The rapid rise to popularity of sociology in the last decade has contributed to this but there are clearly other structural factors which have conspired to effect a new orientation: most notably the emergence of conspicuous youth cultures and of the adolescent group in its own right as a consumption unit of considerable and growing economic interest.

It is not so much that a sociological perspective on the nature of adolescence has overthrown earlier psychological and physiological approaches or in any way invalidated them. It is rather a coalescence of the older with the newer insights which have deepened our understanding of the whole developmental stage as a many-faceted process in which the social elements are often of equal and sometimes even of prime importance. The modern approach which combines sociological with psychological and physiological concepts is undoubtedly a great step forward and one which will obviously become the future orthodoxy. Few authorities have made a richer contribution to this new socio-cultural approach than Professor Wall who, though starting from a mainly psychological base, has consistently emphasised the importance of social influences and expectations as determinants of youthful behaviour. Had this volume not been conceived as a tribute to his work, he himself would have been the more worthy choice as author for this particular chapter. However, as one who has been deeply influenced by Professor Wall's thinking, I welcome the opportunity to act as it were as his deputy, partly because it gives me an occasion to say the kind of things about youth and society that I want to say, but more especially because it enables me, in the role of a contributor, to discharge some of my indebtedness to an original and stimulating scholar.

Social adolescence

The idea has steadily been emerging that there is a phase of social, individual and group life which deservedly could be termed the period of 'social adolescence'. This involves the idea of the young person undergoing a stage of social preparation which is necessary for the future enactment of his or her occupational role: in fact a kind of vocational apprenticeship. As Musgrove (1964) pointed out, youths in this country in the nineteenth century attained adult status earlier than today largely because of their obvious economic value as wage-earners and producers. It is because more skills have to be learned and at much greater depth than hitherto that the learning phase has had to be extended into years which used to be regarded as young manhood and young womanhood. With an ever growing body of scientific and technical knowledge we can expect that this intermediate social apprenticeship phase in which increasing numbers enroll for further and higher education will become even more protracted in the future unless positive steps are taken to restructure the situation. In Britain the lowering of the age of legal maturity in 1969, following the recommendations of the Latey Committee Report, may be seen as one such move to prevent adolescence, as it were, from invading the period of biologically and psychologically accredited adulthood. But such legislation will not of itself be enough to overcome problems which students and apprentices still have to face as a result of their economic dependency and associated low social status. Stresses and strains may indeed be exacerbated by the consequent role confusion which a change in one area can set up in another aspect of a youth's life. This can be illustrated by considering the changes in relationship which will be forced upon school teachers when they are obliged to deal with senior pupils who are fully enfranchised and hence can exert an indirect influence on the very institution which for so long has insisted on its paternalistic role *vis-à-vis* all its scholars. Similarly in universities and colleges of education the old notion of a student being *in statu pupillari* will need to be drastically revised.

We can in fact already see the stirrings of rebellion produced, to some extent, by youth's earlier grasp of autonomy in the demands that college and university students and, more recently, sixth-formers in secondary schools and lycées have been stridently making for a greater share in the management of educational institutions and in reactions against disciplinary codes and procedures.

Similarly, trends towards earlier marriage, especially for girls, will tend to exert dysfunctional pressures on existing institutions. Schoolgirl mothers will become more common, as married students have already become, and considerable tact will have to be employed in dealing with them, all of which suggests that a fresh basis for pupil-teacher and lecturer-student relationships will need to be evolved in the near future unless misunderstanding and lack of sympathy are to increase the risk of aliena-tion.

Another important consequence of longer school life and of protracted 'social adolescence' could well be that different social classes and cultural groups will grow closer to one another in a variety of ways and become much more sympathetic with each other's viewpoints. Prolonged educa-tion and formal training will almost inevitably make for common experi-ences, and, in Britain, the expansion of comprehensive schooling and a projected raising of the school-leaving age until the seventeenth birthday could well work effectively in the same direction. The growing demo-cratic sentiments that are now apparent amongst young people in general may well be the first fruits of such social changes and in time inter-class tensions and hostilities which *inter alia* are the cause of some youthful vandalism and crime might well be reduced. So, at least, we are entitled to hope. At the same time, more common consumption habits seem to tend in the same direction towards a new synthesis between traditional middle-class and working-class cultural behaviour and life styles. The immediate effect of all this may be seen in the blurring of class distinctions in dress and even in leisure-time pursuits. Young artisans and college students often wear similar clothes, behave in comparable ways and often amuse them-selves by dancing and devotion to 'pop' music. So much is this the case that some social commentators have suggested that middle-class standards and values have been undermined by the invasion upwards of working-class attitudes and mores. By the same token, traditional working-class standards are seen by other critics as in process of being vitiated by common values sustained by the mass media and expanding literacy resulting from universal minimal education. However, whatever the short-term effects of this cultural diffusion, in the long run we may expect that one of the significant results will be to lessen inter-generational misunderstandings all round, since these were, in many cases, I suspect, closely associated with social class differences in the first place.

There has also, it is widely agreed, been a change in recent years in sexual behaviour in every social group, but it is perhaps most noticeable that the more permissive atmosphere of society in general, coupled with wider availability of contraception and an emphasis on pleasure as an end in itself (the ethic of the mass media), positively encourages the idea of sexual experience outside and before marriage. Whether moralists like it or not, there is a new attitude of acceptance of sexual experience, even towards sexual experimentation, which is undermining traditional fears and inhibitions and resulting, among other things, in a far more active feminine role in sexual relations. It also generates pressure in the direction of greater equality between the sexes which has obvious consequences for the institutions of marriage and the family and for economic affairs. I am of the opinion, moreover, that the widespread undermining of social authority which is frequently commented on nowadays is partly the outcome of this new pattern of marital relationships which the insistence on equality between the sexes has rapidly been bringing about in the last half-century or so. Children who see their fathers treated as equals, and sometimes even as inferiors, are much less likely to accept authority in other institutions such as school, church, college or work-place. Perhaps the emergence of what is nowadays called 'unisex' clothing and hairstyles is also related to the recent diminution of masculine superiority in most social milieux.

Peer groups

Eisenstadt (1956) and others have pointed to another equally important function which the adolescent phase plays in modern democratic social systems. That is, to give young people experience in coping with egalitarian relationships with their immediate peers and contemporaries apart from the normal setting in which they are invariably subordinate to adults. Having learned in association with parents, teachers and older kinsfolk to come to some kind of terms with authority and to adjust to externally imposed codes of behaviour, they need a period in which they relate to others as equals and so learn to stand on their own feet. Only in age-homogeneous peer groups can true equality be found and thus it is as members of such youth groups that vital steps towards ultimate autonomy and independence have to be made. So the college sorority, the street-corner gang, the orthodox youth club, the students' union, the spontaneous sports team, the 'click', personal friends, mates or pals fulfil an important social and psychological function which must necessarily to some extent make their members feel themselves distinct from other groups and generations. A great amount of emotion is usually invested in peer-group and friendship relationships at the adolescent stage. The group solidarity and companionship often generate a warmth and romanticism which give youth an almost transcendental glow and rapture never to be regained. At such times youth is seen as a self-evident good and the age-grade itself is totemised. The outcome of this kind of excess is often psychological regression of the individuals involved and either political exploitation, as with Fascist youth groups, or economic exploitation, as in profit-motivated capitalist societies.

The creative role of youth

Thus, for a whole variety of reasons youth is seen to be a necessary and socially valuable (one might go even further and say an invaluable) stage in human development. As a result, the attitudes and values which young people acquire during their developmental phase will have a vital, even critical impact on the whole future of society and, ultimately, of civilisation itself. This is probably what is usually meant when people describe university students as the conscience of society, for in a very real sense the new ideas which emerge and the reappraisals that each rising generation make of traditional standards will become socially active in the modified institutions that develop in the future. For example, it was the war-weary and domestically deprived fathers and mothers who, in the nineteen-fifties, produced the permissive children of the sixties who succeeded in giving society a new look and in producing a massive, hedonistically based pop youth culture. The relaxation of parental discipline and the conscious emphasis on friendship as the sole and proper foundation for all relationships within the family, and indeed outside it, has led to criticism and rejection of authority-based relationships already referred to, and to a self-conscious stress being laid upon mutual toleration and a live-and-let-live ethic in all human relationships. This appears to be the foundation upon which teenage morality is substantially based.

In the light of the foregoing analysis it becomes abundantly clear that what may seem in their beginnings as nothing more than campus quarrels and provocations of legitimated authority systems in such a country as the United States may, a decade or so later, prove to be turning points in world attitudes and, because America is so powerful and so important a state, in world politics. In the last analysis it is what men believe that shapes society; in the long run it is philosophies, religions and ideologies which decide our future destiny. The cloud no larger than a man's hand may come to fill the sky. The dreams of brotherhood, the search for genuine equality, the moral rejection of war as the logical extension of politics, which, in however inchoate and cloudy a state, are active in most of the universities of the Western world may yet, in the hindsight of history, be seen as the creative growth-points of a new and emergent moral order.

In a sense post-World War II youth first served notice of discontent on its elders when the beatniks of San Francisco openly rejected and opted out from the materialistic culture which their parents accepted as normal and desirable. That was a score of years ago, and, while drop-out tendencies are by no means a thing of the past, there is a fresh, more life-affirming spirit observable in the vanguard of those seriously committed young people who today have dared to launch what is clearly a middle-class rebellion against bourgeois values and bourgeois culture. While this may still be only a minority and trend-setting movement in Britain, where in any case the social system is not hopelessly frustrating, it may well, in the end, eclipse in importance the greater majority of young people who are clearly law-abiding conformists concerned more with their own standard of living and occupational security than with the great task of setting the world to rights.

Conformist youth

Various research enquiries in recent years have drawn attention to this somewhat tame and uncritical body of youth which identifies with the status quo and in the main happily accepts the standards and values of the parental generation. Douvan and Adelson (1966), in a very comprehensive study of a 3,000-strong group of American adolescents between the ages of fourteen and sixteen, have revealed the remarkable degree of conformity which characterises the majority of teenagers even in a society which must be undergoing continual change. Peck *et al.*'s (1960) Prairie City enquiry also showed that, far from being eclipsed by peer-group and other external influences, a substantial number of young people still turn to their parents for guidance, and above all as models on which to base their own behaviour. Thelma Veness's (1962) study of a group of students attending day-release classes in England confirms the general picture of conformity, realistic aspiration and unadventurousness which the larger studies have highlighted.

It is important to realise, then, when considering the more striking and newsworthy manifestations of adolescence, that the bulk are neither drop-outs nor deviants, neither delinquents nor rebels. Rather are they average run-of-the-mill boys and girls who, as Douvan and Adelson say, 'invoke neither grief nor wonder' and as a consequence 'all too often escape our notice' as social commentators. Such an undistinguished portrait leads those who, like Friedenberg (1962), deplore the vanishing of the 'true adolescent' from the scene, the ardent youth, that is to say, who faces life 'with love and defiance' in his heart, to draw dismal conclusions regarding the future of our civilisation. But more recent events indicate that the creative radicalism of youth and their ability to respond whole-heartedly to big causes are far from being extinct. The young radicals of the university campuses of the USA, Spain, Japan and elsewhere cannot all be dismissed as half-baked anarchists or Maoist and neo-Marxist agitators merely concerned to overthrow the existing régimes. Although there is a touch of bloody-mindedness and hell-raising in some aspects of student demonstrations and unrest, there are also a considerable number of thoughtful and sensitive young men and women who want to break through the corruptions, the hypocrisies and the shams of our politically divided and morally compromised societies in the hope that together they will be able to create a new, more truly democratic and morally sound community for the future. We may quarrel with the methods. We may think that sometimes they are biting the hands that fed them, that they gravely oversimplify the issues and are naïvely unsophisticated, but when young men in France and Czechoslovakia commit public suicide to show their devotion to their ideals we cannot remain unmoved or dismiss such events as merely hysterical.

Service by youth

At a less dramatic level we have seen in recent years how thousands of young people in Britain have risen to the challenge of personal action and involvement in such causes as the elimination of poverty and bad housing, care of the aged and physically handicapped, famine relief and service to refugees. Such institutions in this country as Child Poverty Action, Shelter, Young Volunteers, International Voluntary Service and Oxfam, to name only some of the most widely known of such ventures, have already received loyal and generous support from young people of both sexes and of various social classes. There is probably enough idealistic yeast to leaven the whole adolescent lump and the more ponderous middle-rangers may well in time come to share some of the enthusiasms of the activists and make their own contribution to social reform in terms of realistic com-promise.

    All this is, of course, highly speculative. What is not speculative and is extremely important in any sociological analysis of youth is the idea that individuals are located along a continuum which stretches from rebellion to over-conformity, from activism to quiescence, and that, viewed as a social process, the adolescent and immediately post-adolescent stages contain elements of both change and stability, of tradition and innovation. Education—the process of youthful socialisation into the existing traditions of a culture—must never be completely successful. There must always be room for divergence, for Liam Hudson's 'creative divergers' to pioneer new pathways and break fresh ground. But certain basic tasks remain unchanging and unchangeable. Each generation, as Havighurst and Wall and others have seen, is inevitably faced by the same fundamental problems and is called on to make achievement in relation to three major areas of human growth.

Developmental tasks

Havighurst (1953) in his pioneering essay has listed ten developmental tasks which every youth growing up to maturity in our contemporary industrial culture is obliged to attempt to master. Professor Wall (1955), following Havighurst, speaks of the four main goals which confront those between the ages of thirteen and twenty-five. He lists them in this way: the achievement of

1.   A social self, 'oriented to others, aware of a place in society, of duties as well as privileges, and in general emancipated from egocentric dependence on parents or indeed on others';
2.   A sexual self, 'capable of a range of feeling from friendly indifference to deep involvement with a member of the opposite sex, adequate adjustment in marriage and the ability to found and care for a family';
3.   A working self, 'essential not only to economic independence but as a basis of self-respect and self-knowledge';
4.   'An interpretation of life, philosophical, religious, political, vaguely or clearly formulated, something by reference to which major decisions can be taken and attitudes of others understood.'

As Douvan and Adelson (1966) have pointed out in their very perceptive study of adolescents in American society, there is still a very considerable difference between the ways in which males and females conceptualise their own future roles. Boys tend to be deeply concerned with work and with preparing themselves for their future careers, while girls, though not unmindful of the fact that they will have to take jobs outside the home before, during and after marriage, nevertheless seem to be more deeply concerned with the qualitative and personal aspects of their future lives. In spite of growing egalitarianism, the culturally pre-scribed and generally acceptable male and female roles are still divergent in certain respects. Stress is more on equality of status between men and women than on identity of role. As a result, as Douvan and Adelson have argued, there are two adolescent crises of identity associated with the two different self-images—the masculine and the feminine—and this fact has to be borne in mind whenever we are considering the relationship between developmental tasks, social role-playing and their educational con-comitants.

The achievement of generalised goals may be used to determine the degree of an individual's adult competence but cannot be regarded as a steady and uniform process either within the life of an individual or within the community as a whole. Different strata and milieux will develop different norms and lay emphasis in divergent directions. However, it seems to me that what is envisaged in the schema of both Havighurst and Wall is really an idealisation of middle-class norms. The majority of successful people in modern society would almost certainly accept the values of stable family life, conscientious work and responsible citizenship as the ultimate touchstones of worth and achievement. There is some evidence, however, that such a consensus is under attack and is in some respects strained to the point of change, that anomic influences are leading some people to lose their sense of social commitment, others to doubt the traditional value of, for example, marital stability or commitment to conscientious work and standards of occupational integrity. The super ego, it has been said, is soluble in alcohol: by the same token it may perhaps also be claimed that morality is soluble in affluence.

While it is utterly misleading to believe that there ever was an age in which social and personal standards were of such a uniformly accepted level of excellence that true consensus was achieved and consciously practised, it does seem that our own immediate quarter century following the end of World War II has been characterised by an unusual degree of challenge to authority and concomitant diversity of attitudes and behavi-our which must have exerted a particularly unsettling influence on the young. No generation hitherto has been so widely exposed to the mass media and to the growth of religious scepticism. In the not too distant past it must have been almost unthinkable for governors to appoint agnostics to headships of local authority schools or to find open acknowledgment of spiritual doubt in Religious Knowledge lessons, or the usefulness of the morning assembly for the so-called act of corporate worship being challenged. The more bracing atmosphere of present-day education is almost certainly a gain both for individual autonomy and for religion itself. But it no doubt has made the difficult choices involved in the whole business of growing up rather more difficult and confusing than heretofore.

Self-images of youth

If, following Jung, we employ the concept of the self-image as a conceptual tool in trying to understand the problems of youth, it would seem logical to suppose that the search for a stable personal identity is becoming more complex, if only because the multiple choices open to young people today and their greater degree of exposure to conflicting ideas and values has produced a blurring of the lines which demarcate the fantasy self-image from the ego-ideal and both from the *persona* that is presented to the outer world. Moreover, the self-images are all subject to external influences and, as Jahoda and Warren (1965) have so rightly said: 'Not only the average adult's impression of today's youth will be heavily biased towards teenage violence, teenage sexual licence, teenage fashion, newsworthy adolescent feats of all kinds, but also *the self-image of the teenagers themselves*. Thus in some instances the effects of visibility may well be to make the mythical stereotype based on it come true, owing to acceptance of a version of this stereotype by the very objects of the stereotyped perception.'

The more discussion there is, the greater the exposure to television and newspaper features, to advertisements and almost unlicensed film and stage shows, the greater the psychiatric risks involved in the changes that are coming upon our society. Fresh problems can be seen to be being born as a result of individuals' anxiety about their performance at the various tasks and the manner and extent to which their performances fall short of the supposed norms. While a great deal of adolescent behaviour must, almost by definition, be experimental in character, the fact that youths are expected to make progress in several different spheres of life, coupled with the lack of general agreement regarding norms and standards, contribute powerfully to what is often referred to as the crisis of identity phenomenon. The more sheltered the lives that young people live, the more ordered their existence and the more they are being marked out and groomed for élite status, the less such a crisis is likely to be. However, at the present time we are witnessing one of the most significant and intellectually intriguing of social changes in the rebellion of some members of the potential élite which we have already discussed. Here we can see the emergence of the more refined and numerically much rarer image of youth, not as the upholder of the existing culture but the moulder of the new culture, concerned, as Tawney (1961) put it, 'to make a tradition not to perpetuate one'.

One of the weaknesses of contemporary youthful idealism nevertheless results from the general loss of religious belief and confidence which, in the past, must surely have directed zeal into purely spiritual channels. Nowadays moral values seek more immediate outlets in righting social wrongs as an end in itself. There is also a widespread disbelief amongst the young in the usefulness of orthodox political procedures and, indeed, in the viability of rational policies and methods in public and national life. Faced with growing disenchantment with religious and political leadership and institutions, young people (very afraid of being manipulated) are all too apt to react in an emotional and almost desperate manner. Thus their regenerative idealism and reforming influence is dissipated in unrealistic provocations of authority and in the pursuit of demonstrations which often seem to be undertaken solely for demonstrations' sake—to the ultimate detriment of us all.

Services for youth

Amid all the confusion that exists in modern society, with its rapid rate of change and its conflicts of view-point, its undeniable class differences and inter-generational tensions, somehow young people have got to grow up without breakdown, teachers, parents and youth workers have got to function without sparking off hostility and society itself has got to come to understand what the role of youth is and to accept the teenage period, not as an unfortunate interregnum between two otherwise stable periods but as a necessary, even highly creative and desirable, preparatory phase in which the coming generation prepares itself scholastically, technically and morally to shape the future. A good deal of help is already being given, both through formal and informal channels, by established child-caring institutions such as schools and youth movements and by new ones called into being to meet novel and pressing problems. Much social research has already thrown light upon the developmental phase and we are beginning to understand much more clearly what the growing-up process involves both in psychological and sociological terms. Before we can advance much further or with any great confidence in the direction of offering young people firmer and more reliable help there are a number of issues which are still insufficiently understood. More thought, discussion and, above all, research is called for if we are to make progress in creating *with the active cooperation of young people themselves* more flexible and resilient pedagogical and therapeutic social services.

Sound educational policies rest upon an adequate theory of youth being available and this in turn depends to a considerable extent upon research workers applying themselves to the crucial issues and indicating some of the answers to basic problems. One of these major issues is whether or not the age at which physiological maturity is reached is going to be further reduced in the future. If biological maturity is really advancing at the rate that Tanner (1955) and others have indicated, then the time is not very far off when the period of childhood will be greatly restricted. Should this happen then the social consequences are obvious and considerable: the years of economic dependency must shrink accordingly and the period of juvenile obedience to parental authority must also be curtailed. We shall be obliged to attempt to bring social and economic maturity more into line for the vast majority of young people, not leaving it as we do today for those staying on at school to be wholly dependent while their working-class counterparts enjoy a compromise status in which they are often financially independent but are still adjudged to be legal minors in certain important respects. We are almost certainly moving towards a greater degree of social equality and more and more will tend to treat all members of an age-group alike. In Britain, as we have already said, the granting of the franchise and legal maturity at eighteen is an important step in this direction. The crucial question, however, is where should the dividing line be stabilised? Should we be prepared to grant legal autonomy at seventeen or even sixteen?

The answers to such questions must to a considerable extent depend upon the findings of biological and social research. *A priori* attitudes will only be obstructive. Parental doubts and middle-aged prejudices will in the end be obliged to give way under the pressure of scientific fact. If the years of youth are proving to be so stressful that inter-generational hostility is flaring up in open rebellion, then it may well, to some extent, be due to the fact that during the past few decades we have unwittingly protracted the period of dependency beyond what is psychologically endurable for the more intelligent and highly educated of our young people. But before we can be sure whether this is so we need further research directed, in the main, to finding out whether the adolescent turbulence and open rebellion is a product of such stressful social conditions, if it does, as a matter of fact, result from structural forces in society, or whether it is chiefly caused, as some aver, by political activists, mainly of the left. If the latter is the case, then no amount of restructuring of the

I

role and status of youth will reduce the problem, no earlier transfer of responsibility and autonomy will meet the situation. Political pressures will not be reduced by minor social changes and adjustments. Purely nihilistic or mainly negativistic movements can seldom be met by rational procedures and, in the last analysis, will have to be contained by the exercise of democratic force.

Future status of youth

But the majority of protesting youth is probably idealistic and politically naïve, more disenchanted with the shams of conventional society than hell-bent on its destruction. The criticisms of these young people can probably to a considerable extent be met rationally, by reforms based on scientific understanding. This will mean perhaps, among other things, paying students wages instead of grants, regarding students as young workers whose primary work consists in active preparation to be able at a later date to undertake highly skilled jobs. Similarly we may have to extend something very much like young worker status to pupils in sixth forms and, at the same time, accept the presence of students and older pupils on various committees and disciplinary bodies.

In other words, conventional social institutions will have to bend gracefully before the winds of legitimate change and not merely cede privileges under duress. The tempo of change may be accelerating as a result of rising expectations within all social strata coupled with a general extension of formal educational opportunities. Among the more highly educated youth the development of social studies and courses in sociology have for the first time enabled many young people to understand how their society works and what is wrong with it. The demand for more active participation in planning and in all kinds of decision-making is one outcome of the activities of this more sophisticated new generation with its commitment to humanitarian causes at home and abroad.

These seem to be some of the macroscopic issues which confront us today. In this kind of analysis one is of course talking of broad trends and influences operating in society as a whole and impinging on the sphere of youth in particular. Conventional pedagogy and social work have, almost as a kind of occupational brief, tended to concentrate more on the juvenile misfits and adolescent failures than on the wider social issues and movements. In stable social systems this is perhaps understandable, for there will always be a place for the offer of help and service to disadvantaged groups and troubled individuals. Thus we have developed, and still need, special youth work agencies dedicated to providing appropriate leisure-time pursuits as part of the general educational and recreational framework. These services and youth groups, which may be thought of as primarily designed to prevent adolescent difficulties occurring, have in recent years needed to be supplemented by more specialised services created to meet specific crises arising from such problems as drug addiction, depressive illness, and vagrancy.

At the level of individual psychic malfunctioning, whether produced mainly by individual or social causes, we have come to see that adolescents sometimes require special personal counselling and various schemes of an experimental nature such as the Soho Project in London, and the establishment of student counsellors at colleges and universities have come into existence to meet such critical needs. Similarly, some secondary schools have appointed counsellors to their staff to deal with personal maladjustments and to help young people to understand themselves better in relation to the major developmental tasks which we outlined earlier. For whatever social changes are made, the basic tasks will remain; the problem of achieving a valid personal identity at different psycho-social levels will still have to be met. However much we change the law, individuals will not all mature at the same time or with identical rhythms. It is idle to suggest that full all-round and final maturity will be attained by the age of eighteen or, for that matter, twenty-one. All we can hope for is that round about the eighteenth birthday boys and girls will individually and collectively have made sufficient advances in the direction of ultimate maturity to be reasonably well set on their life's course as to need no more than occasional and specific help. Their judgment, although still subject to change, will be adequate to the normal tasks of living.

Perhaps we may also hope that the coming generation will retain—well into the middle years of life—something of the fire and passion which is still the special prerogative of youth. Even the oversimplified slogan which has been raised at many demonstrations—'Make love, not war'—has something to say to those of us who have yielded our consciences too easily to the sluggish pragmatism of middle-aged moral expediency.

J. M. Tanner

17. Physical aspects of adolescence

For the majority of young persons, the years of puberty are the most eventful ones of their lives so far as their growth and development is concerned. Admittedly, during foetal life and the first year or two after birth developments occurred still faster, and a sympathetic environment was probably even more crucial, but the subject himself was not the fascinated, charmed or horrified spectator that watches the developments, or lack of developments, of adolescence. Growth is a very regular and highly regulated process, and from birth onwards the growth rate of most bodily tissues decreases steadily, the fall being swift at first and slower from about three years. Body shape changes gradually since the rate of growth of some parts (such as the arms and legs) is greater than the rate of growth of others, such as the trunk. But the change is a steady one, a smoothly continuous development rather than any passage through a series of separate stages.

Then, at puberty, a very considerable alteration in growth rate occurs. There is a swift increase in body size, a change in the shape and body composition, and a rapid development of the gonads, the reproductive organs, and the characteristics signalling sexual maturity. Some of these changes are common to both sexes, but most are sex-specific. Boys have a great increase in muscle size and strength, together with a series of physiological changes making them more capable than girls of doing heavy physical work, and running faster and longer. The changes specifically adapt the male to his primitive primate role of dominating, fighting and foraging. Such adolescent changes occur generally in primates, and man lies at about the middle of the primate range both as regards adolescent size-increase and degree of sexual differentiation.

The adolescent changes are brought about by hormones, either secreted for the first time, or secreted in much higher amounts than previously. Each hormone acts on a set of targets or receptors, but these are often not concentrated in a single organ, nor in a single type of tissue. Testosterone, for example, acts on receptors in the cells of the penis, the skin of the face, the cartilages of the shoulder joints and certain parts of the brain. Whether all these cells respond by virtue of having the same enzyme system, or whether different enzymes are involved at different sites is not yet clear. The systems have developed through natural selection, producing a functional response of obvious biological usefulness in societies of hunter gatherers, but of less certain benefit in the culture of invoice-clerk and shop assistant. Evolutionary adaptations of bodily structure usually carry with them an increased proclivity for using those structures in behaviour, and there is no reason to suppose this principle suddenly stops short at twentieth-century man. There is no need to take sides in the current debate on the origins of aggression to realise that a major task of any culture is the channelling of this less specifically sexual adolescent energy into creative and playful activity.

The adolescent changes have not altered, of course, in the last fifteen years, or the last fifty, or probably the last five thousand. Girls still develop two years earlier than boys; some boys still have completed their whole bodily adolescent development before other boys of the same chronological age have begun theirs. These are perhaps the two major biological facts to be borne in mind when thinking of the adolescent's view of himself in relation to his society. The sequence of the biological events remains the same. But there has been one considerable change: the events occur now at an earlier age than formerly. Forty years ago the average British girl had her first menstrual period (menarche) at about her fifteenth birthday; nowadays it is shortly before her thirteenth. Fifty years ago in Britain, social class differences played a considerable part in causing the variation of age of menarche in the population, the less well-off growing up more slowly. Nowadays age at menarche is almost the same in different classes and most of the variation is due to genetic factors. A relationship with number of children in the family persists, however—the more siblings the later the menarche. Probably this represents a complex of environmental, chiefly nutritional, influence.

In this chapter I shall discuss (1) the growth of the body at puberty and its changes in size, shape and tissue composition; (2) sex dimorphism and the development of the reproductive system; (3) the concept of developmental age and the interaction of physical and behavioural advancement; (4) the interaction of genetic and environmental influences on the age of occurrence of puberty and the secular trend towards earlier maturation.

1. Growth of the body at adolescence

The extent of the adolescent spurt in height is shown in figure 1. For a year or more the velocity of growth approximately doubles; a boy is likely to

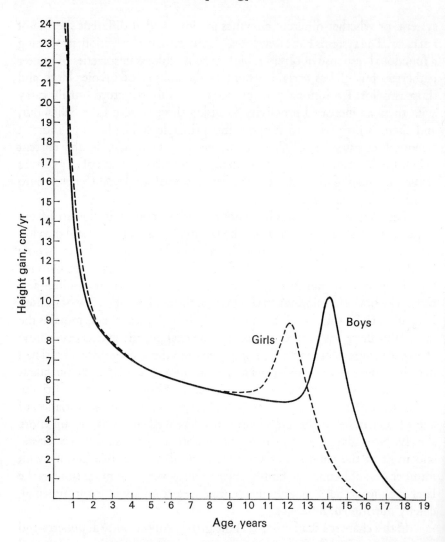

FIGURE I   *Typical individual velocity curves for supine length or height in boys and girls. These curves represent the velocity of the typical boy and girl at any given instant. (From Tanner, Whitehouse and Takaishi 1966.)*

be growing again at the rate he last experienced about age two. The peak velocity of height (PHV, a point much used in growth studies) averages about 10·5 cm/yr in boys and 9·0 cm/yr in girls (with a standard deviation of about 1·0 cm/yr), but this is the 'instantaneous' peak given by a smooth curve drawn through the observations. The velocity over the whole year encompassing the six months before and after the peak is naturally somewhat less. During this year a boy usually grows between 7 and 12 cm and a girl between 6 and 11 cm. Children who have their peak early reach a somewhat higher peak than those who have it late.

The average age at which the peak is reached depends on the nature and circumstances of the group studied. In moderately well-off British or North American children at present the peak occurs on average at about fourteen years in boys, and twelve years in girls. The standard deviations are about 0·9 yr in each instance. Though the absolute average ages differ from series to series the two-year sex difference is invariant.

The adolescent spurt is at least partly under different hormonal control from growth in the period before. Probably as a consequence of this the amount of height added during the spurt is to a considerable degree independent of the amount attained prior to it. Most children who have grown steadily up, say, the 30th centile line on a height chart till adolescence end up at the 30th centile as adults, it is true; but a number end as high as the 50th or as low as the 10th, and a very few at the 55th or 5th. The correlation between adult height and height just before the spurt starts is about 0·8. This leaves some 30 per cent of the variability in adult height as due to differences in the magnitude of the adolescent spurt. So some adolescents get a nasty and unavoidable shock; though probably the effects of early and late maturing (see below) almost totally confuse the issue of final height during the years we are considering.

Practically all skeletal and muscular dimensions take part in the spurt, though not to an equal degree. Most of the spurt in height is due to acceleration of trunk length rather than length of legs. There is a fairly regular order in which the dimensions accelerate; leg length as a rule reaches its peak first, followed by the body breadths, with shoulder width last. Thus a boy stops growing out of his trousers (at least in length) a year before he stops growing out of his jackets. The earliest structures to reach their adult status are the head, hands, and feet. At adolescence, children, particularly girls, sometimes complain of having large hands and feet. They can be reassured that by the time they are fully grown their hands and feet will be a little smaller in proportion to their arms and legs, and considerably smaller in proportion to their trunk.

The spurt in muscle, both of limbs and heart, coincides with the spurt in skeletal growth, for both are caused by the same hormones. Boys' muscle widths reach a peak velocity of growth which is considerably greater than that reached by girls. But since girls have their spurt earlier there is actually a period, from about $12\frac{1}{2}$ to $13\frac{1}{2}$ years, when girls on average have larger muscles than boys of the same age.

Simultaneously with the spurt in muscle there is a loss of fat in boys, particularly in fat on the limbs. Girls have a velocity curve of fat identical in shape to that of boys; that is to say their fat accumulation, going on in both sexes from about age six, decelerates. But the decrease in velocity in girls is not sufficiently great to carry the average velocity below zero, that is, to give an absolute loss. Most girls have to content themselves with a temporary go-slow in fat accumulation. As the adolescent growth spurt draws to an end fat tends to accumulate again in both sexes.

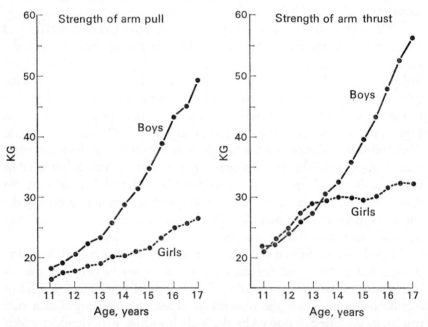

FIGURE 2   *Strength of arm pull and arm thrust from ages elven to seventeen. Mixed longitudinal data, 65-95 boys and 66-93 girls in each age-group. (From Tanner 1962; data from Jones 1949.)*

The marked increase in muscle size in boys at adolescence, leads to an increase in strength, illustrated in figure 2. Before puberty boys and girls are similar in strength for a given body size and shape; after, boys are much stronger, probably due to developing more force per gram of muscle as well as absolutely larger muscles. They also develop larger hearts and lungs relative to their size, a higher systolic blood pressure, a lower resting heart-rate, a greater capacity for carrying oxygen in the blood, and a greater power for neutralising the chemical products of muscular exercise such as lactic acid (see Tanner 1962, p. 168). In short, the male becomes at

adolescence more adapted for the tasks of hunting, fighting, and mani-
pulating all sorts of heavy objects, as is necessary in some forms of food-
gathering.

It is as a direct result of these anatomical and physiological changes
that athletic ability increases so much in boys at adolescence. The popular
notion of a boy 'outgrowing his strength' at this time has little scientific
support. It is true that the peak velocity of strength is reached a year or so
later than that of height, so that a short period may exist when the
adolescent, having completed his skeletal and probably also muscular
growth, still does not have the strength of a young adult of the same body
size and shape. But this is a temporary phase; considered absolutely, power,
athletic skill and physical endurance all increase progressively and rapidly
throughout adolescence. It is certainly not true that the changes accompanying adolescence enfeeble, even temporarily. If the adolescent
becomes weak and easily exhausted it is for psychological reasons and not
physiological ones.

2. Sex dimorphism and the development of the reproductive system

The adolescent spurt in skeletal and muscular dimensions is closely related
to the rapid development of the reproductive system which takes place at
this time. The course of this development is outlined diagramatically in
figure 3. The solid areas marked *breast* in the girls and *penis* and *testis* in the
boys represent the period of accelerated growth of these organs and the
horizontal lines and the rating numbers marked *pubic hair* stand for its
advent and development (details of ratings in Tanner 1962). The sequence
and timings given represent in each case average values for British boys
and girls; to give an idea of the individual departures from the average,
figures for the range of age at which the various events begin and end are
inserted under the first and last point of the bars. The acceleration of penis
growth, for example, begins on average at about age $12\frac{1}{2}$ years, but sometimes as early as $10\frac{1}{2}$ and sometimes as late as $14\frac{1}{2}$. The completion of penis
development usually occurs at about age $14\frac{1}{2}$ but in some boys is at $12\frac{1}{2}$ and
in others at $15\frac{1}{2}$. There are a few boys, it will be noticed, who do not begin
their spurts in height or penis development until the earliest maturers have
entirely completed theirs. At ages 13, 14 and 15 there is an enormous
variability within any group of boys, who range all the way from
practically complete maturity to absolute pre-adolescence. The same is
true of girls aged 11, 12 and 13.

The psychological and social importance of this difference in the

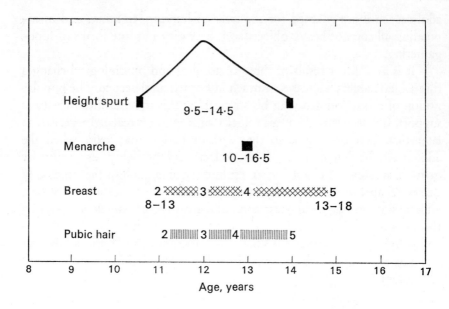

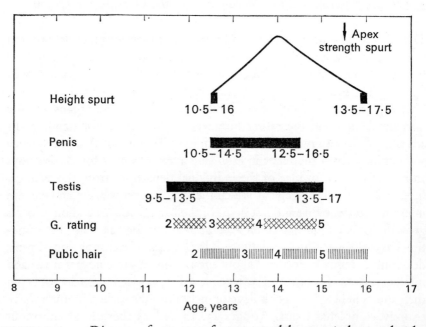

FIGURE 3   *Diagram of sequence of events at adolescence in boys and girls.
The average boy and girl are represented: the range of ages within which each
event charted may begin and end is given by the figures placed directly below its
start and finish. (From Marshall and Tanner 1970.)*

tempo of development, as it has been called, is very great, particularly in boys. Boys who are advanced in development are likely to dominate their contemporaries in athletic achievement and sexual interest alike. Conversely the late developer is the one who all too often loses out in the rough and tumble of the adolescent world; and he may begin to wonder whether he will ever develop his body properly or be as well endowed sexually as those others he has seen developing around him. A very important part of the educationist's and the doctor's task at this time is to provide information about growth and its variability to pre-adolescents and adolescents and to give sympathetic support and reassurance to those who need it.

The *sequence* of events, though not exactly the same for each boy or girl, is much less variable than the age at which the events occur. The first sign of puberty in the boy is usually an acceleration of the growth of the testes and scrotum with reddening and wrinkling of the scrotal skin. Slight growth of pubic hair may begin about the same time, but is usually a trifle later. The spurts in height and penis growth begin on average about a year after the first testicular acceleration. Axillary hair appears on average some two years after the beginning of pubic hair growth; that is, when pubic hair is reaching stage 4. The remainder of the body hair appears from about the time of first axillary hair development until a considerable time after puberty. The ultimate amount of body hair an individual develops seems to depend largely on heredity, though whether because of the kinds and amounts of hormones secreted or because of the reactivity of the end-organs is not known.

Breaking of the voice occurs relatively late in adolescence; it is often a gradual process and so not suitable as a criterion of puberty. The change in pitch accompanies enlargement of the larynx and lengthening of the vocal cords, caused by the action of testosterone on the laryngeal cartilages. There is also a change in quality of timbre which distinguishes the voice (more particularly the vowel sounds) of both male and female adults from that of children. This is dependent on the enlargement of the resonating spaces above the larynx, due to the rapid growth of the mouth, nose and maxilla which occurs during adolescence.

In the skin the sebaceous and apocrine sweat glands, particularly of the axillae and genital and anal regions, develop rapidly during puberty and give rise to a characteristic odour; the changes occur in both sexes but are more marked in the male. Enlargement of the pores at the root of the nose and the appearance of comedones and acne, whilst liable to occur in either sex, are considerably commoner in adolescent boys than girls, since the underlying skin changes are the result of androgenic activity.

In some boys (between a fifth and a third of most groups studied) there is a distinct enlargement of the breast (sometimes unilaterally) about midway through adolescence. This usually regresses again after about one year.

In girls the appearance of the 'breast bud' is as a rule the first sign of puberty, though the appearance of pubic hair precedes it in about one-third. The uterus and vagina develop simultaneously with the breast. The labia and clitoris also enlarge. Menarche, the first menstrual period, is a late event in the sequence. Though it marks a definitive and probably mature stage of uterine development, it does not usually signify the attainment of full reproductive function. The early cycles may be more irregular than later ones and in some girls, but by no means all, are accompanied by dysmenorrhea. They are often anovulatory, that is, un-accompanied by the shedding of an egg. Thus there is frequently a period of adolescent sterility lasting a year to eighteen months after menarche; but it cannot be relied on in the individual case. Similar considerations may apply to the male, but there is no reliable information about this. On average girls grow about 6 cm more after menarche, though gains of up to twice this amount may occur. The gain is practically independent of whether menarche occurs early or late.

Normal variations in pubertal development

The diagram of figure 3 must not be allowed to obscure the fact that children vary a great deal both in the rapidity with which they pass through the various stages of puberty and in the closeness with which the various events are linked together. At one extreme one may find a perfectly healthy girl who has not yet menstruated though she has reached adult breast and pubic hair ratings and is already two years past her peak height velocity; at the other a girl who has passed all the stages of puberty within the space of two years. Details of the limits of what may be considered normal can be found in the papers of Marshall and Tanner (1969, 1970).

In girls the interval from the first sign of puberty to complete maturity varies from $1\frac{1}{2}$ to 6 years. From the moment when the breast bud first appears to menarche averages $2\frac{1}{2}$ years but may be as little as six months or as much as $5\frac{1}{2}$ years. The rapidity with which a child passes through puberty seems to be independent of whether puberty is occurring early or late. There is some independence between breast and pubic hair developments, as one might expect on endocrinological grounds. Menarche usually occurs in breast stage 4 and pubic hair stage 4 but in about 10 per cent of girls occurs in stage 5 for both, and occasionally may occur in stage 2 or even 1 of pubic hair. Menarche invariably occurs after peak height velocity is passed, so the tall girl can be reassured about future growth if her periods have begun.

In boys a similar variability occurs. The genitalia may take any time between two and five years to pass from G2 to G5, and some boys complete the whole process while others have still not gone from G2 to G3. Pubic hair growth in the absence of genital development is very unusual in normal boys, but in a small percentage of boys the genitalia develop as far as stage 4 before the pubic hair starts to grow.

The height spurt occurs relatively later in boys than in girls. Thus there is a difference between the average boy and girl of two years in age of peak height velocity, but of only one year in the first appearance of pubic hair. The PHV occurs in very few boys before genital stage 4, whereas 75 per cent of girls reach PHV before breast stage 4. Indeed, in some girls the acceleration in height is the first sign of puberty; this is never so in boys. A small boy whose genitalia are just beginning to develop can be unequivocally reassured that an acceleration in height is soon to take place, but a girl in the corresponding situation may already have had her height spurt.

The development of sex dimorphism

The differential effects on the growth of bone, muscle and fat at puberty increase considerably the difference in body composition between the sexes. Boys have a greater increase not only in the length of bones but in their thickness, and girls have a smaller loss of fat. The most striking dimorphisms however are the man's greater stature and breadth of shoulders and the woman's wider hips. These are produced chiefly by the changes and timing of puberty but it is important to remember that sex dimorphisms do not only arise at that time. Many appear much earlier. Some, like the external genital difference itself, develop during foetal life. Others develop continuously throughout the whole growth period by a sustained differential growth rate. An example of this is the greater relative length and breadth of the forearm in the male when compared with whole arm length or whole body length.

Part of the sex difference in pelvis shape antedates puberty. Girls at birth already have a wider pelvic outlet. Thus the adaptation for childbearing is present from a very early age. The changes at puberty are concerned more with widening the pelvic inlet and broadening the much more noticeable hips. It seems likely that these changes are more important in attracting the males' attention than in dealing with its ultimate product.

These sex-differentiated morphological characters arising at puberty —to which we can add the corresponding physiological and perhaps psychological ones as well—are secondary sex characteristics in the straightforward sense that they are caused by sex hormone or sex-differential hormone secretion and serve reproductive activity. The penis is directly concerned in copulation, the mammary gland in lactation. The wide shoulders and muscular power of the male, together with the canine teeth and brow ridges in Man's ancestors, developed probably for driving away other males and ensuring peace from other animals, an adaptation which soon becomes social.

A number of traits persist, perhaps through another mechanism known to the ethologists as ritualisation. In the course of evolution a morphological character or a piece of behaviour may lose its original function and, becoming further elaborated, complicated or simplified, may serve as a sign stimulus to other members of the same species, releasing behaviour that is in some way advantageous to the spread or survival of the species. It requires little insight into human erotics to suppose that the shoulders, the hips and buttocks, and the breasts (at least in a number of widespread cultures) serve as releasers of mating behaviour. The pubic hair (about whose function the medical textbooks have always preserved a cautious silence) probably survives as a ritualised stimulus for sexual activity, developed by simplification from the hair remaining in the inguinal and axillary regions for the infant to cling to when still transported, as in present apes and monkeys, under the mother's body. Similar considerations may apply to axillary hair, which is associated with special apocrine glands which themselves only develop at puberty and are related histologically to scent glands in other mammals. The beard, on the other hand, may still be more frightening to other males than enticing to females. At least ritual use in past communities suggests this is the case; but perhaps there are two sorts of beards.

The initiation of puberty

The manner in which puberty is initiated has a general importance for the clarification of developmental mechanisms. Certain children develop all the changes of puberty, up to and including spermatogenesis and ovulation, at a very early age, either as the result of a brain lesion or as an isolated developmental, sometimes genetic defect. The youngest mother on record was such a case, and gave birth to a full-term healthy infant by Caesarian section at the age of five years eight months. The existence of precocious puberty and the results of accidental ingestion by small children of male or female sex hormones indicates that breasts, uterus and penis will respond to hormonal stimulation long before puberty. Evidently an increased end-organ sensitivity plays at most a minor part in pubertal events.

The signal to start the sequence of events is given by the brain, not the pituitary. Just as the brain holds the information on sex, so it holds information on maturity. The pituitary of a newborn rat successfully grafted in place of an adult pituitary begins at once to function in an adult fashion, and does not have to wait till its normal age of maturation has been reached. It is the hypothalamus, not the pituitary, which has to mature before puberty begins. Small amounts of sex hormones circulate from the time of birth and these inhibit the pre-pubertal hypothalamus from producing gonadotrophin releasers. At puberty the hypothalamic cells appear to become less sensitive to sex hormones. The small amount of sex hormones circulating then fails to inhibit the hypothalamus, gonadotrophins are released, these stimulate the production of testosterone by the testis or oestrogen by the ovary. The level of the sex hormone rises until the same feedback circuit is re-established, but now at a higher level of gonadotrophins and sex hormones. The concentration of sex hormones is now high enough to stimulate the growth of secondary sex characteristics and support mating behaviour.

3. Developmental age and the interaction of physical and behavioural advancement

Children vary greatly in their tempo of growth. The effects are most dramatically seen at adolescence, but they are present at all ages from birth and even before. Girls, for example, do not suddenly become two years ahead of boys at adolescence; on the contrary they are born with slightly more mature skeletons and nervous systems, and gradually increase their developmental lead (in absolute terms) throughout childhood.

The concept of *developmental* age, as opposed to *chronological* age, is a very important one. To measure developmental age we need some way of determining the percentage of the child's growth process which has been attained at any time. In retrospective research studies, the percentage of final adult height may be very effectively used; but in the clinic we need something that is immediate in its application. The difficulty about using height, for example, is that different children end up at different heights, so that a tall-for-his-age twelve-year-old may either be a tall adult in the making with average maturational tempo, or an average adult in the making with an accelerated tempo. Precisely the same applies to the child who scores above average on most tests of mental ability.

To measure developmental age we need something which ends up the same for everyone and is applicable throughout the whole period of growth. Many physiological measures meet these criteria in whole or in part. They range from the number of erupted teeth to the percentage of water in muscle cells. The various developmental 'age' scales do not necessarily coincide, and each has its particular use. By far the most generally useful, however, is skeletal maturity or *bone age*. A less important one is dental maturity.

Skeletal maturity is usually measured by taking a radiograph of the hand and wrist (using the same radiation exposure that a child inevitably gets, and to more sensitive areas, by spending a week on holiday in the mountains). The appearances of the developing bones can be rated and formed into a scale; the scale is applicable to boys and girls of all genetic backgrounds, though girls on average reach any given score at a younger age than boys. Skeletal maturity is closely related to the age at which puberty occurs, that is, to maturity measured by secondary sex characteristic development. Thus the range of *chronological age* within which menarche may normally fall is about to 10 to $16\frac{1}{2}$ years, but the corresponding range of skeletal age for menarche is only 12 to $14\frac{1}{2}$. Evidently the physiological processes controlling progression of skeletal development are in most instances closely linked with those which initiate the events of adolescence. Furthermore, children tend to be consistently advanced or retarded during their whole growth period, or at any rate after about age three.

Dental maturity partly shares in this general skeletal and bodily maturation. At all ages from six to thirteen, children who are advanced skeletally have on average more erupted teeth than those who are skeletally retarded. But this relationship is not a very close one, and quantitatively speaking it is the relative independence of teeth and general skeletal development which should be emphasised. There is some general factor of bodily maturity creating a tendency for a child to be advanced or retarded as a whole; in his skeletal ossification, in the percentage attained of his eventual size, in his permanent dentition, doubtless in his physiological reactions, and possibly in the results of his tests of ability. But not too much should be made of this general factor; and especially it should be noted how very limited is the loading, so to speak, of brain growth in it. There is little justification in the facts of physical growth and development for the concept of 'organismic age' in which almost wholly disparate measures of developmental maturity are lumped together.

Physical maturation, mental ability and emotional development

Clearly the occurrence of tempo differences in human growth has profound implications for educational theory and practice. This would especially be so if advancement in physical growth were linked to any significant degree with advancement in intellectual ability and in emotional maturity.

There is good evidence that in the European and North American school systems children who are physically advanced towards maturity score on average slightly higher in most tests of mental ability than children of the same age who are physically less mature. The difference is not great, but it is consistent and it occurs at all ages that have been studied, that is, back as far as $6\frac{1}{2}$ years. Similarly the average intelligence test score of post-menarcheal girls is higher than the score of pre-menarcheal girls of the same age (refs in Tanner 1962, 1966). Thus in age-linked examinations physically fast-maturing children have a significantly better chance than slow-maturing children.

It is also true that physically large children score higher than small ones, at all ages from six onwards. In a random sample of all Scottish eleven-year-old children, for example, comprising 6,440 pupils, the correlation between height and score in the Moray House group tests was 0.25 ± 0.01 which leads to an average increase of $1\frac{1}{2}$ points Terman-Merrill IQ per inch of stature. A similar correlation was found in London children. The effects can be very significant for individual children. In ten-year-old girls there was a nine-point difference in IQ between those whose height was above the 75th percentile and those whose height was below the 15th. This is two-thirds of the standard deviation of the test score.

It was usually thought that both the relationships between test score and height and between test score and early maturing would disappear in adulthood. If the correlations represented only the effects of co-advancement both of mental ability and physical growth this might be expected to happen. There is no difference in height between early- and late-maturing boys when both have finished growing. But it is now clear that, curiously, at least part of the height-IQ correlation persists in adults (Tanner 1966). It is not clear in what proportion genetic and environmental factors are responsible for this.

There is little doubt that being an early or a late maturer may have repercussions which may be considerable. There is little enough solid information on the relation between emotional and physiological development, but what there is supports the commonsense notion that emotional attitudes are clearly related to physiological events.

The boy's world is one where physical powers brings prestige as well as success, where the body is very much an instrument of the person. Boys who are advanced in development, not only at puberty but before as well, are more likely than others to be leaders. Indeed this is reinforced by the

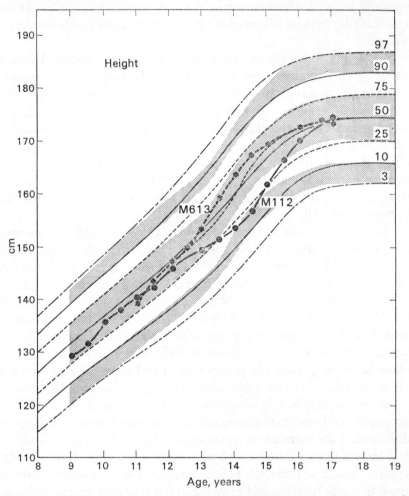

FIGURE 4   *Height attained of two boys, one with an early and the other with a late adolescent spurt. Note how at age eleven and again at age seventeen years the boys are the same height. (From Tanner 1961.)*

fact that muscular, powerful boys on average mature earlier than others and have an early adolescent growth-spurt. The athletically built boy not only tends to dominate his fellows before puberty but by getting an early start he is in a good position to continue that domination. The unathletic, lanky boy, unable perhaps to hold his own in the pre-adolescent rough and tumble, gets still further pushed to the wall at adolescence, as he sees others shoot up while he remains nearly stationary in growth. Even boys several years younger now suddenly surpass him in size, athletic skill, and perhaps, too, in social graces. Figure 4 shows the height curves of two boys, the first an early-maturing muscular boy, the other a late-maturing lanky one. Though both boys are of average height at age eleven, and together again at average height at seventeen, the early maturer is considerably taller during the peak of puberty.

At a much deeper level the late developer at adolescence may sometimes have doubts about whether he will ever develop his body properly and whether he will be as well endowed sexually as those others he has seen developing around him. The lack of events of adolescence may act as a trigger to reverberate fears accumulated deep in the mind during the early years of life.

It may seem as though the early maturers have things all their own way. It is indeed true that most studies of the later personalities of children whose growth history is known do show early maturers as more stable, more sociable, less neurotic and more successful in society, at least in the United States (see Mussen and Jones 1957). But early maturers have their difficulties also, particularly the girls in some societies. Though some glory in their new possessions, others are embarrassed by them. The early maturer too has a longer period of frustration of sex drive and of drive towards independence and the establishment of vocational orientation.

Little can be done to reduce the individual differences in children's tempo of growth, for they are biologically rooted and not significantly reducible by any social steps we may take. It therefore behoves all teachers, psychologists and paediatricians to be fully aware of the facts and alert to the individual problems they raise.

4. Trend toward large size and earlier maturation

The rate of maturing and the age at onset of puberty are dependent on a complex interaction of genetic and environmental factors. Where the environment is good, most of the variability in age at menarche in a population is due to genetic differences. In France in the 1950s the mean difference for identical twins was two months, while that between non-identical twin sisters was eight months (Tisserand-Perier, cited in Tanner 1962). In many societies puberty occurs later in the poorly-off, and in most societies investigated, children with many siblings grow less fast than children with few.

During the last hundred years there has been a striking tendency for children to become progressively larger at all ages (Tanner 1968). This is known as the 'secular trend'. The magnitude of the trend in Europe and America is such that it dwarfs the differences between socio-economic classes.

The data from Europe and America agree well: from about 1900, or a little earlier, to the present, children in average economic circumstances have increased in height at age five to seven by about 1 to 2 cm each decade, and at ten to fourteen by 2 to 3 cm each decade. Pre-school data show that the trend starts directly after birth and may, indeed, be relatively greater from age two to five than subsequently. The trend started, at least in Britain, a considerable time ago, because Roberts, a factory physician writing in 1876, said that 'A factory child of the present day at the age of nine years weighs as much as one of ten years did in 1833 ... each age has gained one year in forty years.' The trend in Europe is still continuing at the time of writing, but there is some evidence to show that in the United States the best-off sections of the population are now growing up at something approaching the fastest possible speed.

During the same period there has been an upward trend in adult height, but to a considerably lower degree. In earlier times, final height in man was not reached till twenty-five years or later, whereas now it is reached at seventeen or eighteen. Data exist, however, which enable us to compare fully grown men at different periods. They lead to the conclusion that in Western Europe men increased in adult height little if at all from 1760 to 1830, about 0·3 cm per decade from 1830 to 1880, and about 0·6 cm per decade from 1880 to 1960. The trend is apparently still continuing in parts of Europe, though not in the best-off section of American society, nor in Oslo and London.

Most of the trend toward greater size in children reflects a more rapid maturation; only a minor part reflects a greater ultimate size. The trend toward earlier maturing is best shown in the statistics on age at menarche. A selection of the best data is illustrated in figure 5 (the sources are detailed in Tanner 1962). The trend since 1850 shows menarche as occurring between three and four months per decade earlier in average sections of Western European populations. Well-off persons show a trend of about half this magnitude, having never been so retarded in menarche as the worse-off.

The causes of the secular trend are probably multiple. Certainly better nutrition is a major one, and perhaps in particular more protein and calories in early infancy. A lessening of disease may also have contributed. Hot climates used to be cited as a potent cause of early menarche, but it seems now that their effect, if any, is considerably less than that of nutrition. The annual mean world temperature rose from 1850 to 1940 (when it began to fall again); the polar ice caps have been melting and the glaciers

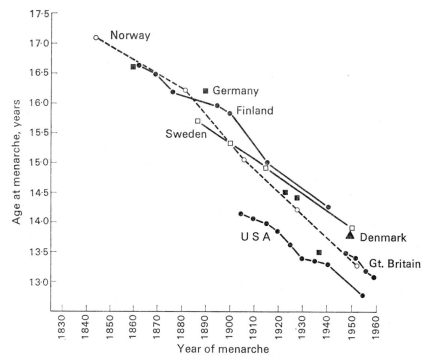

FIGURE 5   *Secular trend in age at menarche 1830-1960. (Sources of data and method of plotting detailed in Tanner 1962.)*

retreating, but on present evidence it seems unlikely that this general warming–up has contributed significantly to the earlier menarche of girls.

Some authors have supposed that the increase psycho-sexual stimulation consequent on modern urban living has contributed, but there is no positive evidence for this. Girls in single-sex schools have menarche at exactly the same age as girls in co-educational schools, but whether this is a fair test of difference in psycho-sexual stimulation is hard to say.

References

How children learn new skills

AMARIA, P., BIRAN, L. A. and LEITH, G. O. (1961) 'Individual versus co-operative learning.' *Educ. Res.*, **V**, 11, 2-3.

BALES, R. F. *et al.* (1952) 'Channels of communication in small groups.' *Am. Soc. Rev.*, **16**, 4, 461-8. (Based on ARGYL, M. *The Scientific Study of Social Behaviour*. London: Methuen.)

BLOOM, B. S. *et al.* (1956) *Taxonomy of Educational Objectives*, Handbook I: 'Cognitive Domain'. New York: David McKay.

BLOOM, B. S. (1968) *Learning for Mastery*. University of California, Center for Study of Evaluation.

CARROLL, J. (1963) *A Model of School Learning*. New York: Teachers College Record 64.

CLAPAREDE, E. (1930) *L'éducation fonctionnelle*. Neuchâtel: Delachaux et Niestlé.

DE GREVE, M. and VAN PASSEL, F. (1968) *Linguistique et enseignement des langues étrangères*. Brussels: Labor; Paris: Nathan.

FOSHAY, A. W. *et al.* (1962) *Educational Achievements of Thirteen-Year-Olds in Twelve Countries*. Hamburg: UNESCO Institute for Education.

GUILLAUME, P. (1936) *La formation des habitudes*. Paris: Presses Universitaires de France.

HOTYAT, F. (1965) *Les tâches après la class dans l'enseignement moyen et normal*. Brussels: Editions de l'Institut de Sociologie.

KRATHWOHL, D. R., BLOOM, B. S. and MASIA, B. B. (1964) *Taxonomy of Educational Objectives*, Handbook II: 'Affective Domain'. New York: David McKay.

KRUEGER, W. (1894) 'Experimental study of memory.' *Psychol. Rev.*

LE NY, J. F., DE MONTPELLIER, G., OLERON, G. and FLORES, C. (1964) 'Apprentissage et memoire.' In FRAISSE, P. and PIAGET, J. (eds) *Traité de psychologie experimentale*. Paris: Presses Universitaires de France.

MANDLER, G. (1967) 'Organisation and Memory.' In *The Psychology of Learning and Motivation*. London: Academic Press.

NEILSEN, R. (1951) *Le developpment de la sociabilité chez l'enfant*. Neuchâtel: Delachaux et Niestlé.

PIAGET, J. (1947) *La psychologie de l'intelligence.* Paris: Armand Colin. (*See also his other works on genetic psychology.*)

ROBAYE, F. (1957) *Niveaux d'aspiration et d'expectation, critères de personnalité.* Paris: Presses Universitaires de France.

WITTROCK, M. C. (1969) *The Evaluation of Instruction. Cause and Effect Relations in Naturalistic Data.* University of California, Center for Study in Education.

The purposes of futurologic studies in education

BELL, D. (1967) (ed.) 'Toward the year 2000: Work in Progress.' *Daedalus*, **96**, 639-1226.

COOMBS, P. H. (1968) *The World Educational Crisis: A Systems Analysis.* New York: Oxford University Press.

HELMER, O. *et al.* (1966) *Social Technology.* New York: Basic Books.

HUSEN, T. and BOALT, G. (1968) *Educational Research and Educational Change: The Case of Sweden.* New York: Wiley.

KENISTON, K. (1960) *The Uncommitted: Alienated Youth in American Society.* New York: Harcourt, Brace and World.

KENISTON, K. (1968) *Young Radicals: Notes on Committed Youth.* New York: Harcourt, Brace and World.

MARKLUND, S. (1966) 'Educational reform and research in Sweden.' *Educ. Res.*, **9**, 1, 16-21.

MARKLUND, S. (1968) 'Training teachers for the schools of today.' *Int. Rev. Educ.*, **14**, 432-45.

MARKLUND, S. (1969) 'School organization, school location and student achievement.' *Int. Rev. Educ.*, **15**, 295-320.

MARKLUND, S. and SÖDERBERG, P. (1967) *The Swedish Comprehensive School.* London: Longman.

Swedish National Board of Education (1965) *Läroplan för gymnasiet* (*Gymnasium* curriculum). Stockholm: Government Printing Office.

Swedish National Board of Education (1969) *Tonåringen och livsfrågorna* (The teenager and the basic problems of life). Stockholm: Government Printing Office.

Swedish State Report (1958) *Lärarbrist och läraröverskott* (Shortage and surplus of teachers). Stockholm: Government Printing Office.

Swedish State Report (1964) *Skolans försörjning med lärare* (Providing teachers for the schools). Stockholm: Government Printing Office.

US National Science Board (1969) *Knowledge into Action: Improving the Nation's Use of the Social Sciences.* Report of the Special Commission on the Social Sciences. Washington, DC: US Government Printing Office.

US Office of Education, Pilot Policy Research Center (1967) *A Predictive Study: Attitudes and Values of Future Decision-Makers.* Progress Report, Vol. 3, Western Behavioral Sciences Institute, La Jolla, California.

ZIEGLER, W. L. and MARIEN, M. M. (1969) *An Approach to the Future—Perspective in American Education.* Syracuse, New York: Educational Policy Research Center.

Affective consequences of school achievement

ANTTONEN, R. G. (1969) 'Longitudinal study in mathematics attitude.' *J. educ. Res.*, **62**, 467-71.

ATKINSON, J. W. and FEATHER, N. T. (1966) (eds) *A Theory of Achievement Motivation.* New York: Wiley.

BARAHENI, M. N. (1962) 'Inquiry into attitudinal concomitants of success and failure at school.' *Educ. Res.*, **5**, 63-8.

BLOOM, B. S. (1964) *Stability and Change in Human Characteristics.* New York: Wiley.

BORMUTH, J. R. (1970) *On the Theory of Achievement Test Items.* Chicago: University of Chicago Press.

BOWER, E. M. (1962) 'Mental health in education.' *Rev. educ. Res.*, **32**, 441-54.

ENGEL, M. (1959) 'The stability of self-concept in adolescence.' *J. abnorm. soc. Psychol.*, **58**, 211-15.

ERIKSON, E. H. (1963) *Childhood and Society.* New York: Norton.

FLEMMING, C. W. (1925) 'A detailed analysis of achievement in high school.' *Teachers College Contributions to Education*, **196**, 35-47. New York: Bureau of Publications, Teachers College, Columbia University.

FRANDSEN, A. N. and SESSIONS, A. D. (1953) 'Interests and school achievement.' *J. educ. psychol. Measur.*, **13**, 94-101.

GLASER, R. and NITKO, A. J. (1970) *Measurement in Learning and Instruction.* Learning Research and Development Center, University of Pittsburgh.

HICKLIN, W. J. (1962) 'A study of long-range techniques for predicting patterns of scholastic behavior.' Unpublished Ph.D. dissertation, University of Chicago.

HUSEN, T. (1967) (ed.) *International Study of Educational Achievement in Mathematics: A Comparison of Twelve Countries.* Volumes I and II. New York: Wiley.

HUSEN, T. (1969) *Talent, Opportunity and Career.* Stockholm: Almquist and Wiksell.

KHAN, S. B. (1969) 'Affective correlates of academic achievement.' *J. educ. Psychol.*, **60**, 216-21.

KURTZ, J. J. and SWENSON, E. J. (1951) 'Student, parent, and teacher attitude toward student achievement in school.' *School Review*, **59**, 273-9.

MICHAEL, W. B., BAKER, D. and JONES, R. A. (1964) 'A note concerning the predictive validities of selected cognitive and non-cognitive measures for freshmen students in a liberal arts college.' *J. educ. psychol. Measur.*, **24**, 373-5.

NEALE, D. C. (1969) 'The role of attitudes in learning mathematics.' *The Arithmetic Teacher*, **16**, 631-40.

PAYNE, M. A. (1963) 'The use of data in curricular decisions.' Unpublished Ph.D. dissertation, University of Chicago.

POPHAM, W. J. and HUSEK, T. R. (1969) 'Implications of criterion-referenced measurement.' *J. educ. Measur.*, **6**, 1-9.

RUSSELL, I. L. (1969) 'Motivation for school achievement: measurement and validation.' *J. educ. Res.*, **62**, 263-6.

SEARS, P. S. (1963) *The effect of classroom conditions on the strength of achievement motive and work output of elementary school children.* Cooperative Research Project Number OE 873, Stanford University, Stanford, California.

STRINGER, L. A. and GLIDEWELL, J. C. (1967) *Early Detection of Emotional Illness in School Children: Final Report.* Missouri: St Louis County Health Department.

TORSHEN, K. (1969) 'The relation of classroom evaluation to students' self-concepts and mental health.' Unpublished Ph.D. dissertation, University of Chicago.

WHITE, R. W. (1959) 'Motivation reconsidered: the concept of competence.' *Psychol. Rev.*, **66**, 297-333.

WYMAN, J. B. (1924) 'On the influence of interest on relative success.' Unpublished Ph.D. dissertation, Stanford University.

The epidemiology of handicapping conditions of educational concern

BIRCH, H. G. *et al.* (1970) *Mental Subnormality in the Community: A Clinical and Epidemiological Study.* Baltimore: Williams and Wilkins.

Committee on Local Authority and Allied Personal Social Services (1968) *The Seebohm Report.* London: HMSO.

DAVIE, R., BUTLER, N. R. and GOLDSTEIN, H. (1972) *From Birth to Seven.* London: Longman.

Department of Education and Science (1968) *Psychologists in Education Services* (Summerfield Report). London: HMSO.

DOUGLAS, J. W. B. (1964) *The Home and the School.* London: MacGibbon and Kee.

INGRAM, T. T. S., JAMESON, S., ERRINGTON, J. and MITCHELL, R. G. (1962) 'Living with Cerebral Palsy: a study of school leavers suffering from cerebral palsy in Eastern Scotland.' *Clinics in Developmental Medicine*, 14. Spastics Society and Heinemann.

LEWIS, E. O. (1929) *Report of the Mental Deficiency Committee*, Part IV. London: HMSO.

MAXWELL, J. (1953) *Social Implications of the 1947 Scottish Mental Survey.* London: University of London Press.

MAXWELL, J. (1961) *The Level and Trend of National Intelligence.* London: University of London Press.

MILLER, F. J. W., COURT, S. D. M., WALTON, W. S. and KNOX, E. G. (1960) *Growing up in Newcastle*. London: Oxford University Press.

MOORE, T. (1966) 'Difficulties of the ordinary child in adjusting to primary school.' *J. child Psychol. Psychiat.*, **7**, 1, 17-38.

PRINGLE, M. L. K., BUTLER, N. R. and DAVIE, R. (1966) *11,000 Seven-Year-Olds*. London: Longman.

RUTTER, M. (1966) *Children of Sick Parents: an Environmental and Psychiatric Study*. Maudsley Monograph No. 16. London: Oxford University Press.

RUTTER, M., GRAHAM, P. and YULE, W. (1970) *Neurological Disorders in Childhood: A Study in a Small Community*. London: Heinemann.

RUTTER, M., TIZARD, J. and WHITMORE, K. (1970) *Education, Health and Behaviour*. London: Longman.

SPENCE, J., MILLER, F. J. W. and COURT, S. D. M. (1964) *A Thousand Families in Newcastle upon Tyne—An Approach to the Study of Health and Illness in Children*. London: Oxford University Press.

TIZARD, J. and GRAD, J. C. (1961) *The Mentally Handicapped and their Families: A Social Survey*. Maudsley Monograph No. 7. London: Oxford University Press.

YULE, W. (1967) 'Predicting reading ages on Neale's Analysis of Reading Ability.' *Br. J. educ. Psychol.*, **37**, 2, 252-5.

The treatment of maladjusted pupils : research and experiment 1960-69

ACKERMANN, N. W. (1958) *The Psychodynamics of Family Life*. New York: Basic Books.

ARBUCKLE, D. S. (1967) (ed.) *Counseling and Psychotherapy: an Overview*. New York: McGraw-Hill.

Association of Psychiatric Social Workers (1963) *Relationship in Casework*. London.

Association of Teachers of Maladjusted Children (1967) *Therapeutic Education* (June 1967). London.

BALBERNIE, R. (1966) *Residential Work with Children*. Oxford: Pergamon.

BALOW, B. (1966) 'The emotionally and socially handicapped.' *Rev. educ. Res.*, **36**, 120-33.

BARTLETT, E. F. (1970) 'Survey of day units for the maladjusted child.' Unpublished dissertation, University College of Swansea.

BERGIN, A. E. (1967) 'An Empirical Analysis of Therapeutic Issues'. Ch. 9 in ARBUCKLE, D. S. (ed.) *op. cit.*

BETTELHEIM, B. (1950) *Love is Not Enough*. Illinois: Free Press of Glencoe.

BETTELHEIM, B. (1955) *Truants from Life*. Illinois: Free Press of Glencoe.

BREGER, L. and MCGAUGH, J. L. (1965) 'Critique and reformulation of "learning-theory" approaches to psychotherapy and neurosis.' *Psychol. Bull.*, **63**, 5, 338-58.

CAPLAN, G. (1961) *An Approach to Community Mental Health*. London: Tavistock.

CHAZAN, M. (1963) 'Maladjusted pupils: trends in post-war theory and practice.' *Educ. Res.*, **6**, 1, 29-41.

CHAZAN, M. (1968) 'Children's Emotional Development.' In BUTCHER, H. J. (ed.) *Educational Research in Britain*, **1**. London: University of London Press.

CHAZAN, M. (1969) 'Maladjustment and reading difficulties I: Recent research and experiment.' *Rem. Educ.*, **4**, 3, 119-23.

CLYNE, M. B. (1966) *Absent*. London: Tavistock.

Committee on Local Authority and Allied Personal Social Services (1968) *The Seebohm Report*. London: HMSO.

DAVIDSON, S. (1961) 'School phobia as a manifestation of family disturbance: its structure and treatment.' *J. child Psychol. Psychiat.*, **1**, 270-87.

Department of Education and Science (1968) *Psychologists in Education Services* (Summerfield Report). London: HMSO.

Department of Education and Science (1971) *Statistics of Education, 1970*, Part I. London: HMSO.

DUPONT, H. (1969) (ed.) *Educating Emotionally Disturbed Children*. New York: Holt, Rinehart and Winston.

ENGELN, R., KNUTSON, J., LAUGHY, L. and GARLINGTON, W. (1968) 'Behaviour modification techniques applied to a family unit—a case study.' *J. child Psychol. Psychiat.*, **9**, 245-52.

EYSENCK, H. J. and RACHMAN, S. (1965) *The Causes and Cures of Neurosis*. London: Routledge and Kegan Paul.

FENICHEL, C. (1966) 'Psycho-Educational Approaches for Seriously Disturbed Children in the Classroom.' In KNOBLOCK, P. (ed.) *Emotionally Disturbed Children*. New York: Syracuse University Press.

FISCHER, I. (1968) 'The Relevance of Behaviour Therapy for the Understanding and Treatment of Psychotic Children.' In MITTLER, P. J. (ed.) *Aspects of Autism*. London: BPS.

FOULKES, S. H. and ANTHONY, E. J. (1965) *Group Psychotherapy: the Psychoanalytic Approach.*. Harmondsworth: Penguin (2nd edn).

GITTLEMAN, M. (1965) 'Behaviour rehearsal as a technique in child treatment.' *J. child Psychol. Psychiat.*, **6**, 251-5.

GLAVIN, J. P. and QUAY, H. C. (1969) 'Behaviour disorders.' *Rev. educ. Res.*, **39**, 1, 83-102.

GRANT, Q. R. (1962) 'Psychopharmacology in childhood emotional and mental disorders.' *J. Paediat.*, **61**, 626-37.

GRAY, W. and NOBLE, F. C. (1968) 'The School Counsellor and the School Psychologist.' In ADAMS, J. F. (ed.) *Counselling and Guidance: a Summary View*. New York: Macmillan.

HARING, N. G. and PHILLIPS, E. L. (1962) *Educating Emotionally Disturbed Children*. New York: McGraw-Hill.

HEWETT, F. M. (1967) 'Educational engineering with emotionally disturbed children.' *Except. Child.*, **33**, 459-67.

HOWELLS, J. G. (1963) *Family Psychiatry*. Edinburgh: Oliver and Boyd.

JONES, A. (1970) *School Counselling in Practice*. London: Ward Lock Educational.

KOUNIN, J. S., FRIESEN, W. V. and NORTON, A. (1966) 'Managing emotionally disturbed children in regular classrooms.' *J. educ. Psychol.*, **57**, 1-13.

LENHOFF, F. G. (1960) *Exceptional Children*. London: Allen and Unwin.

LEVITT, E. E. (1957) 'The results of psychotherapy with children.' *J. consult. Psychol.*, **21**, 189-95.

LEVITT, E. E. (1963) 'Psychotherapy with children; a further evaluation.' *Behav. Res. Ther.*, **1**, 45-51.

LEWIS, W. W. (1967) 'Project Re-Ed: Educational Intervention in Discordant Child Rearing Systems.' In COWEN, E. L., GARDNER, E. A. and ZAX, M. (eds) *Emergent Approaches to Mental Health Problems*. New York: Appleton-Century-Crofts.

LOCKYER, L. and RUTTER, M. (1969) 'A five to fifteen year follow-up study of infantile psychosis III: Psychological aspects.' *Br. J. Psychiat.*, **115**, 865-82.

LYTTON, H. and CRAFT, M. (1969) *Guidance and Counselling in British Schools—a discussion of current issues*. London: Arnold.

MACLAY, I. (1967) 'Prognostic factors in child guidance practice.' *J. child Psychol. Psychiat.*, **8**, 3/4, 207-15.

MCKERRACHER, D. W. (1967) 'Alleviation of reading difficulties by a simple operant conditioning technique.' *J. child Psychol. Psychiat.*, **8**, 1, 51-6.

MEYER, V. and CHESSER, E. S. (1970) *Behaviour Therapy in Clinical Psychiatry*. Harmondsworth: Penguin.

MHAS, O. (1970) *Group Counselling*. New York: Holt, Rinehart and Winston.

MORSE, W. C. and DYER, C. W. (1963) 'The emotionally and socially handicapped.' *Rev. educ. Res.*, **33**, 109-25.

National Association for Mental Health (1970) *School Counselling*. London.

NEWTON, M. R. and BROWN, R. D. (1967) 'A Preventive Approach to Developmental Problems in School Children.' Ch. 21 in BOWER, E. M. and HOLLISTER, W. G. (eds) *Behavioural Science Frontiers in Education*. New York: Wiley.

PATTERSON, B. R., MCNEAL, S., HAWKINS, N. and PHELPS, R. (1967) 'Reprogramming the social environment.' *J. child Psychol. Psychiat.*, **8**, 3/4, 181-95.

PETRIE, I. R. J. (1962) 'Residential treatment of maladjusted children: a study of some factors related to progress in adjustment.' *Br. J. educ. Psychol.*, **32**, 29-37.

PRINGLE, M. L. K., BUTLER, N. R. and DAVIE, R. (1966) *11,000 Seven-Year-Olds*. London: Longman.

ROBINS, L. N. (1966) *Deviant Children Grown Up*. Baltimore: Williams and Wilkins.

ROE, M. C. (1965) *Survey into Progress of Maladjusted Pupils*. London: ILEA.

Royal Medico-Psychological Association, Child Psychiatry Section (1966) 'Report on schools and hostels for maladjusted children.' *Br. J. Psychiat.*, **112**, 484, 321-8.

RUTTER, M. and GRAHAM, P. (1966) 'Psychiatric disorder in 10- and 11-year-old children.' *Proc. R. Soc. Med.*, **59**, 382-7.

RUTTER, M., GREENFIELD, D. and LOCKYER, L. (1967) 'A five to fifteen year follow-up study of infantile psychosis II: Social and behavioural outcome.' *Br. J. Psychiat.*, **113**, 1183-99.

RUTTER, M. and LOCKYER, L. (1967) 'A five to fifteen year follow-up study of infantile psychosis I: Description of sample.' *Br. J. Psychiat.*, **113**, 1169-82.

RUTTER, M. et al. (1967) 'A tri-axial classification of mental disorders in childhood. An international study.' *J. child Psychol. Psychiat.*, **10**, 41-61.

SCHIFF, S. and KELLAM, S. G. (1967) 'A community-wide mental health programme of prevention and early treatment in first grade.' *Psych. Research Report* 21, American Psychiatric Association, 92-102.

SHAW, O. L. (1965) *Maladjusted Boys*. London: Allen and Unwin.

SHEPHERD, M., OPPENHEIM, A. N. and MITCHELL, S. (1966) 'Childhood behaviour disorders and the child guidance clinic: an epidemiological study.' *J. child Psychol. Psychiat.*, **7**, 1, 39-52.

SHIELDS, R. W. (1962) *A Cure of Delinquents—the Treatment of Maladjustment*. London: Heinemann (2nd edn 1971).

SLAVSON, S. R. (1943) *An Introduction to Group Therapy*. New York: Commonwealth Fund.

SLOANE, H. N., JOHNSTON, M. N. and BIJOU, S. W. (1967) 'Successive modification of aggressive behaviour and aggressive fantasy play by management of contingencies.' *J. child Psychol. Psychiat.*, **8**, 3/4, 217-26.

THOULESS, R. H. (1969) *Map of Educational Research*. Slough: NFER.

TOD, R. J. N. (1968) *Disturbed Children. Papers on Residental Work*, Volume 2. London: Longman.

ULLMAN, L. and KRASNER, L. (1965) *Case Studies in Behaviour Modification*. New York: Holt, Rinehart and Winston.

University of London Institute of Education (1973) 'The "problem" child and the psychological services.' *London Educational Review*, Summer 1973.

VALETT, R. (1966) 'A social reinforcement technique for the classroom management of behaviour disorders.' *Except, Child.*, **33**, 3, 185-9.

WAHLER, R. G., WINKEL, G. H., PETERSON, R. F. and MORRISON, D. C. (1965) 'Mothers as behaviour therapists for their own children.' *Beh. Res. Ther.*, **3**, 113-24.

WALTON, D. (1961) 'Experimental psychology and the treatment of a ticqueur.' *J. child Psychol. Psychiat.*, **2**, 148-55.

WARREN, W. (1965) 'A study of adolescent psychiatric inpatients and the outcome six or more years later. Part 1, Clinical histories and hospital findings. Part II, The follow-up study.' *J. child Psychol. Psychiat.*, **6**, 1-17 and 141-60.

WERRY, J. S., WEISS, G., DOUGLAS, V. and MARTIN, J. (1966) 'Studies on the hyperactive child: the effect of chlorpromazine upon behaviour and learning ability.' *J. child Psychiat.*, **5**, 292-312.

WHELAN, R. J. (1966) 'The Relevance of Behaviour Modification Procedures for Teachers of Emotionally Disturbed Children.' In KNOBLOCK, P. (ed.) *Intervention Approaches in Educating Emotionally Disturbed Children*. New York: Syracuse University Press.

WHELAN, R. and HARING, N. (1966) 'Modification and maintenance of behaviour through systematic application of consequences.' *Except. Child.*, **32**, 281-9.

WILLIAMS, D. (1969) 'Maladjustment and reading difficulties III: Remedial treatment.' *Rem. Educ.*, **4**, 3, 129-33.

WILLIAMS, N. (1961) 'Criteria for Recovery of Maladjusted Children in Residential Schools.' Unpublished M.Ed. thesis, University of Durham.

WING, J. K. (1966) (ed.) *Child Autism: Clinical, Educational and Social Aspects*. Oxford: Pergamon.

WOLFF, S. (1961) 'Symptomatology and outcome of pre-school children with behaviour disorders attending a child guidance clinic.' *J. child Psychol. Psychiat.*, **2**, 269-75.

WOLFF, S. (1969) *Children Under Stress*. Harmondsworth: Penguin.

YULE, W. (1969) 'Maladjustment and reading difficulties II: The findings of the Isle of Wight studies.' *Rem. Educ.*, **4**, 3, 124-8.

Advances in remedial education

BANNATYNE, A. (1971) *Language, Reading and Learning Disabilities*. Springfield, Ill.: Thomas.

BATEMAN, B. (1965) 'An educator's view of a diagnostic approach to learning disorders.' In HELLMUTH, J. (ed.) *Learning Disorders*. Seattle: Special Child Publications.

BARTLETT, D. and SHAPIRO, M. B. (1956) 'Investigation and treatment of a reading difficulty in a dull child with severe psychiatric disturbance.' *Br. J. educ. Psychol.*, **26**, 180-90.

Board of Education (1932) *Handbook of Suggestions for Teachers*. London: HMSO.

Board of Education (1937) *The Education of Backward Children*. London. HMSO.

BRENNAN, W. K. (1971) 'A policy for remedial education.' *Rem. Educ.*, **6**, 1, 7-11

BRENNER, N. W. and GILLMAN, S. (1968) 'Verbal intelligence, visuo-motor ability and school achievement.' *Br. J. educ. Psychol.*, **38**, 1, 75-8.

BURT, C. (1937) *The Backward Child*. London: University of London Press.

CASPARI, I. E. (1973) 'Educational Therapy.' In VARMA, V. P. (ed.) *Psychotherapy Today*. London: Constable.

CASPARI, I. E. (In press) 'Anxiety about Learning.' In VARMA, V. P. (ed.) *Anxiety in School Children*. London: Pitman Medical.

CLARK, M. (1970) *Reading Difficulties in School*. Harmondsworth: Penguin.

CORDTS, A. D. (1965) *Phonics for the Reading Teacher*. New York: Holt, Rinehart and Winston.

COTTERELL, G. (1972) 'A case of severe learning disability.' *Rem. Educ.*, **7**, 1, 5-9.

CRANE, A. R. (1959) 'An historical and critical account of the accomplishment quotient idea.' *Br. J. educ. Psychol.*, **29**, 252-8.

DE HIRSCH, K. and JANSKY, J. J. (1966) 'Early prediction of reading, writing and spelling ability.' *British Journal of Disorders of Communication*, **1**, 2, 99-108.

Department of Education and Science (1971) *Slow Learners in Secondary Schools.* Education Survey 15. London: HMSO.

Department of Education and Science (1972) *Severe Reading Difficulties.* London: HMSO.

FROSTIG, M. (1964) *The Frostig Developmental Test of Visual Perception.* Palo Alto, California: Consulting Psychologist Press.

FROSTIG, M. (1968) 'Testing as a Basis for Educational Therapy.' In LORING, J. (ed.) *Assessment of the Cerebral Palsied Child.* London: Spastics Society and Heinemann.

GRAHAM, N. C. (1970) 'The language of educationally subnormal children.' Unpublished report, University of Birmingham.

GULLIFORD, R. (1971) *Special Educational Needs.* London: Routledge and Kegan Paul.

HEWETT, F. (1964) 'A hierarchy of educational tasks for children with learning disorders.' *Except. Child.* **34**, 4, 207-14.

INGLIS, A. and CONNEL, E. (1964) *The Teaching of Handwriting.* London: Nelson.

INGRAM, T. T. S. (1960) 'Paediatric aspects of specific developmental dysphasia, dyslexia and dysgraphia.' *Cerebral Palsy Bulletin*, **2**, 254-76.

JOHNSON, D. J. and MYKLEBUST, H. R. (1967) *Learning Disabilities.* New York: Grune and Stratton.

KIRK, S. A. and KIRK, W. D. (1971) *Psycholinguistic Learning Disabilities: diagnosis and remediation.* Urbana: University of Illinois Press.

KIRK, S. A., MCCARTHY, J. J. and KIRK, W. D. (1968) *The Illinois Test of Psycholinguistic Abilities.* Urbana: University of Illinois Press (rev. edn).

LAWRENCE, D. (1971) 'The effect of counselling on retarded readers.' *Educ. Res.*, **13**, 2, 119-24.

LEWIS, E. O. (1931) *Reorganisation and the Retarded Child.* London: National Union of Teachers.

LYTTON, H. (1968) 'Selection for remedial education.' *Rem. Educ.*, **3**, 2, 66-9.

MERRITT, J. (1969) 'Reading skills re-examined.' *Special Education*, **58**, 1, 18-22.

MITTLER, P. (1970) (ed.) *The Psychological Assessment of Mental and Physical Handicaps.* London: Methuen.

MORRIS, J. M. (1966) *Standards and Progress in Reading.* Slough: NFER.

PETERS, N. (1967) 'The influence of reading methods on spelling.' *Br. J. educ. Psychol.*, **37**, 1, 47-53.

PHILLIPS, C. J. (1958) 'Retardation and the use of tests.' *Educ. Rev.*, **11**, 1, 16-30.

PHILLIPS, C. J. (1968) 'The future of remedial education services.' *Rem. Educ.*, **3**, 2, 70-3.

PRESLAND, T. (1970) *Applied Psychology and Backwardness in Handwriting.* Broadstone, Dorset: Association of Educational Psychologists.

PRINGLE, M. L. K., BUTLER, N. R. and DAVIE, R. (1966) *11,000 Seven-Year-Olds.* London: Longman.

REID, J. (1966) 'Learning to think about reading.' *Educ. Res.,* **9**, 1, 56-62.

REYNELL, J. K. (1969) *Reynell Developmental Language Scales.* Slough: NFER.

ROBERTS, G. R. and LUNZER, E. A. (1968) 'Reading and learning to read.' In LUNZER, E. A. and MORRIS, J. F. (eds) *Development in Human Learning.* London: Staples.

RUTTER, M., TIZARD, J. and WHITMORE, K. (1970) *Education, Health and Behaviour.* London: Longman.

SAMPSON, O. (1969) 'Remedial Education Services.' *Rem. Educ.,* **4**, 3-8 and 61-5.

SCHONELL, F. J. (1942) *Backwardness in the Basic Subjects.* Edinburgh: Oliver and Boyd.

SCHONELL, F. J. (1957) *Diagnosis and Remedial Teaching in Arithmetic.* Edinburgh: Oliver and Boyd.

SCHONFIELD, D. (1956) 'Special difficulties at a reading age of 8+.' *Br. J. educ. Psychol.,* **26**, 2, 39-50.

TANSLEY, A. E. (1967) *Reading and Remedial Reading.* London: Routledge and Kegan Paul.

VERNON, P. E. (1958) 'The relation of intelligence to educational backwardness.' *Educ. Rev.,* **11**, 1, 7-15.

WARD, J. (1971) 'On the concept of criterion-reference measurement.' *Br. J. educ. Psychol.,* **40**, 3, 314-21.

WEDELL, K. (1968) 'Perceptual-motor difficulties.' *Special Education,* **57**, 25-30.

WEDELL, K. (1970) 'Diagnosing learning difficulties.' *Journal & Newsletter, Association of Educational Psychologists,* **2**, 7, 23-9.

WEPMAN, J. (1958) *Auditory Discrimination Test.* Chicago: Language Research Association.

YOUNGHUSBAND, E., BIRCHALL, D., DAVIE, R. and PRINGLE M. L. K. (1970) *Living with Handicap.* London: National Children's Bureau.

Brain-damaged children: psychological and educational implications

ABERCROMBIE, M. L. J. (1964a) 'Perceptual and Visuomotor Disorders in Cerebral Palsy.' *Clinics in Dev. Med.* No. 11. London: Spastics Society and Heinemann.

ABERCROMBIE, M. L. J. *et al.* (1964b) 'Visual Perceptual and Visuomotor Impairments in Physically Handicapped Children.' *Percept. mot. Skills,* Monogr. Supp. 3, Vol. V, No. 18.

ABERCROMBIE, M. L. J. (1965) 'On Drawing a Diamond.' Article in Penguin Science Survey B.

ABERCROMBIE, M. L. J. (1968) 'Some notes on spatial disability: movement, intelligence quotient and attentiveness.' *Dev. Med. & Child Neurol.*, **10**, 2, 206-13.

BAX, M. and MACKEITH, R. (1963) (eds) 'Minimal Cerebral Dysfunctioning.' *Clinics in Dev. Med.* No. 10. London: Spastics Society and Heinemann.

BIRCH, H. G. (1964) *Brain Damage in Children. The Biological and Social Aspects.* Baltimore: Williams and Wilkins.

BIRCH, H. G. (1965) 'Auditory visual integration, intelligence and reading ability in school children.' *Percept. mot. Skills*, Monogr. 20.

BORTNER, M. (1968) (ed.) *Evaluation and Education of Children with Brain Damage.* Springfield, Ill.: Thomas.

BOWLEY, A. H. (1969) 'Reading difficulty with minor neurological dysfunctioning.' *Dev. Med. & Child Neurol.*, **11**, 4, 493-503.

BRENNER, M. W. and GILLMAN, S. (1966) 'Visual motor ability in schoolchildren: a survey.' *Dev. Med. & Child Neurol.*, **8**, 6, 686-703.

BROWN, R. I. (1965) 'The effects of varied environmental stimulation on the performance of subnormal children.' *J. clin. Psychol.*, **7**, 25-261.

BROWN, R. I. and SEMPLE, L. (1970) 'Effects of unfamiliarity on the overt verbalization and perceptual motor behaviour of nursery school children.' *Br. J. educ. Psychol.*, **40**, 3, 291-8.

CASHDAN, A. and JEFFREE, D. M. (1966) 'The influence of home background on the development of severely subnormal children.' *Br. J. med. Psychol.*, **39**, 4, 313-18.

CHALFANT, C. J. and SCHEFFELIN, M. A. (1970) *Central Processing Dysfunctions in Children. Phase Three of a Three Phase Project.* US Nat. Instit. of Neurologic. Diseases and Stroke. Monogr. No. 9.

CLEMENTS, S. D. and PETERS, J. F. (1962) 'Minimal brain dysfunction in school age children.' *Archs. gen. Psychiat.*, **6**, 185-197.

CLEMENTS, S. D. (1966) *Minimal Brain Dysfunction in Children. Phase One of a Three Phase Project.* US Nat. Instit. of Neurologic. Diseases and Stroke. Monogr. No. 3, US Dept. of Health, Educ. and Welfare.

CONNOLLY, K. (1968) 'The application of operant conditioning to the measurement and development of motor skills in children.' *Dev. Med. & Child Neurol.*, **10**, 6, 697-705.

CONNOLLY, K. and JONES, B. (1970) 'A developmental study of afferent-reafferent integration.' *Br. J. Psych.*, **61**, 2, 259-66.

CRAWFORD, J. E. (1964) *Children with Subtle Perceptual Motor Difficulties.* Pittsburg: Stanwix House.

CRUICKSHANK, W. M. et al. (1957) *Perception in Cerebral Palsy, a Study in Figure Background Relationship.* New York: Syracuse University Press (rev. edn 1965).

CRUICKSHANK, W. M. et al. (1961) *A Teaching Method for Brain Injured and Hyperactive Children.* New York: Syracuse University Press.

K

CRUICKSHANK, W. M. (1966) (ed.) *The Teacher of Brain Injured Children: a Discussion of the Bases for Competency.* New York: Syracuse Univ. Press.

CRUICKSHANK, W. M. (1966) *Cerebral Palsy: its Implications and Community Problems.* New York: Syracuse University Press.

CRUICKSHANK, W. M. (1967) *The Brain Injured Child in Home, School and Community.* New York: Syracuse University Press.

CRUICKSHANK, W. M. (1968) 'Educational Implications of Psychopathology in Brain Injured Children.' In LORING, J. (ed.) *op. cit.*

DINNAGE, R. (1971) *The Handicapped Child: Research Review, Vol. I.* London: Longman and National Children's Bureau.

FIELD, J. G. (1960) 'Two types of tables for use with Wechsler's Intelligence Scales.' *J. clin. Psychol.,* **16**, 6, 3-8.

FRANCIS-WILLIAMS, J. (1970) *Children with Specific Learning Difficulties.* Oxford: Pergamon.

FROSTIG, M. *et al.* (1964) *The Marianne Frostig Developmental Test of Visual Perception.* Palo Alto, California: Consulting Psychologists Press.

FROSTIG, M. (1968) 'Testing as a Basis for Educational Therapy.' In LORING, J. (ed.) *op. cit.*

GALLACHER, J. J. (1960) *The Tutoring of Brain Injured Mentally Retarded Children.* Springfield, Ill.: Thomas.

GRAHAM, F. K. *et al.* (1962) 'Development three years after perinatal anoxia.' *Psychol. Monogr.,* **76**, No. 3.

GRAHAM, F. K. *et al.* (1963) 'Brain Injury in the preschool child, some developmental considerations.' *Psychol. Monogr.,* **77**, 10, 1-16.

HEWETT, S. with J. and E. NEWSON (1970) *The Family and the Handicapped Child.* London: Allen and Unwin.

HORN, J. and QUARMBY, D. (1970) 'The problem of older non-readers.' *Special Education,* **59**, 3, 23-5.

HUTT, C. *et al.* (1964) 'Arousal and childhood autism.' *Nature,* **204**, 908-9.

HUTT, S. J. *et al.* (1963) 'A method of studying children's behaviour.' *Dev. Med. & Child Neurol.,* **5**, 3, 233-45.

HUTT, S. J. and HUTT, C. (1964) 'Hyperactivity in a group of epileptic (and some non-epileptic) brain-damaged children.' *Epilepsia,* **5**, 334-51.

HUTT, S. J. and HUTT, C. (1970) (eds.) *Behaviour Studies in Psychiatry.* Oxford: Pergamon.

JOHNSON, D. D. and MYKLEBUST, H. R. (1967) *Learning Disabilities: Educational Principles and Practice.* New York: Grune and Stratton.

KEPHART, N. C. (1960) *The Slow Learner in the Classroom.* Columbus, Ohio: Merrill.

LANSDOWN, R. (1970) *A Study of the Frostig Programme for the Development of Visual Perception used in the Ordinary Primary School.* London Borough of Waltham Forest.

LORD, E. E. (1930) 'A study of mental development of children with lesions in the CNS.' *Genet. Psychol. Monogr.,* **7**, 365-486.

LORING, J. (1968) (ed.) *The Assessment of the Cerebral Palsied Child for Education.* London: Spastics Society and Heinemann.

NIELSEN, H. H. (1966) *A Psychological Study of Cerebral Palsied Children.* Copenhagen: Munksgaard.

PAINE, R. S. *et al.* (1968) 'A study of minimal cerebral dysfunctioning.' *Dev. Med. & Child Neurol.,* **10,** 4, 505-20.

PIAGET, J. and INHELDER, B. (1956) *The Child's Conception of Space.* London: Routledge and Kegan Paul.

PRINGLE, M. L. KELLMER (1964) *The Emotional and Social Adjustment of Physically Handicapped Children.* Slough: NFER Occas. Pub. No. 11.

REYNELL, J. (1969) *Infant and Young Children's Language Scales, Manual and Test Material.* Slough: NFER.

RUTTER, M., GRAHAM, P. and YULE, W. (1970) 'A Neuropsychiatric Study in Childhood.' *Clinics in Dev. Med.* Nos. 35 and 36. London: Spastics Society and Heinemann.

RUTTER, M., TIZARD, J. and WHITMORE, K. (1970) *Education, Health and Behaviour.* London: Longman.

SCHULMAN, J. L. *et al.* (1965) *Brain Damage and Behaviour.* Springfield, Ill.: Thomas.

SLOAN, W. (1955) 'The Lincoln Oseretzky Motor Developmental Scale.' *Genet. Psychol. Monogr.,* **51,** 183.

STOTT, D. H. (1966) 'A general test of motor impairment for children.' *Dev. Med. & Child Neurol.,* **8,** 5, 523-31.

STRAUSS, A. A. and KEPHART, N. C. (1955) *Psychopathology and Education of the Brain-Injured Child. Vol. II.* New York: Grune and Stratton.

STRAUSS, A. A. and LEHTINEN, L. E. (1947) *Psychopathology and Education of the Brain-Injured Child. Vol. I.* New York: Grune and Stratton.

TANSLEY, A. E. (1967) *Reading and Remedial Reading.* London: Routledge and Kegan Paul.

THOMAS, A., CHESS, S. and BIRCH, H. G. (1968) *Temperament and Behaviour Disorders in Children.* New York: University Press.

THOMPSON, D. A. and JOHNSON, J. D. (1971) 'Teaching machines for the very handicapped: the Touch-Tutor at Hawksworth Hall.' *Special Education,* **60,** 1, 11-12.

TYSON, M. (1963) 'Pilot study of remedial visuomotor training.' *Special Education,* **52,** 4, 22-5.

TYSON, M. (1970) 'The Design of Remedial Programmes.' Ch. 22 in MITTLER, P. (ed.) *The Psychological Assessment of Mental and Physical Handicaps.* London: Methuen.

WALL, W. D. (1955) *Education and Mental Health.* Paris: UNESCO; London: Harrap.

WALTON, J. N., ELLIS, E. and COURT, S. D. (1962) 'Clumsy children, a study of developmental apraxia and agnosia.' *Brain,* **84,** 603.

WECHSLER, D. (1958) *The Measurement and Appraisal of Adult Intelligence.* Baltimore: Williams and Wilkins.

WEDELL, K. (1960) 'The visual perception of cerebral palsied children.' *J. child Psychol. Psychiat.*, **1**, 215-27.

WEDELL, K. (1968) 'Perceptual motor difficulties.' *Special Education*, **57**, 4, 25-30.

WEDELL, K. (1973) *Learning and Perceptuo-Motor Disabilities in Children*. London: Wiley.

WHITING, H. *et al.* (1969) 'A clinical evaluation of the Stott test of motor impairment.' *Br. J. soc. clin. Psychol.*, **8**, 270-4.

WILLIAMS, M. (1970) *Brain Damage and the Mind*. Harmondsworth: Penguin.

WOLF, J. M. (1969) (ed.) *The Results of Treatment in Cerebral Palsy*. Springfield, Ill.: Thomas.

Mobility training for children in British schools for the blind

ANNETT, J. (1969) *Feedback and Human Behaviour*. Harmondsworth: Penguin.

College of Teachers of the Blind (1968) *Mobility Guidance*. Nottingham Univ.

GRAY, P. G. and TODD, J. A. (1968) *Mobility and Reading Habits of the Blind*. (SS 386). London: HMSO.

LEONARD, J. A. (1968) Report on a conference on the Mobility of Blind Persons with special emphasis on the Long Cane Technique. July 1968. Southern Regional Association for the Blind.

LEONARD, J. A. and NEWMAN, R. C. (1967) 'Spatial orientation in the blind.' *Nature*, **215**, 1413-14.

SENDEN, V. (1960) *Space and Sight*. London: Methuen.

THORNTON, W. (1968) *Cure for Blindness*. London: Hodder and Stoughton.

Advances in the education of hearing-handicapped children

BEAGLEY, H. A. and KELLOGG, S. E. (1969) 'A comparison of evoked response and subjective auditory thresholds.' *Int. Audiol.*, **8**, 345.

CORNETT, R. O. (1970) 'Effects of Cued Speech upon Language and Speech Patterns of the Aurally Handicapped Child.' Stockholm, Sweden: International Congress on Education of the Deaf.

DALE, D. M. C. (1967) *Applied Audiology for Children*. Springfield, Ill.: Thomas.

DALE, D. M. C. (1968) *Deaf Children at Home and at School*. London: University of London Press.

DALE, D. M. C. (1971) *Language Development for Deaf Children Through Social Studies*. Washington DC: Alexander Graham Bell Association for the Deaf.

DAVIS, H. *et al.* (1946) 'The selection of hearing aids.' *Laryngoscope*, **56**, 85-63

DAVIS, H. and ONISHI, S. (1969) 'Maturation of auditory evoked potentials.' *Int. Audiol.*, **8**, 371.

Department of Education and Science (1967) *Education Survey I: Units for Partially Hearing Children*. London: HMSO.

Department of Education and Science (1968) *The Place, if any, of Fingerspelling and Signing in the Education of Deaf Children*. London: HMSO.

DOCTOR, P. V. (1970) 'Educational Impact—The 1964-65 Rubella Epidemic in the United States.' Stockholm: Int. Cong. Ed. of Deaf.

EWING, A. W. G. and EWING, I. R. (1958) *New Opportunities for Deaf Children.* London: University of London Press.

EWING, A. W. G. and EWING, E. C. (1968) *Teaching Deaf Children to Talk.* Manchester: University Press.

HARDY, W. (1971) 'Speech for the Deaf Child: Knowledge and Trends.' In CONNOR, L. E. (ed.) *Speech for the Deaf Child.* Washington DC: A. G. Bell Assn.

JOHANNSON, B. (1966) 'The use of the transposer for the management of the deaf child.' *Int. Audiol.,* **5**, 362-72.

RAPIN, I. and GRAZIANIH, L. M. (1969) 'Summated auditory evoked responses for audiometry.' *Int. Audiol.,* **8**, 371.

SILVERMAN, S. R. and DAVIS, H. (1960) *Hearing and Deafness—A Guide for Laymen.* New York: Rinehart and Winston.

SPENCER, L. M. (1970) 'The construction of a test of the intelligibility of the speech of deaf children.' Unpublished Ph.D. thesis, University of London.

US Department of Health, Education and Welfare (1965) *Education of the Deaf.* Washington DC: Government Printing Office.

VERNON, P. E. (1969) *Intelligence and Cultural Environment.* London: Methuen.

The education of gifted children

BURT, C. (1961) 'The gifted child.' *Br. J. statist. Psychol.,* **14**, 2, 123-39.

BURT, C. (1962a) 'The gifted child.' In BEREDAY and LAUWERYS (eds) *The Year Book of Education.* London: Evans.

BURT, C. (1962b) 'Critical notice: Creativity and Intelligence, by J. W. Getzels and P. W. Jackson.' *Br. J. educ. Psychol.,* **12**, 292-8.

BURT, C. (1963) 'Is intelligence normally distributed?' *Br. J. statist. Psychol.,* **16**, 2, 175-90.

Department of Education and Science (1968) *Education of Gifted Children.* London: HMSO.

HOLLINGWORTH, S. (1942) *Children Above 180 I.Q.* New York: World Book Co.

PRINGLE, M. L. K. (1970) *Able Misfits.* London: Longman/Nat. Children's Bureau.

ROSENTHAL, R. and JACOBSON, L. (1970) *Pygmalion in the Classroom. Teacher expectation and pupils' intellectual development.* New York: Holt, Rinehart and Winston.

Scottish Education Department (1965) *Primary Education in Scotland.* Edinburgh: HMSO.

TERMAN, L. M. et al. (1925) *Genetic Studies of Genius. Vol. 1, Mental and Physical Traits of a Thousand Gifted Children.* California: Stanford University Press.

TERMAN, L. M. et al. (1959) *Genetic Studies of Genius. Vol. 5, The Gifted Group at Mid-Life.* California: Stanford University Press.

WALL, W. D. (1960a) 'Highly intelligent children I. The psychology of the gifted.' *Educ. Res.*, **II**, 2, 101-11.

WALL, W. D. (1960b) 'Highly intelligent children II. The education of the gifted.' *Educ. Res.*, **II**, 3, 207-17.

Advances in training educational psychologists

BURT, C. (1969) 'Psychologists in the education services.' *Bull. Br. psychol. Soc.*, **22**, 1-12.

CURR, W. (1969) 'Critical notice of Psychologists in Education Services.' *Br. J. educ. Psychol.*, **39**, 92-6.

CURRIE, J. M. (1969) 'Psychologists in education services: teaching experience.' *Bull. Br. psychol. Soc.*, **22**, 89-91.

Department of Education and Science (1968) *Psychologists in Education Services*. London: HMSO.

FROST, B. P. (1969) Letter to the editor, *Bull. Br. psychol. Soc.*, **22**, 258-9.

KEIR, G. (1953) 'Symposium on psychologists and psychiatrists in the child guidance service III. A history of child guidance.' *Br. J. educ. Psychol.*, **22**, 5-29.

Ministry of Education (1955) *Report of the Committee on Maladjusted Children*. London: HMSO.

MOORE, R. B. W. (1969) 'The nature of educational psychology in school psychological and child guidance services.' *Bull. Br. psychol. Soc.*, **22**, 185-7.

MORRIS, J. (1969). Unpublished contribution to the symposium on Psychologists in Education Services, held by the Education Section of the British Psychological Society at Roehampton, September 1969.

MURRELL, K. F. H. (1969) 'Specialization in psychology at undergraduate level in university education.' *Bull. Br. psychol. Soc.*, **22**, 189-92.

NISBET, J. (1962) 'The Scottish Bachelor of Education Degree: a follow-up.' *Bull. Br. psychol. Soc.*, **15**, 27-8.

RUTTER, M., TIZARD, J. and WHITMORE, K. (1970) *Education, Health and Behaviour*. London: Longman.

TRAXLER, A. J. (1967) 'State certification of school psychologists: recent trends.' *Am. Psychol.*, **22**, 8, 660-6.

The draw-a-man test (Machover) at adolescence

MACHOVER, K. (1949) *Personality Projection in the Drawing of the Human Figure*. Springfield, Ill.: Thomas.

OSTERRIETH, P. A. (1968) 'Étude de l'âge apparent des personnages dessinés par les enfants et les adolescents des deux sexes.' Proceedings of the VI Congrè International Rorschach, Paris, 1965, **IV**, 651-7.

OSTERRIETH, P. A. and CAMBIER, A. (1963) 'Vers une utilisation plus rigoureuse et plus exhaustive du dessin en psychologie: quelques jalons.' *Bulletin de Psychologie*, Paris, No. 225, **XVII**, 248-52.

OSTERRIETH, P. A. and CAMBIER, A. (1969) 'Essai d'investigation rigoureuse du dessin chez l'enfant.' *Revue de Neuropsychiatrie infantile*, Paris, No. 617, 393-409.

Intellectual aspects of adolescence

CONNELL, R. W. (1971) *The Child's Construction of Politics*. Melbourne: The University Press.

GOLDMAN, J. (1964) *Religious Thinking from Childhood to Adolescence*. London: Routledge and Kegan Paul.

INHELDER, B. and PIAGET, J. (1958) *The Growth of Logical Thinking*. London: Routledge and Kegan Paul.

KIMBALL, R. L. (1968) *A Background Concept Study in Malawi*. Domasi: Science Centre.

LOVELL, K. and SLATER, A. (1960) 'The growth of the concept of time: a comparative study.' *J. child Psychol. Psychiat.*, **1**, 179-90.

ORTON, A. (1970) 'A cross-sectional study of the development of the mathematical concept of function in secondary school children of average and above-average ability.' M.Ed. Thesis, University of Leeds.

PELUFFO, N. (1967) 'Culture and cognitive problems.' *Int. J. Psychol.*, **2**, 187-98.

PIAGET, J. (1946) *Le Développement De La Notion De Temps Chez L'Enfant*. Paris: Presses Univer. Translated 1969, *The Child's Conception of Time*. London: Routledge and Kegan Paul.

PIAGET, J. *et al.* (1968) *Épistemologie et Psychologie De La Fonction*. Paris: P.U.F.

TABACK, S. F. (1969) 'The child's concept of limit.' Ph.D. Thesis, Teachers College, Columbia University.

THOMAS, H. L. (1969) 'An analysis of stages in the attainment of a concept of a function.' Ph.D. Thesis, Teachers College, Columbia University.

Emotional and moral aspects of adolescence

ARGYLE, M. (1967) *The Psychology of Interpersonal Behaviour*. Harmondsworth: Penguin.

ARGYLE, M. (1969) *Social Interaction*. London: Methuen.

AUSUBEL, D. P. (1966) 'Maturation and learning in adolescent development.' *Int. J. educ. Sci.*, **1**, 47-60.

BRUNER, J. S. (1960) *The Process of Education*. New York: Vantage Books.

BRUNER, J. S. (1965) 'The Growth of Mind.' In TORRANCE, E. P. and WHITE, W. F. (eds) *Issues and Advances in Educational Psychology*. New York: Peacock.

BRUNER, J. S. (1966) *Towards a Theory of Instruction*. New York: Norton.

BULL, N. J. (1969) *Moral Judgement from Childhood to Adolescence*. California: Sage.

CARSTAIRS, G. M. (1963) *This Island Now*. Harmondsworth: Penguin.

CORRY, J. (1967) 'Current Sexual Behaviour and Attitudes.' In BRECHER, R. and BRECHER, E. (eds) *An Analysis of Human Sexual Response*. London: André Deutsch.

DURKHEIM, E. (1952) *Suicide*. London: Routledge and Kegan Paul.

ELKIN, F. (1960) *The Child and Society: The Socialization Process*. New York: Random Press.

EPPEL, E. M. and EPPEL, M. (1966) *Adolescents and Morality*. London: Routledge and Kegan Paul.

ERIKSON, E. H. (1950) *Childhood and Society*. New York: Norton (rev. edn 1963).

ERIKSON, E. H. (1968) *Identity*. London: Faber.

FIRTH, R. (1951) *Elements of Social Organization*. New York: Watts.

GESELL, A. *et al.* (1946) *The Child from Five to Ten*. London: Hamish Hamilton.

GESELL, A. *et al.* (1956) *Youth, the Years from Ten to Sixteen*. London: Hamish Hamilton.

GINSBERG, M. (1956) *On the Diversity of Morals*. London: Heinemann.

GOLD, M. and DOUVAN, E. (1969) *Adolescent Development*. Rockleigh, NJ: Allyn and Bacon.

GREET, K. G. (1966) (ed.) *Sex and Morality*. London: S.C.M. Press.

HADINGHAM, E. (1970) (ed.) *Youth Now*. Kingston Grammar School, Surrey.

HALLORAN, D. J., ELLIOTT, P. and MURDOCK, G. (1970) *Demonstrations and Communication: A Case Study*. Harmondsworth: Penguin.

HAVIGHURST, R. J. (1953) *Human Development and Education*. London: Longman.

HERON, A. (1963) (ed.) *Towards a Quaker View of Sex*. Friends Home Service Committee.

Independent Television Authority (1970) *Religion in Britain and Northern Ireland*. London.

KELLY, G. A. (1955) *The Psychology of Personal Constructs*. New York: Norton.

KAY, W. (1968) *Moral Development*. London: Allen and Unwin.

KING, R. K. (1969) *Values and Involvement in a Grammar School*. London: Routledge and Kegan Paul.

KINSEY, A. C. *et al.* (1948) *Sexual Behaviour in the Human Male*. London and Philadelphia: Saunders.

KINSEY, A. C. *et al.* (1953) *Sexual Behaviour in the Human Female*. London and Philadelphia: Saunders.

KLUCKHOHN, C. (1951) 'Values and Value-Orientations in the Theory of Action: An exploration in Definition and Classification.' In PARSONS, R. and SHILS, E. (eds) *Towards a General Theory of Action*. Harvard: University Press.

KOHLBERG, L. (1968) *The Acquisition and Development of Values*. Bethesda, Maryland: National Institute of Child Health.

MASLOW, A. H. (1962) *Towards a Psychology of Being*. London: Van Nostrand.

MAYER, P. and MAYER, I. (1970) 'Socialization by Peers.' In *Socialization, the Approach from Social Anthropology*. London: Tavistock.

MAYS, J. B. (1965) *The Young Pretenders.* London: Michael Joseph.

MILLER, D. (1967) 'The Adolescent Mind.' *New Education*, **3**, 2, 16.

MEAD, M. (1970) *Culture and Commitment.* London: Bodley Head.

MUSGROVE, F. (1964) *Youth and the Social Order.* London: Routledge and Kegan Paul.

NIBLETT, W. R. (1968) (ed.) *Moral Education in a Changing Society.* London: Faber.

OTTO, H. A. and OTTO, S. T. (1969) 'A New Perspective of the Adolescent.' In RODGERS, D. (ed.) *Issues in Adolescent Psychology.* New York: Appleton-Century-Crofts.

PARSONS, T. and BALES, R. F. (1956) *Family, Socialization and Interaction Process.* London: Routledge and Kegan Paul.

PETERS, R. S. (1959) *Authority, Responsibility and Education.* London: Allen and Unwin.

PETERS, R. S. (1966) *Ethics and Education.* London: Allen and Unwin.

PIAGET, J. (1932) *The Moral Judgment of the Child.* London: Routledge and Kegan Paul.

RODGERS, C. R. (1961) *On Becoming a Person.* London: Constable.

ROSENBERG, M. (1965) *Society and the Adolescent Self-Image.* Princeton: University Press.

SANDSTRÖM, C. I. (1961) *The Psychology of Childhood and Adolescence.* Harmondsworth: Penguin.

SCHOFIELD, M. (1965) *The Sexual Behaviour of Young People.* London: Longman.

Schools Council (1969) *Enquiry* 1. London: HMSO.

THOMPSON, H. S. (1967) *Hell's Angels.* Harmondsworth: Penguin.

WALL, W. D. (1948) *The Adolescent Child.* London: Methuen.

WALL, W. D. (1968) *Adolescents in School and Society.* Slough: NFER.

WILSON, J., WILLIAMS, N. and SUGARMAN, B. (1967) *Introduction to Moral Education.* Harmondsworth: Penguin.

Social aspects of adolescence

DOUVAN, E. and ADELSON, J. (1966) *The Adolescent Experience.* New York: Wiley.

EISENSTADT, S. N. (1956) *From Generation to Generation.* London: Routledge and Kegan Paul.

FRIEDENBERG, F. (1962) *The Vanishing Adolescent.* New York: Dell.

HAVIGHURST, R. J. (1953) *Human Development and Education.* London: Longman.

JAHODA, M. and WARREN, N. (1965) 'The Myths of Youth.' *Sociology of Education*, **38**, 2, 138-49.

MUSGROVE, F. (1964) *Youth and the Social Order.* London: Routledge and Kegan Paul.

PECK, R. F. *et al.* (1960) *The Psychology of Character Development.* New York: Wiley.

TANNER, J. M. (1955) *Growth at Adolescence*. Oxford: Blackwell.
TAWNEY. R. H. (1961) *The Acquisitive Society*. London: Fontana.
VENESS, T. (1962) *School Leavers*. London: Methuen.
WALL, W. D. (1955) *Education and Mental Health*. Paris: UNESCO; London: Harrap.

Physical aspects of adolescence

DONOVAN, B. T. and VAN DER WERF TEN BOSCH, J. J. (1965) *Physiology of Puberty*. London: Arnold.
FALKNER, F. (1960) 'Child development: an international method of study.' *Annal. paediat.*, Suppl. No. 72.
FALKNER, F. (1966) *Human Development*. London: Saunders.
MARSHALL, W. A. and TANNER, J. M. (1969) 'Variations in the pattern of pubertal changes in girls.' *Arch. Dis. Childh.*, **44**, 291.
MARSHALL, W. A. and TANNER, J. M. (1970) 'Variations in the pattern of pubertal changes in boys.' *Arch. Dis. Childh.*, **45**, 13.
MUSSEN, P. H. and JONES, M. C. (1957) 'Self-concepting motivations and inter-personal attitudes of late- and early-maturing boys.' *Child Dev.*, **28**, 243-56.
TANNER, J. M. (1961) *Education and Physical Growth. Implications of the study of children's growth for educational theory and practice*. London: University of London Press.
TANNER, J. M. (1962) *Growth at Adolescence*. Oxford: Blackwell (2nd edn).
TANNER, J. M. (1966) 'Galtonian eugenics and the study of growth.' *Eugen Rev.*, **58**, 122-35.
TANNER, J. M. (1968) 'Earlier maturation in man.' *Scient. Am.*, **218**, 21-7.
TANNER, J. M. (1968) 'Growth and endocrinology of the adolescent.' In GARDNER, L. (ed.) *Endocrine and Genetic Diseases of Childhood*. Philadelphia and London: Saunders.
TANNER, J. M., WHITEHOUSE, R. H. and TAKAISHI, M. (1966) 'Standards from birth to maturity for height, weight/height velocity and weight velocity: British children 1965.' *Arch. Dis. Childh.*, **41**, 454-71.

Index